The Rugby League
Coaching Manual

THE RUGBY LEAGUE COACHING MANUAL

Phil Larder

Director of Coaching, the Rugby League
National Coaching Scheme

LINE DRAWINGS AND DIAGRAMS
BY KEN TRANTER

PUBLISHED FOR THE RUGBY FOOTBALL LEAGUE BY

HEINEMANN KINGSWOOD

Heinemann Kingswood
Michelin House
81 Fulham Road London SW3 6RB

LONDON   MELBOURNE
AUCKLAND

First published 1988

0434 98133 8 (cased)
0 434 98149 4 (paperback)

Typeset by Graphicraft Typesetters Ltd, Hong Kong
Printed in Great Britain by
Redwood Burn Limited, Trowbridge, Wiltshire
Designed by Geoff Green

To my wife, Anne,
for the many reasons she must know so well,
and of course Matt, Dids and Anna,
who give us so much pleasure

Contents

List of Illustrations

KEY TO THE DIAGRAMS

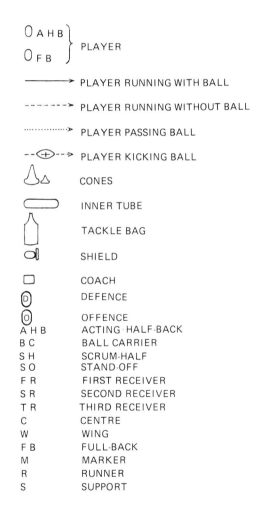

◯ A H B ◯ F B	PLAYER
⟶	PLAYER RUNNING WITH BALL
- - - - - ➤	PLAYER RUNNING WITHOUT BALL
⋯⋯⋯⋯➤	PLAYER PASSING BALL
- - ⊕ - -➤	PLAYER KICKING BALL
cones	CONES
INNER TUBE	INNER TUBE
tackle bag	TACKLE BAG
shield	SHIELD
▭	COACH
Ⓓ	DEFENCE
Ⓞ	OFFENCE
A H B	ACTING·HALF-BACK
B C	BALL CARRIER
S H	SCRUM-HALF
S O	STAND-OFF
F R	FIRST RECEIVER
S R	SECOND RECEIVER
T R	THIRD RECEIVER
C	CENTRE
W	WING
F B	FULL-BACK
M	MARKER
R	RUNNER
S	SUPPORT

Acknowledgements

My thanks go to all who made this publication possible. In Australia, especially, I should like to thank Frank Stanton and the 1982 Kangaroos who opened my eyes to how the game could be played; Alan Davidson and the Rothmans National Sports Foundation for opening their doors to me; Peter Corcoran, National Director of Coaching, for his many ideas, and Kris, his wife, for her warm-hearted hospitality; Frank Johnson, New South Wales State Coaching Director, for his rugby knowledge, commonsense and those 'pavlovas'; and Jack Gibson, Ron Massey, Mick Souter, and others at Cronulla for putting me on the right path.

In the United Kingdom I should like to thank Les Bettinson, David Oxley and others at the Rugby Football League; Tom Keaveney and Maurice Oldroyd of the British Amateur Rugby League Association; Robin Barron and the Sports Council; Sue Campbell and the National Coaching Foundation for information and their scholarship; and the British Association of National Coaches, the Bolton Health Studios, Paul Fitzpatrick, Derek Wyatt, Tony Pocock, Margot Richardson and Alma Thomas.

My thanks go also to those who have passed through the Rugby League National Coaching Scheme, for their ideas and inspiration, and its regional coaches Maurice Bamford, Garth Budge, Eric Fitzsimons, Clive Griffiths, Arthur Keegan, Dennis McHugh, Ken Newby, the late Geoff Peggs, Bev Risman, Barry Smith, Graham Starkey and David Wright for their determination, passion and commitment. And of course to my parents, who introduced me to the greatest game of all.

All the photographs in this book, except eight, are published by kind permission of the Andrew Varley Picture Agency. The exceptions are the frontispiece and no. 81 from Eddie Rolmanis; nos. 8, 9, 10 and 18 from Dennis Hussey; no. 19 from Chris Hardy; and no. 28 from the *Wigan Observer*.

Foreword

Rugby League is an expanding game. Each season more and more new clubs join the thriving leagues organized by the British Amateur Rugby League Association and each winter week-end the professional clubs contest matches unsurpassed in entertainment value, skill and excitement.

Under its dedicated and energetic director, Phil Larder, the National Coaching Scheme has played an important part not only in helping to bring about notable improvements in the way the game is now played in this country but has also encouraged the clearly discernible growth in the game's popularity. It is fitting, therefore, that Phil Larder should be the author of this important book.

The coach is teacher and tactician, mentor and motivator. He bears a heavy responsibility for developing the all-round skills of players at every level. Tactical appreciation, decision-making, mastery of unit and team skills, physical conditioning and the use of videos and statistics – these are all essential elements which go to make up the modern Rugby League coach.

It has been clear for a long time that an authoritative and comprehensive working handbook was urgently needed if potential coaches were to assimilate the necessary skills, and established coaches were to revise and polish their ideas, in the light of modern thinking. This superb publication answers these needs admirably.

It will surely become required reading for any coach whether he be in charge of the most junior amateur team or the most glamorous professional club. I heartily commend this book to all who wish to broaden their knowledge of the sport which proudly styles itself 'the man's game for all the family'.

DAVID OXLEY
Secretary-General,
The Rugby Football League

Preface

I am sure that everyone in Rugby League will welcome the publication of this coaching manual by the Director of Coaching, Phil Larder. Having worked closely with Phil since his appointment in 1982, I know well the degree of dedication that has been necessary to write this manual, which I believe will become the bible of all coaches, students and connoisseurs of the game.

At BARLA we recognise that coaching is vital to the development of the 13-a-side code, and it is essential to keep abreast of the progress that is being made in the modern field of coaching, fitness and technical expertise. To this end we actively encourage all coaches to qualify through the National Coaching Scheme and particularly those involved with youth and junior rugby. It is pleasing to report that over 2,000 coaches have qualified through the Scheme in recent years. For the first time in the game's history, Rugby League football is now on the curriculum of P.E. colleges and institutes of higher education throughout the country, and courses are held for many metropolitan councils and education offices through local physical education advisers.

BARLA's national and regional development plans, approved and supported by the Sports Council and by local authorities, have placed special emphasis on the importance of a successful coaching structure since its formation in 1973. It is, therefore, with a great deal of satisfaction and pride that we welcome the publication of this book.

BARLA strongly recommends all its clubs to make this manual compulsory reading for coaches, players and members, as we all strive to improve the skills and enjoyment of the greatest game of all – Rugby League football.

MAURICE OLDROYD
National Administrator,
The British Amateur Rugby League Association

Introduction

Although this book is aimed primarily at the Rugby League coach, it should be of interest also to players, referees, administrators, spectators and all who are attracted to the game.

For the coach it will be a much needed reference book. Individuals may not agree with everything they are about to read, but I hope the information will help to improve their coaching technique, whatever age group they work with. More important, the manual should act as a catalyst and stimulate the coach to widen his outlook.

It is far too easy for a coach to accept his first coaching position – perhaps offered because of his playing ability – and then simply use methods that were successful years ago when he was an impressionable young player. At best this is lazy, and shows a scant disregard for his elevation to coach. At the worst it is treason, and the direct cause of our playing standards having entered a dark tunnel in the 1970s and early 1980s, from which we are just now beginning to emerge.

There are even greater ramifications for the junior coach. If he treats his young charges as small adults, and uses methods and techniques more appropriate to senior players, then they may never forgive him;

and they could be lost from our sport, or even from all sports, for ever.

Coaches have to realize that the world does not stand still, and that recent advances in sport have been greater than in any other walk of life. Science has brought with it improved training methods and modern technology, while man in his quest for perfection has made greater demands on his body, with greater sacrifices of time and effort. Improvements in performance have been considerable.

In every measurable sport, records have tumbled. Nowhere is this more true than in the power events, where the modern technology of strength acquisition has had a staggering effect. Similar improvements have been made in the skilled sports. Television coverage has made the nation increasingly aware of improved performances in world gymnastics, and who will forget the exhibitions of ice-skating perfection of Torvill and Dean?

Such improvement is a direct result of good coaching, and good coaching means receiving up-to-date information with an open and enquiring mind – a mind that is aware of developments within its own sport and able to fuse those developments with changes in other sports and in other countries into an improved coaching method.

The modern approach is even more relevant to Rugby League football where recent rule changes, particularly the introduction of the limited-tackle rule, the handover rule and the sharp reduction in the number of scrummages, have dramatically changed the way the game is played.

I should like to think that this book will assist coaches of all age groups by providing them with much needed and valuable information. It will also help to make them more aware, I hope, and that, added to the invaluable experience of many thoughtful and enquiring individuals, should help to improve coaching and playing standards throughout the game.

PHIL LARDER

The author – after a hard day's coaching at the Lilleshall National Sports Centre in the summer of 1985.

Paul Dixon, Halifax and Great Britain, runs strongly into the Hull defence during their 1988 Challenge Cup semi-final.

Section 1

COACHING

Encourage beginners to have fun, to run at the opposition with the ball and to tackle fearlessly.

The role of the coach

1   Successful coaching
2   The game: the ingredients of success
3   Man management: a)   know yourself
                      b)   know your players
4   The learning process
5   Organization and planning
6   Observation and analysis

1   SUCCESSFUL COACHING

Coaches, when asked to describe their duties, might list this wide range of roles:

As a teacher – imparting new knowledge and skills
As a conditioner – improving fitness
As a motivator – generating a positive, confident and decisive approach
As a disciplinarian – determining a system of rewards and punishments and fostering correct attitudes
As a manager and administrator – providing good organization
As a publicity agent – creating public interest
As a social worker – counselling and advising
As a friend – supporting and sustaining
As a scientist – using analysis, evaluation and synthesis
As a student – being willing to listen and learn

Perhaps it is as technicians that most coaches are happiest. Certainly a Rugby League coach must have a comprehensive knowledge of the game. He must know all the techniques, the skills, the various tactics and strategies, and he has to communicate that knowledge to each individual in the squad.

This is not easy. Each player is different from the next, and all demand individual attention. The coach must make an in-depth study of them all, but even then he will have problems unless he has knowledge of the learning process, and the skills of a teacher.

Coaching is an involved and complex process, often performed under extreme pressure; and an ability to control emotions in periods of stress is an essential coaching discipline.

2   THE GAME: THE INGREDIENTS OF SUCCESS

Coaches need to have their own concept of how the game should be played, and how that vision can best be achieved. The essential ingredients of success are:

Attitude
Mental toughness
Physical conditioning
Skill
Games awareness and decision-making
Tactical planning.

Attitude

More and more people are discovering that Rugby League is a most enjoyable team game, and it is no surprise that the number of teams within the British Amateur Rugby League Association continues to rise each year. Most players simply play for the enjoyment and comradeship of the game itself, and are not interested in extensive and exhausting physical conditioning programmes.

However, there are those, as in every sport, who are striving for excellence. They must be prepared to make sacrifices of both time and effort. Skill, games awareness, tactical understanding and physical conditioning have to be established and developed. All are important in themselves and provide links in the chain of success. If a link fails, the whole chain will be broken. Yet Rugby League – even professionally – is only a part-time sport. Most clubs train twice or at most three times a week. By necessity the sessions are held in the evening after a hard day's work. Thus club training is restricted to between four and six hours a week, scarcely time to get through the work that needs to be done. Many coaches readily accept this and prepare a list of priorities which usually includes physical conditioning, tap-plays and unopposed team practice. Skills practices, the development of games awareness and the understanding of the major principles of play are often ignored.

Those striving for excellence in any sport need total dedication. To reach the top in athletics, Daley Thompson, Steve Ovett, Sebastian Coe and Steve Cram have had to make exceptional sacrifices. Cynics will no doubt point out that for these stars it has been financially worthwhile, but for every Daley Thompson there are hundreds of athletes throughout the country, fired by a burning desire for excellence, who are making similar sacrifices.

Those mixing with athletes and coaches from other sports – particularly when attending the Rugby League coaching courses at the Loughborough Summer School or at the National Sports Centres – are staggered to learn that the average club gymnast, athlete and swimmer, with personal ambition, trains every day, twelve months of the year. To do anything else would invite failure. These performers are true amateurs, receive no financial reward, and are usually in full-time employment. To achieve excellence they realize and accept that such commitment is essential.

Are we therefore guilty of selling Rugby League short? Should we insist that those striving for excellence should be equally committed?

It would certainly seem that our top performers need much greater commitment to the game than merely attending the club training sessions. Thankfully, more and more of them do now recognize this

1   Shaun Edwards (Wigan and Great Britain) has the total commitment necessary to reach the top.

and are taking responsibility for their own conditioning. Once this has been established there will be more time available to develop the other ingredients for success.

Coaches therefore need players of the correct attitude, who:

1   Arrive early for training

2   Have a positive attitude to the club, team coach and colleagues
3   Listen and learn
4   Train hard
5   Are loyal, stable and reliable
6   Do not abuse themselves by smoking, excessive drinking or late nights
7   Eat correctly
8   Train on non-training days
9   Play hard but within the rules
10 Give 100% plus effort in the game
11 Encourage others, particularly when the going is tough
12 Have a will to win, and hunger for success.

As far as attitude is concerned, it is the junior and youth coaches who hold the key to Great Britain's future success. If they establish the correct attitudes in their young players then Rugby League in Britain will have a sound foundation on which to build for the future.

Mental toughness

Every sport has examples of individuals freezing on the important occasion. When the stage is set for them to perform at their best they become over-anxious, and their skills, decision-making, concentration and self-confidence desert them. The reason for their poor performance has nothing to do with their physical ability. The problem is mental: mental toughness and mental preparation are now recognized as major attributes of sporting success.

In an attempt to boost confidence and determination, and inject 'steel' into the players' performance, many coaches are content simply to use such well-worn phrases as: 'When the going gets tough, the tough get going,' 'It's not the size of the dog in the fight, but the size of the fight in the dog,' and, 'If I can beat a guy in his mind, everything falls into shape,' but the more imaginative now tend to seek the help of sports psychologists.

Anxiety is the principal factor which has to be overcome. According to many sports psychologists there are four different types of situation which induce anxiety. These are: fear of physical harm, ego threat, fear of punishment, and fear of inanimate objects. The last two are scarcely relevant to Rugby League, although it has been known for some players to cringe as they pass the coach's bench.

Anxiety can be controlled and overcome by a process of relaxation, concentration and visualization as discussed in the Appendix. Without a correct mental approach the highest levels of performance can never be reached. Equally, with determination, ambition, dedication, hard work and correct coaching, standards of excellence can be achieved, but in the final analysis it is the team best prepared mentally which wins the game.

Physical conditioning

In the past there has been some confusion about the relation of physical conditioning to success in Rugby League football. It was the American football coach, Vincent Lombardi, who said 'fatigue makes cowards of us all', a theory which can also be related to Rugby League.

The success of the 1978 Australian Kangaroos was explained by many observers in Britain as being a direct result of their superior physical conditioning.

2   Rod McKenzie, conditioner to the Rugby Football League, 1981–87.

It is greatly to be credit of the Rugby League Council that decisive steps were taken to overcome this problem. Rod McKenzie, a lecturer at Carnegie School of Physical Education, Leeds Polytechnic, was appointed as 'Rugby League conditioner'. Rod not only held lectures with the club coaches, but also embarked upon an extensive fitness programme with the Great Britain squad during the summer of 1982 in preparation for the next Kangaroo tour.

Despite the positive influence of McKenzie, the 1982 Kangaroos were even more successful than their predecessors. They not only won the Test series 3–0 but were the first overseas touring party to win all their games, often with displays of outstanding skill. They proved that while high standards of physical fitness are certainly necessary to play winning Rugby League football, fitness is but one of the ingredients of success.

However, during the last decade, many British Rugby League coaches have certainly failed to prepare their players physically. Many have neglected to study modern developments in strength, speed and power training. Few understood that endurance is the foundation on which to build, and few accepted the value of a flexibility programme. Few were capable of producing individual and well-balanced training programmes and far too many ran their teams in a haphazard way until they looked tired, and relied upon that as an adequate conditioning programme. It is little wonder that in the middle 1970s and early 1980s Britain fell so far behind the Australians.

Rugby League football is probably the most physically demanding of all team games and while physical fitness may be only one of the ingredients of success, it is still vitally necessary for coaches to be fully conversant with all the principles of fitness which are necessary in Rugby League.

Skill

Rugby League is a game of skill, and the skilled performer not only entertains the crowd but often enables his team to win the game. Consider the varied skills involved in timing the defence-splitting pass, executing the perfect tackling technique which sends an opponent crashing to the ground, the precision kick to the corner for the chasing winger and the deft side-step which wrong-foots the would-be tackler.

3   Lee Crooks (Leeds, formerly Hull, and Great Britain) is regarded as one of the most skilled forwards in the world.

One of the qualities of Rugby League is that all the players should be proficient in all the major skills. Coaches of all age groups, therefore, should spend time each week. encouraging all their players to perfect all the skills of the game. In the same way that a week-end motorist reacts more slowly on the road by comparison with a top rally driver, the player who continuously practises skills will react more quickly and more precisely than one who does not.

All Rugby League players understand the important principles of possession and the necessity of picking up a loose ball, which in itself is relatively simple. The player who has practised picking up a loose ball in training sessions will react far quicker in a match situation than one who has not.

Certainly the more complex skills of timing a pass, precision kicking and catching a 'bomb' under pressure require continuous practice. A respected coach, involved with a young and comparatively inexperienced Under-19 team, once said that school and Under-13 teams were the places to practise skills, and that coaches of the older players had more important duties to perform. One wonders what he would think of the training programmes adopted by world-class gymnasts, and of the tens of hours a week spent on skills practice by the ice skaters Torvill and Dean? The acquisition of skill is an ongoing thing, and although the junior coach will devote more hours to it than the senior coach, skills training should be a part of every player's weekly training programme.

Games awareness and decision-making

Though it is important for players to perfect their individual skills, which would certainly guarantee success in such sports as gymnastics, coaches must remember that in Rugby League a high level of skill must be accompanied by the ability to make the correct decisions.

Study the facts:

1   In a game of eighty minutes of Rugby League, the ball is out of play for approximately thirty minutes and in play for approximately fifty minutes.
2   Out of the fifty minutes in which the ball is in play, in an even game each team will control the ball for twenty-five minutes.
3   On average, therefore, individual team members will control the ball for less than two minutes each, and be involved in tackling for less than two minutes each.

Question: What is the player doing for the other forty-six minutes the ball is in play?
Answer: Making decisions and judgements.

It is important that players in the atmosphere of intense competition make correct decisions and choices. There is little value in a player with a high level of skill using it incorrectly. For example, a centre with a high level of handling skills is doing little for himself or his team if, when breaking down the field with the gap on the outside, he turns his

winger inside and into the cover. It is immaterial how well the pass is executed; he has chosen the wrong option and a try-scoring opportunity has been lost.

Decision-making should be developed at an early age, and practices devised for training sessions which encourage players to think and make decisions. There is little value in a coach criticizing a player from the touch-line for an error in judgement, then forgetting about it during the mid-week training sessions only to be reminded by the player making a similar error in the next game. A more positive approach would be to make a detailed study of each player's performance in the game. This can be helped by the use of match statistics and in some cases a study of the match video. A breakdown of skill and errors of judgement can then be discussed with the specific players concerned.

Once the player recognizes the mistake, he can be helped to correct the fault in training clinics specifically designed to create similar situations. The player can then be guided through the process of correct decision-making by the coach.

A perfect example of this was provided by John Fieldhouse in his Test début against the 1985 touring

4   John Fieldhouse (St Helens, formerly Widnes, and Great Britain) was the Whitbread player of the series against New Zealand in 1985.

Kiwis. Fieldhouse had all the attributes of success; he was strong, fast, brave, skilful with a high work-rate. He had been on the fringe of international selection but had been repeatedly overlooked because of a tendency to lose possession at vital times. Despite the fact that control of the ball was to be one of the major strategies of the series, Fieldhouse was selected. Maurice Bamford and the Great Britain coaching team worked hard in every session with him, making him realize the importance of possession and then testing him in pressure situations. The coaching he received had a positive effect. In the three-match series he controlled the ball well and produced an outstanding performance which deservedly won him the Whitbread Trophy award as the player of the series.

Tactical planning

Many coaches would define tactics as the set moves to be used during a game from tap-plays and scrums.

There is, however, more to tactics than developing a series of plays which are used irregularly in the game. Set moves are no more than the decorations of the game and should not be perfected until the basic foundations have been developed:

Control of the ball
Support play
Defence
Tactical kicking.

These four principles of play form an ideal foundation of any team's tactical preparation and should be given a large proportion of the training time available. Once these have been developed, set moves can be devised in an attempt to open up the opposition's defences, and a tactical plan produced.

3   MAN MANAGEMENT:

(a)   Know yourself

Man management is an essential aspect of coaching and it is imperative that the coach has a positive effect on his players, particularly as they are often working in an atmosphere of stress.

The coach needs to be able to control his own emotions, and to ensure that he obtains a positive response from the players at all times. To do this, he has to understand himself, try to eradicate his weaknesses and develop his strengths. At no time is this more true than on match days and in the build-up to important games.

A coach must know how he reacts in moments of stress. A high degree of self-control is necessary because his moods are highly contagious, and will have a bearing on the atmosphere in the dressing-room.

The coach should also be fully in control of himself during the game. Substitutes, reserves, injured players on the sideline and perhaps even those on the pitch will be aware of the coach's behaviour. Officials, spectators, relations and friends of the players will be able to study the coach's reactions, as will those from the visiting team. The coach's behaviour will have an important influence on the respect in which he is held in the game, and any comments, particularly those of a personal nature, will be remembered and probably conveyed to the team after the game.

It is natural for the coach – particularly one who is highly motivated – to be carried away by the excitement and traumas of the conflict. But he cannot afford such luxuries for he has a most important role to play. It is during the game that team and player analysis is important, and even if he can study the game video afterwards, he still has to try to improve his team's performance at half-time. Indeed, this is his only opportunity to influence the game once it has begun, by modifying the game plan and passing on constructive advice to the players. The danger is that too much information will be conveyed. The players can only absorb so much in this short time and there is a danger of their 'switching off' if the coach goes overboard.

Similar situations arise before the game. Most people involved with sport now think that motivation is a long-term process and cannot be fully achieved in the half-hour prior to the game or competition. Thankfully the days of the pre-match 'rant and rage' are dead and buried. It is far better for the coach to appear calm and completely in control of himself: he will certainly insist that his players must be in control

5 The author sits alongside Maurice Bamford (Great Britain's coach from 1984–86) and Les Bettinson (the Great Britain team manager) during the first Test against Australia in 1986. Notice the emotional control and deep concentration as the action is analysed.

of every situation, and should set the example himself. Motivation is different for each individual. Prior to the game, therefore, the coach will need to ensure that each player is gently steered to his own optimum level of commitment.

The end of the game can be a traumatic time, in particular if errors have been made and the game lost. The coach could be in an emotional state and must be aware of the dangers of making harsh criticisms. Immediately after the game, the players are unlikely to respond positively to any form of inquest and it is usually advisable to wait until the first training session afterwards.

It is important for the coach to realize that if he expects his players to improve, he must set an example himself. He should never be too proud to ask for help – only a fool thinks he knows it all. Coaches should meet regularly with one another to discuss training methods and to hear of new developments.

Others from inside or outside their sport may have discovered solutions to problems bothering them: help others and be helped.

Knowing what you do not know is almost as important as knowing what you do. Coaches are expected to wear many hats and they cannot be experts in all of them. Coaches should seek out people with knowledge; they should listen and learn. They should sit down and assess their own strengths and where they need to improve. They should beware of taking the easy way out. They would not expect that of their players, and should not accept it of themselves.

3   MAN MANAGEMENT:

(b)   Know your players

The coach of the junior team has a very different ta

than that of the open-age coach. The first step in getting to know the players, therefore, is to understand the needs and requirements of their particular age group.

The major aim of the junior coach is to help each individual member of his squad to develop to his full potential in an enjoyable atmosphere. In order to do this, the coach obviously has to make a detailed study of each of them. By analysing their strengths and weaknesses and by creating a personal relationship with them, he will be ideally placed to help their development.

The senior coach is assessed by his win/lose record, so it is important that his team plays to its maximum ability. In order to do this each individual within the team must perform well.

The senior coach, therefore, should also make a detailed study of each member of the squad. He will need to establish a personal relationship with each player, recognizing that each will be affected by outside factors – home, family, work, friends, other team members – as well as inside – health, fitness, diet, emotion, mood. Individuals are complex and there are no standard approaches which can be applied to each player or performer.

It is especially important for coaches to be able to communicate well with, and to motivate, the teams they are responsible for:

1 **Communication.** The coach should spend time talking with each member of his squad. He should take an interest in their personal lives and try to understand their worries, fears, hopes and desires. Once the coach begins to build a picture of each individual he will be in a position to develop a strategy for dealing with each of them.

2 **Motivation.** To motivate the players to perform at their best is a most important coaching skill. Motivation is an individual process as individuals all react differently to stimuli. Just as some team members need to be stimulated before competitions, others need to be calmed down. Only by understanding each player can the coach hope to bring them to the correct level of arousal.

3 **Mutual respect.** It is important also for the coach to gain the respect of his players. The surest way of doing this is by respecting them. The coach should never chastise an individual in front of others, or ridicule his team after defeat.

4   THE LEARNING PROCESS

Coaches of all age levels should find the following points of value:

1 **Interest.** A player who is not interested has a closed mind and will not learn. Attempts should be made to ensure that each coaching session is both interesting and enjoyable.

2 **Enthusiasm.** Enthusiasm is infectious. Coaches should enthuse about the game, the club, the team and the individuals within the team. The players too should be encouraged to be enthusiastic: enthusiastic people want to do more, not less.

3 **Set a good example.** Players learn by watching, but it is essential that they see correct techniques. The responsibility of outstanding players and coaches in establishing standards for young players cannot be overemphasized.

4 **Practice.** There is a saying that practice makes perfect, but this does not always apply to coaching. Players perfect what they practise, so if they are practising an incorrect technique this incorrect technique will become a habit. This has serious implications for coaches, for they must ensure that all practices are carried out with correct technique. Only perfect practice makes perfect.

5 **Knowledge of results.** The more progress a player can be seen to be making, the more he is likely to be encouraged to practise. Like medicine, we may not always like it, but if there is clear evidence that it is doing us good we will continue to take it. Correct practice involves setting players performance targets so that progress can be measured, and this task belongs entirely to the coach.

6 **Challenges.** Players improve by being set more difficult tasks and by playing with and against

better players, the proviso always being that the task is not too difficult nor the players too good. Coaches must set these challenges carefully, calculating the probability of success.

7   Faith.   At the end of the day, players will not achieve more than they think is possible. The question is, what is possible? Many of us underestimate our abilities. Coaches should inspire players to try harder and to aim higher.

8   Encouragement.   Players learn more from encouragement than criticism. Praise effort, good results and improvement. The encouragement can be by words, a smile or a wink or nod of the head. The coach should never underestimate praise.

Criticism, of course, is often necessary, but this should never be personal, sarcastic or cutting, and is very often best delivered in private. Immediately after criticizing a player, the coach should make every effort to boost confidence again.

9   Coach positively.   Players perform at their best when they are confident they can handle the situation and are fully confident of their own ability. It is necessary for the coach to be sensitive to their feelings. Children are developing their self-image, which is an important stage in growing up. The coach must recognize this in order to help develop their self-confidence, and not ridicule, over-criticize, or show up any of them. Ego and self-confidence are equally important to the adult, and coaches who over-criticize are travelling a dangerous path.

It is far better to adopt the approach, 'We shall win more games if we master catching a high ball. Remember to concentrate intently on the ball and keep those elbows together. Let me watch you practise that now,' than 'The two bombs you dropped last week cost us the game. Go over there and practise catching a high ball.'

5   ORGANIZATION AND PLANNING

At the end of the season it is important that the coach finds time to reflect on and analyse the work that he and his players have done throughout the year. This analysis is the first step in planning the work for the coming season. Just as the work for the next match begins the minute the players walk off the pitch, the work for the next season begins the minute the season is over.

After reflection, the coach should plan his next campaign. It helps to write down the aims and objectives and then list each step that has to be taken. Do the players have to be fitter? Faster? Stronger? Do the tactics have to be revised or explained? Should new moves be introduced? Have the players to improve their skills, the understanding of what to do in any given situation, or has the coach to improve team spirit and player confidence?

Whichever options the coach selects, they must be well thought out, planned and organized. If winning the championship is the aim, perhaps attitude in the dressing-room is the key. Certain players may have to be released, and others brought in to replace them. If increased fitness is the answer, work must begin immediately: the close season is the time to improve stamina, strength, speed and suppleness.

Perhaps the coach requires more time with his players. The answer could be to give his players responsibility for their own fitness preparation, thereby ensuring that there is more time available on club training nights to perfect the skills, decision-making and tactics that have been missing in the previous season.

An extract from the notes prepared by the coaching staff for the Great Britain team management after the 1986 Kangaroos tour as part of the preparation for the 1988 Lions tour of Australasia is set out on pages 12 and 13 and shows the sort of guidelines that should be prepared.

Once the problems have been identified the coach must begin to plan and organize the year. On what date should preparation begin? How many club sessions are going to take place during each part of the season? What is the emphasis going to be? Do the players need advice on individual training programmes? How can the tactics be revised? Does the team need to improve its kicking game? Defence? Control of the ball or support play? When is work on this going to start? What steps are to be taken? Do the players fully understand the strategies of the coach? Do they make correct decisions on the pitch under

Attitude

The marked improvement must be continued and intensified.

Areas of priority:

a) Intense close season preparation - 6 day per week programme

b) Reduce alcohol intake

c) Improve diet

d) Improve professionalism and commitment

Mental Toughness

a) Our players require a more intense competition within the English League to rival that in Sydney.

b) My idea of using a sports psychologist has not been supported. Therefore I need to attend a sports psychology course (Malcolm & Les?).

c) Every effort must be made to improve the self-confidence of our players. "We will get our act together and do it".

d) Mental toughness will be an important consideration when the touring party is selected.

Physical Conditioning

Improvement needs to be intensified.

a) Encourage internationals to spend the close season at home rather than play in Australia. (Difficult because of the size of some contracts, i.e. Lee Crooks, Garry Schofield).

b) Embark on an intense close season preparation. Main aim - strength; subsidiary - stamina, speed, suppleness.

c) Incorporate new fitness levels to an increase in work rate and speed about the pitch.

d) 6 day per week programme.

e) Encourage all clubs to adopt the same.

f) Encourage BARLA and ESRL to put all outstanding players on a similar programme (i.e. centres of excellence).

Skill

a) Internationals. From the Player Report sheets completed after all the internationals, draw up a list of each player's strengths and weaknesses.

Close season - develop strengths and eradicate errors.

b) Clubs. Encourage clubs to do the same. (Professional club conference May 16 and 17).

c) Future Professionals. BARLA's ten centres of excellence. Identify each player's deficiencies and improve.

Games Awareness and Decision-Making

a) Internationals v Australia. Australia reduce the time we have to make decisions. The Tests are faster than club games.

Training - make time a consideration, create situations to increase speed of thought.

b) Influence the Rugby League Council via Les and David Howes to insist that we have pre-Test games in Sydney (and Brisbane).

c) Encourage the RFL to increase intensity of Division 1.

Tactics

a) Defence

Improve

i)   Commitment
ii)   Attitude - pressurise rather than stop
iii) Work rate
iv)   Marker duties
v)   Speed of the defensive line
vi)   Defensive line going up and through rather than up and stop
vii) Drift

b) Control of the Ball

Major concern. Percentage success rate has been

NZ - 72%   62%   60%
F - 43%   63%
Aussie - 58%   55%   65%
F - 54%   68%
Average 60%
Aim 75%. Must achieve at least 70%. Emphasise in training.

c) Support

i) Every attack must be supported. Continue to improve support play of backs when forwards driving, particularly stand-off and centres.

ii) Set pieces. Every player hitting the line must be supported.

iii) All breaks - immediate support.

iv) Work on shields in every session. Supporting the tackled player.

d) Kicking Game

i) Must play game in opponents' half.
Concentration upon - kick (Joe)
                          chase

ii) Short kicking game, particularly
    a) Chip and chase
    b) Grubber in goal and chase

iii) Defending the kick

pressure? If not, why not? Could it be that they do not fully understand the coach's strategy? If not, how is this understanding to be developed, nurtured and improved?

Step by step the coach should plan his route to improvement and success. First of all a general plan for the year must be mapped out, perhaps with the year divided into close-season, pre-season, early-season, mid-season, and end-of-season preparation. Once the season has been subdivided, each section must be analysed. What is going to be the main theme during each one?

The coach is now on the way to improvement. Using this general plan he can now begin to analyse the work for each week and for each individual coaching session. Using all his experience and knowledge, decisions can be made which ensure that training sessions throughout the season dovetail into each other. Each step should be written down for future reference and be used as a guideline. Once the season has started, everyday problems may cause the plan to be changed but those initial guidelines are important.

Coaches of junior sides need to realise that they may have a different team each year. As the strengths and weaknesses of each team will differ, what worked one year may not work the next.

The points listed below may be of value to all coaches:

1 **Planning**. Each coaching session should be well planned. The coach should first consider what is to be the main objective of the session and then begin to structure the content, ensuring that there is a fine balance of all the relevant factors. Facilities, equipment, and number of participants should all be taken into consideration.

2 **Arrive early**. By arriving at each coaching session early, the coach not only presents the correct image to his squad, but has time to overcome any unforeseen problems and to organize the equipment which is to be used. Perhaps even more important than this is that it enables the coach to focus his mind on the work to be done, particularly necessary if the coaching session comes at the end of a working day.

3 **Organizing the squad**. The coach should keep the organization simple. If sessions are going fairly well, new ideas should be introduced gently. Having decided what to do the coach now has to decide how to do it, and this often necessitates the group being divided into sub-groups. The problems of selecting sub-groups can be avoided by playing the 'number game'. The whole group runs round the space available, the coach shouts a number, and the group rushes to form groups of that number. This is fun for groups of all ages and avoids those embarrassing moments for the coach when he loses count of his squad and for individuals when selecting partners. If certain individuals need to be in particular ability groups, the coach should work those out beforehand, but must be prepared to adjust them if one or two miss the session.

The best group size depends on what is to be done and the ability of the players. For example, piggy-in-the-middle, 2 against 1 (two people with the ball against one trying to intercept it) is good if the players are competent. Otherwise, the coach may have to revert to a 3 v. 1 or even a 4 v. 1 situation. If a session takes the form of starting in sub-groups and building up to a full group, numbers should be selected that allow easy progression. For example, if working in threes, it is relatively easy to move to 3 against 3 and then on to 6 against 6. It would be much harder to start in fives, move to 3 against 3 and finish with 8 against 8.

4 **Facilities**. The facilities should always be checked before every session to ensure that they are in adequate condition. If space allows, it is an advantage to have grids marked adjacent to the playing area. These are usually ten-metre squares for children; fifteen-metre squares for adults are most frequently provided.

5 **Equipment**. It is often the case that teams which make annual presentations of trophies and medals to virtually all team members cannot afford enough equipment. Obviously rugby balls are the priority. As an absolute minimum a coach needs to have one ball for every four players, and with junior teams the ratio should be one ball between two

players. Size is also important: juniors should use size 3 or size 4, depending on their age.

Marker cones are invaluable as coaching aids and each club should have at least two dozen. Large inner tubes, too, can help to improve both individual and team defence, and in making conditioning specific. Used inner tubes can usually be bought very cheaply, although they may take time to accumulate. Always remember to make them safe by covering the metallic valve with thick foam and carpet. This important safety factor should be checked each time they are used. Tackle shields and tackle bags are also valuable for all age groups (see pages 73 and 74).

Equipment should be checked before each session. There is nothing worse than having the whole squad ready and eager to go, then spending time searching for the missing pump necessary to inflate the balls.

6   Voice.   Communication by speaking is a skill in itself. Its importance is greatly underestimated just as the difficulty of speaking to a group is greatly overestimated. The difference between speaking in front of one person and speaking in front of thousands is almost entirely one of confidence. Coupled with confidence should be the ability to speak effectively. There are certain ground rules for effective communication which coaches should understand:

Be convinced that there is something of value to say. If there is any doubt, the best advice is to keep quiet.

Think before speaking. Even a short time spent in considering what to say and how best to say it will pay dividends.

Be certain of the meaning of words. Misuse of words inevitably leads to misunderstanding.

Avoid jargon – particularly professional jargon. The majority of people will not understand jargon and its use can only lead to confusion.

Speak clearly in terms of volume and speed. In varying the speed, try also to vary the pitch. This makes the presentation more compelling.

Speak concisely. Short words are better than long words and one word is better than two. This greatly assists clarity. It also assists in reducing the complicated to simple proportions.

Make all instructions positive. Instructions should be affirmative, i.e. 'Do this' rather then 'Don't do that'.

Watch the group while speaking. This is compelling and helps the group to concentrate on what is being said.

When addressing the group, ensure that they can all see and hear you. Make sure they are not facing any distractions. If there are any, they should be behind the group.

7   Safety.   The problems of safety must be recognized. Make sure the training area is free from glass, holes and other hazards. Be careful not to leave rugby balls where players can stand on them. In frosty conditions ensure the surface is flat and safe. The junior coach, above all, should be aware of the dangers of pitting small children against those more physically mature.

8   Assess what is going on.   During each session stand back and try to assess what is going well, what is going badly, and what is needed for next time. The coach should not be afraid to make mistakes. It is often said that a good coach is not someone who does it right all the time, but is someone who recognizes when it goes wrong and spends time thinking how to put it right for the next time.

The sort of notes a coach should make as soon as possible after a session are summarized on page 16. This will enable him to build up a notebook with reminders of useful activities and modifications.

6   OBSERVATION AND ANALYSIS

Perhaps the most important coaching duty is the improvement of performance. The junior coach will set about this task in a vastly different way to the senior coach, and these methods will be discussed more specifically in later chapters. However, there are a few common factors:

1   Observation.   Once the individuals have been organized, briefed and are working in a training atmosphere, it is necessary for the coach to step back and concentrate on the work being done.

2 Analysis. Is the group well organized, and working safely to achieve the required objectives? Are members of the group technically proficient and making the correct decisions? The coach should cast a critical eye over each player and analyse his performance. It is important that he is fully aware of what he expects from each player, has the ability to observe faults and then by careful analysis forms in his own mind a procedure for correction.

<u>Coaching Notes</u>

Date: Friday 20.9.85

7.00 Discussion   M.B.

Maurice emphasised importance of sessions.
Apologised for the inconvenience, but stressed that this was essential final preparation before the 3 day camp prior to the First Test.
Players commitment excellent, although those from Hull and Widnes anticipated problems.

7.30. Warm up and flexibility.
  Theme - "Control of the Ball"
        a). Union Jack
        b). Stretching
        c). 3 v 1
        d). 4 v 4

8.00. Pattern 1. <u>Unopposed</u>
        6 plays from a tap 30 metres out.

8.20. Defence
        a). Importance (M.B.)
        b). Double Marker (Think left. Think right.) (P.L.)
        c). Blind side drift (M.B.)
        d). Line Defence - incorporating Bomb receive (P.L.)

8.50 Individual Tackling Drills - Bags   M.B./P.L.

<u>Comments</u>

  Spirit & confidence - high. (Week at Lilleshall good for spirit)
  Pattern 1 - need to work on support, particularly drop off 1 & 2
        (use centres)
  Blind Side Drift - improving.
  Tackle Drill - some players still hitting with upper arm
        instead of shoulder.

<u>Suggestion</u>
  Next week. Emphasis - close support - (use centres)

Coaching the junior player

1 Major considerations
2 Knowing the children's capabilities
3 The aims of the junior coach
4 Coaching method
5 The coaching session

1 MAJOR CONSIDERATIONS

1 Rugby League has much to offer children and young people. Apart from the joy of playing the game itself, Rugby League helps children to gain confidence in their own abilities, the chance to work in co-operation with others and can give them an understanding of competition. It also provides an opportunity to experiment with physical and emotional boundaries in a healthy and safe environment. In short it gives children and young people the chance to develop some of the skills needed for living in our society. Why then do so many young talented athletes drop out of the game, indeed out of sport generally? There is evidence that some of them are put off by the nature of their interaction with coaches.

2 Many unqualified people coach. Amateur Rugby League is one of the fastest growing team sports in the country. Its governing body, the British Amateur Rugby League Association, is encouraging all amateur clubs to run youth teams. More and more of them comply, with the result that administrators, players, parents and friends are being encouraged to coach youngsters. Many of these people, although enthusiastic and well meaning, do not fully understand the needs and desires of the children they coach.

3 Many junior coaches copy professional coaches. Many coaches naturally copy the work of those at the top of the tree. But the professional coach is coaching talented, committed adults, whilst the junior coach is coaching children, who need a completely different approach.

2 KNOWING THE CHILDREN'S CAPABILITIES

The most important aspect of coaching is to have a detailed knowledge of the individuals in the squad. This is particularly relevant to youngsters as they develop and change so quickly.

Coaches need to be aware of the growth process, especially the effects of puberty. This term derives from the Latin *pubertus*, meaning age of manhood, and is usually considered to date from the onset of menstruation in girls and the emergence of pubic hair in boys. However, these two easily observable changes are each only a small part of a complex process involving many body functions. Puberty is accompanied by changes not only in the reproductive system and in the secondary sexual characteristics of the individual, but in the functioning of the heart and thus of the cardio-vascular system, in the lungs which in turn affect the respiratory system, in the size and strength of many of the muscles of the body, and so on. Puberty, therefore, must be seen as an event in the physical life of the body with wide-ranging implications.

6 The effects of puberty and the growth spurt: two pupils from Brigshaw Comprehensive School, both aged 13, typify the problem. Michael Roberts is 5 ft. 11 in. tall, James Faulker 4 ft. 6 in.

One of the many physical changes associated with puberty is the 'growth spurt'. This term is usually taken to refer to the accelerated rate of increase in height and weight that occurs during early adoles-

cence. It is essential to bear in mind, however, that there are considerable individual differences in the age of onset and duration of the growth spurt in perfectly normal children. This is a fact which parents and adolescents themselves frequently fail to appreciate and which causes a great deal of unnecessary anxiety. In boys the growth spurt may begin as early as ten years of age, or as late as sixteen, while in girls the same process can begin at seven or eight, or not until twelve, thirteen or even fourteen. For the average boy, though, as the maturation graph in Diagram 1 makes clear, rapid growth begins at about thirteen, and reaches a peak somewhere during the fourteenth year.

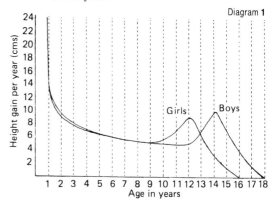

Comparable ages for girls are eleven for the onset of the growth spurt, and twelve for the peak age of increase in height and weight.

The following are the factors which should give coaches most concern:

1 Physical

The physical differences between an early developer and a late developer, both aged thirteen, can often be equivalent to four years' growth. The physically mature child will not only be bigger and stronger, but will also be faster and have higher levels of endurance. The slow developer, particularly when competing in a physical game like Rugby League, can often be at such a physical disadvantage that he loses interest in all sport. On the other hand an early developer when asked to play with boys his own size, but naturally much older, is placed at an emotional disadvantage.

A strong argument can be made, therefore, for dividing leagues by maturation levels (taking both age and size into consideration). Coaches should also take care in not type-casting children at too early an age. It is often a mistake to assume that the big thirteen-year-old will eventually play in the second row. It is more likely that he is an early developer, and that the other pupils will have caught up and even overtaken him by the age of fifteen. A better idea than early speculation is to teach all the skills to all the players and let them experiment with playing positions until they find the one that suits them best.

2   Emotional

Children, particularly adolescents, are not only sensitive but critical of their changing physical self. It is necessary for them to be made fully aware of the growth spurt, and for them to realize that all their friends will experience similar changes sooner or later. It is equally important for the coach, particularly in the intimate atmosphere of the dressing-room, to treat all physical changes as normal, and to make sure that none of the team is ridiculed in any way.

3   THE AIMS OF THE JUNIOR COACH

By comparison with the junior coach, the senior coach has a relatively simple aim – to produce a winning team. The junior coach has a far wider and more important role. He has to remember that the youngsters in his care will spend a lot of time thinking about him, dwelling on the phrases he has used, the words he has spoken and the gestures he has made. He has the ability to make them happy and elated, or unhappy and depressed. Many coaches have an even greater influence on young players than their parents do. This is an awesome responsibility which they should never underestimate. The coach will often influence the personality, character and emotions of the youngsters in his charge.

The major aims of the junior coach are therefore:

1   To develop positively the self-image of each child.   The children are building up a picture of themselves and that image is one of the most important parts of growing up. The coach, in recognizing this, should deliberately boost the confidence of every child in his charge. The coach should certainly not:

> ridicule
> over-criticize
> make public the shortcomings of any of his charges.

2   To develop an interest in and enthusiasm for Rugby League.   It is important that the coach develops in the children a love of and interest in Rugby League. This is achieved by creating an atmosphere of enthusiastic enjoyment. Fear of criticism and ridicule will drive children away from the team and perhaps away from the sport for ever.

3   To develop each child's maximum potential.   The most successful coach is the one who can help each player achieve his full potential:

(a)   Be aware of the make-up of each individual player.
(b)   Be flexible in the approach to each individual.

Increased awareness can help to increase the coach's effectiveness. This is far more important than winning the cup at the end of the season.

Each coaching session should be enjoyable, the atmosphere relaxed, with the coaching emphasis being placed upon skill acquisition and the development of games awareness and decision-making. The game should never be more important than the individual, otherwise the children will be exploited.

Winning – how important is it?

The nature of Rugby League makes it one of the most competitive team games. At senior level this is one of its strengths; most adults can handle the additional pressure of winning and enjoy the competition.

Children are also competitive, but it is important for coaches, parents and administrators to realize that children only enjoy competition on their terms. Adult competition places them under far too much pressure. Remember children enjoy playing at sport; when it becomes too serious the results can be harmful.

Some of the disadvantages of intense competition for children are:

1 **Inferiority complex.** Only one team can win the cup and, therefore, all the others are losers. When the results of games become so important the losers often feel that they have let down the team, the coach, their parents and themselves. This negative feeling often makes them feel inferior.

2 **Coaching is for the team and not the individual.** In a highly competitive structure the emphasis of the coaching often swings away from the individual to the team. At the end of the year the young players have often learnt no more than to play a small part in the team plan.

3 **Pressure affects the coach, parent, and spectator.** When winning becomes so important the coach is often placed under a lot of pressure. This pressure is passed on to the players with the result that:

(a) They become afraid of making mistakes so their performances become inhibited.
(b) The coach relies too much on the better players and the reserves and substitutes are hardly used.
(c) The players hear hurtful and negative comments from the touchline expressed in a most abrasive way. Though these are often made by the coach and parents in the heat of the moment, they can have a profoundly harmful effect on the child concerned.

4 COACHING METHOD

1 Use the positive approach

Coaching can aim to influence people in two main ways: *The positive approach* – designed to strengthen desirable behaviour by motivating people to perform in a desirable way. *The negative approach* – attempts to eliminate negative behaviour through punishment

and criticism. The motivating factor in this approach is fear.

Both approaches are used by coaches – but the positive approach is preferable. It works, and promotes an enjoyable atmosphere.

The positive approach is characterized by the liberal use of reward and encouragement. The most effective way to build desirable behaviour is to use the 'reward power' the coach has. The single most important difference between coaches to whom children respond most favourably and those to whom they respond least favourably is the frequency with which the coaches reward desirable behaviour.

Rewards can include:

A pat on the back
A smile
Clapping
Verbal praise
A friendly nod
A thumbs-up sign, and so on.

Look for positive things – reward them and they will increase. Praise little things others might not notice. Give rewards sincerely – this gives the children something to strive for. Have realistic expectations – reward consistently when children reach them. Reward positive things immediately – this way the reward is more effective.

When coaches choose to reward is of critical importance. Only one team can win, the others lose. If the coach emphasizes that the players played their best, then all can be winners. Therefore, reward effort as much as results, for children have complete control over how much effort they make, and only a limited control over the outcome of their efforts. Do not take efforts for granted – let the children know how much, as a coach, their efforts are appreciated and valued.

2 Use encouragement

This is an important part of the positive approach to coaching. Most children are already motivated to develop skills and play well; encouragement helps to increase their natural enthusiasm.

Encourage effort – do not demand results.

Use encouragement selectively – it has to mean something.

Be supportive.

Never give encouragement in a sarcastic or degrading manner, which irritates and frustrates players.

Be realistic, base encouragement on reasonable expectations for 8-year-olds, 12-year-olds, and so on. If expectations are impossible to reach, children may feel like failures when they cannot reach the goals which have been set for them. Encouraging effort rather than outcome can help to avoid this problem.

Encouragement can become contagious and build team unity. It communicates enthusiasm and rubs off on the team. Encourage immediately after a mistake, when the players need it most of all. Corrective instruction can be given also if handled properly, but always avoid giving corrective instruction in a hostile manner.

Motivation takes several forms. Some children try to achieve the goals because of a desire simply to succeed, so such children perform well under pressure. Others are motivated primarily by fear of failure. Such children dread critical situations because of the possibility of failure and disapproval.

3 Correct use of criticism

Players occasionally require criticism before they will improve, but it is important that their mistakes are pointed out tactfully and constructively. Rather than tell players they are doing something wrong, tell them how to do it correctly.

4 Communication

No matter how refined a coach's technical knowledge becomes, if he is unable to communicate or interact effectively with the players it will be useless. This is particularly true when dealing with children, so

1 Remember that communication is a two-way process. Keep the lines of communication open and always be aware of opportunities for having a positive impact on the players.

2 Treat the children as individuals and respond accordingly. Be aware which children have high and low self-esteem, requiring different methods of communication. Do not talk too much and be prepared to listen. How you speak is important; control your tone of voice.

5 Gaining players' respect

Respect must be earned, not demanded. Show respect for yourself, for the children, for others – parents, opponents and officials. Be credible: if you ask the players to be smart, be smart yourself.

Above all, show the children that, as a coach, you can teach them to develop their skills, and that you are willing to make the effort to do so. Be a fair and considerate leader by showing them that you care about them as individuals, and that you are glad to be coaching them.

6 Maintaining order and discipline

Coaches need to understand the behaviour of children, who are not miniature adults. Pre-adolescents and adolescents are establishing their independence and personal identity. In this way they test the limits imposed by the coaches.

Children need clearly defined limits and a positive structure. They do not like unpredictability and inconsistency. Coaches can utilize this need by creating a well-defined situation in which children can have plenty of freedom and fun within reasonable limits.

There is much evidence that children are more willing to live by rules when they have had a hand in formulating them, and they have made a public commitment to abide by them. The advantage is that if the rules are truly team rules, when someone breaks them it is not the individual versus the coach's rules, but the breaking of their own team rules. This can play an important role in building team unity.

7 Creating a good learning atmosphere

Players expect coaches to help them satisfy their desire to become as skilled as possible. Therefore coaches need to establish their role as a teacher as soon as they can and to set up a learning (rather than competitive) situation in which they can help the children to develop their abilities.

Give instruction in a positive manner, be clear, precise and, if possible, show how to do things correctly. Emphasize the good things that will happen if the children carry out a practice or skill correctly. Do not focus on the bad things that will occur if the practice or skill is not done correctly. Motivate children to make the good things happen; do not build on the fear of a mistake.

Reward effort and progress towards the desired performance; be patient, and do not expect or demand more than maximum effort.

It is important that every child is recognized at least once during each practice game; average players need attention just as much as the stars and problem children. As a coach, ask yourself how often you speak to individual children: you will discover that some get very little attention.

Give support to all players, especially if they have had a rough practice or a bad game. Do not let children leave feeling like a loser or at cross-purposes with the coach.

8   The coach and the parent

The parent can be an important ally, not only to the team but also to the club. It is often the parent who helps to transport the team, and with a little persuasion it is the enthusiastic parent who helps to buy the new kit and generally assists with the overall running of the club.

Some parents, however, by placing their children under too much pressure can have a negative effect upon them and ruin all the work the coach has done. Useful guidelines for parents are:
1   Do not force an unwilling child to take part in sport; he is not playing to satisfy your ambitions. Children and young people are involved in organized sport for their enjoyment – not yours. Emphasize enjoyment and fun.
2   Encourage your child always to play by the rules.
3   Teach your child that effort and teamwork are as important as victory, so that the result of each game is accepted without undue disappointment. Turn defeat into victory by helping your child to improve his skills and to learn a positive sporting attitude. Never ridicule or shout at your child for making a mistake or losing a competition.
4   Children learn best by example. Applaud good play by your team and by members of the opposing team. Set an example by being friendly to the parents of the opposition! Do not question publicly the officials' judgement and never their honesty, and support all efforts to remove verbal and physical abuse at all times.
5   Recognize the value and importance of coaches. They give their time and resources to provide guidance for your child.

5   THE COACHING SESSION

The aims of the junior coach should be to:
1   Develop positively the self-image of every child.
2   Develop an enthusiastic interest in the sport.
3   Develop each child's potential to the maximum.

Maximum potential

To understand this, it helps to study international performers. After all, they are at the top of the tree, and that is where we should be heading. What makes them so good?

1   **Physical**: Rugby League is a hard, exciting, collision sport; strength, speed and power are all vital ingredients, but they alone will not guarantee success. As these will develop at a later age (15 +), the junior coach should concentrate upon other aspects of each child's development.

2   **Mental**: The correct attitude will make an average player good, and a good player outstanding. Dedication, determination, and mental toughness are needed to reach maximum potential. Such attitudes develop in the young child from enjoyment, the competitive spirit, and the natural desire to do well. The coach should gently foster correct attitudes. To

set too high a standard at too young an age can do irreparable damage. Remember the key, enjoyment – and foster other qualities gently.

3   **Skill:**   Children need to master the fundamental skills of Rugby League at an early age. They should be able to run, catch, pass, tackle, evade and have the ability to perform all the other skills which make Rugby League such an exciting sport. Some educationalists will tell us that all we have to do is give children a ball and all will develop naturally. If only this were true! Incorrect habits are most difficult to unlearn, so correct technical instruction at an early age is the key to success. The teaching of technique and skill is, therefore, the major aims of the junior coach, though children often find the learning of skills boring and have difficulty concentrating for any length of time.

4   **Decision-making:**   Technique, however, is only a means to an end, and is not enough in itself. An international can perform skilfully in the international arena, despite the pressure of the occasion and the opposition. Furthermore, the international performer has developed the ability to be in the right place, doing the right things, and all at the right time. This correct selection of options, and rapid decision-making, can best be developed by practising the skills in realistic situations under the eye of a knowledgeable coach.

An understanding of the learning capacity of children at different ages will help the junior coach to draw up an ideal training programme.

Six- and seven-year-olds

Character at six

1   High physical activity, boisterous and self-centred
2   Continuously opposes then makes overtures towards parents
3   Verbally aggressive, but sensitive about being called names
4   Dawdles but impatient with others
5   Has difficulty relating to parents

6   Forms erratic friendships
7   Works and plays in spurts; does not know when to stop but tires easily.

Character at seven

1   Greater mental activity: almost brooding as compared to a six-year old
2   Less self-centred, more concerned with the reaction of others to him
3   Sensitive, often ashamed of himself
4   More polite, likes to help at home
5   Has close friendships
6   Persistent and careful with work. Better understanding of how much he can do.

Physical characteristics

1   Boys are more forceful than girls, but do not move as well
2   Can pass with correct weight transference
3   Better balance but still cannot complete complex balancing acts.

Visual perception

1   Tendency to overestimate speed of objects and movements
2   Consequent difficulty in catching moving objects. About the age of seven, children will be able to catch about two out of every five balls thrown at them when standing still.

The coaching session

1   The children: Soon become tired, cannot concentrate for long periods, tend to play on their own, and do not combine well. They have difficulty in catching balls that have been kicked.
2   Equipment: There should be as much as possible with one ball of suitable size for each player.
3   The session: The length should not exceed twenty to thirty minutes. Each specific skills practice should not last for more than five minutes.
4   Aim: Skills training particularly passing and

catching, and to assist the development of balance, agility, co-ordination, and speed.

5   The coach: Each lesson should be fun, which requires knowledge of children of this age group. The children like to invent their own rules.

Eight- and nine-year-olds

Character at eight

1   Very outgoing and curious
2   More self-conscious
3   Critical and self-evaluative, likes to compare himself with others
4   Highly critical of parents
5   Friendships within same sex most important
6   Social interests may interfere with school-work.

Character at nine

1   Outgoing, curious
2   Confident
3   Involved in personal interests
4   Still self-evaluating, but can admit mistakes without feeling threatened
5   Better relationships at home
6   Close friendships
7   Persistent and absorbed
8   Academic achievement important.

Physical characteristics

1   Develops a good deal of strength
2   Plays a lot of different games
3   Passing develops and becomes more proficient
4   Becomes much better at running.

Visual perception

1   Eight-year-olds may have difficulty in determining where a ball may land when kicked to them. They tend to react too quickly and consequently misjudge where the ball may land.
2   Nine-year-olds will perceive the difficulty of this problem. They will react more slowly and con-

sequently become more accurate in their judgements of where the ball may land.

Social development

1   Eight-year-olds form larger groups. More complex rules are understood.
2   Nine-year-olds can play six- or seven- side, and understand complex but modified rules.

The coaching session

1   The children are more energetic, concentrate for longer periods, and combine better with others. Small-sided games are now possible.
2   Equipment: there should be as much as possible, of dimensions and texture suitable to the age group.
3   The session: the length should nor exceed thirty to forty-five minutes. Specific skills should not be practised for more than seven minutes.
4   Aim: development of skills and of speed, strength, agility, and co-ordination. Children enjoy partner work, particularly pulling and pushing.
5   The coach: requires knowledge of children of this age group. It is a good idea to group the children by ability. Each lesson should be enjoyable, promoting skills acquisition.

Ten- and eleven-year-olds

Character at ten

1   Stable and at ease with the world
2   Sex differences emerging
3   More self-satisfied
4   Likes almost everyone in the family
5   Closer friendships
6   Likes organized clubs
7   Enjoys school, has responsible work habits.

Character at eleven

1   High physical activity (big appetite)
2   Intense curiosity
3   Not quite at ease with self or others

4   New doubts and tensions as adolescence approaches
5   Conflicts with adults
6   Friendships very important
7   Personal and social interests overwhelming
8   Often has difficulty in sustaining interest in school-work.

Physical characteristics

1   All basic motor skills fully developed into adult pattern
2   Can run faster than younger children
3   Boys continue to develop in strength.

Visual perception

1   Children of this age can catch a ball kicked high and over a great distance
2   Can understand the concepts of space.

The coaching session

1   The children are very energetic, enjoying team games and mixing with others. Concentration is good and they can understand the rules. Their need for personal skill intensifies and is now related to the proper game.
2   Equipment: the size and structure are reduced, but are a modification of the real thing.
3   The session: the length should not exceed forty-five to sixty minutes. Each specific skill practice should last for ten minutes.
4   Aim: the children work in small groups. Teaching of fundamental skills can become more advanced with the introduction of games awareness and decision-making.
5   The coach will observe, analyse and begin to improve performance.

Twelve- and thirteen-year-olds

Character at twelve

1   Outgoing and open; begins to realize that he is no longer a child

2   Less self-centred
3   Capable of self-criticism
4   Participates less in family activities as friends become more important
5   Difficult in school; more interested in expressing self than in working with others.

Physical characteristics

Continuing development in strength, speed, and basic skills.

Visual perception

Capable children can cope with all the skills.

The coaching session

1   The children have extensive reserves of energy, play with friends and find teams important. Maturation age is becoming obvious, leadership qualities develop as well as competitive and co-operative behaviour patterns. These children require precise rules.
2   Equipment: still use as much as possible, of modified size but closer to adult standards.
3   The session: should last for not more than sixty to ninety minutes; skills practice should not exceed ten to fifteen minutes.
4   Aim: skills training under pressure; understanding of the game and decision-making can be fully developed.
5   The coach must be aware of maturation levels, control competition to appropriate levels and develop the children's self-image.

Fourteen- and fifteen-year-olds.

The coaching session

1   The children still need emphasis on skill, games awareness and decision-making. Physical fitness now needs consideration. They are capable of playing the game, but maturation levels must not be forgotten. Tactical appreciation can be developed.

2 Equipment: by the age of fifteen, they should play with normal equipment.

3 The session: should nor last longer than sixty to eighty minutes. Each specific skills practice should last fifteen minutes.

4 Aim: skills training under pressure; fitness – particularly stamina, speed and strength linked to skill (no heavy weights until 16 +); games awareness and decision-making, with tactical understanding.

5 The coach must be aware of maturation levels, build up tactical understanding, and improve physical fitness, although that is subsidiary to development of skills.

The coaching session – an example

This is suitable for eleven- and twelve-year-old children. Variations previously explained have to be made for younger children:

1 Warm-up, five minutes
2 Small-sided game, ten minutes
3 Skills development, fifteen minutes
4 Game, twenty minutes
5 Warm-down, five minutes
6 Discussion, five minutes.

Warm-up, five minutes

1 Every coaching session should begin with activity. Running of one form or another is the first essential step, but this should not yet be explosive running, and the ball can obviously be used: even the warm-up should be specific.

2 General stretching movements should follow with particular attention being paid to the hamstrings.

3 Partner work (lifting, pulling, pushing) is strengthening, and also prepares the children for body contact.

4 If any particular muscle groups are to be worked, ensure they are thoroughly warmed up (the shoulders, for example, before tackling).

Small-sided games, ten minutes

Children enjoy being actively involved, and become bored when watching. Thus an essential part of the session is to divide the playing area into grids and to play small-sided games. One ball between six children allows each child to be around the ball for longer periods of time than one ball between twenty-six, and development will therefore be quicker. It is a good idea to set special rules, perhaps emphasizing a point brought out in the previous session, but all small-sided games should be closely related to Rugby League.

The coach should be actively involved in improving performance. But the golden rule must be remembered, 'Children can learn by listening, learn more by watching, but most of all by doing.' Do not talk for too long, and encourage the development of correct habits.

Skills development, fifteen minutes

When introducing a new skill establish a pattern of organization so that the children are immediately aware that they are in a learning situation.

1 Organization: ask them to come in from the games and form a semi-circle round you. Any distractions should be behind them. Make eye contact, be enthusiastic, demand their full attention.

2 Introduction: introduce the skill in simple, clear language. Explain why the skill is important.

3 Demonstration.

It is necessary for the children to have a visual picture of the skill. Demonstrate it perfectly. If a member of the group can perform the skill perfectly, by all means let him demonstrate. The use of a very short video at the beginning of the session can also be of value, but to take the group inside at this stage would be time-consuming. During the demonstration use key points and ensure that all the children have a clear picture of the complete movement. If necessary, demonstrate from different angles and for left handers as well as right if appropriate. Do not talk too much:

Demonstrate perfectly
Use key points
Be thorough but brief.

4   Group practice: allow the group to practise the skill immediately after the demonstration while the vision is fresh in their minds. Create an atmosphere of hard work in which the children want to learn, and are not stifled by fear of making mistakes. Give them a feeling of success. Most of them should be able to perform the skill success-fully; if not it should have been broken down and introduced in a more simple form.

Once the class is working, stand well back and observe:

Is the group well organized?
Are they working correctly?
Are they repeating mistakes?

5   Correction of faults: stand back and observe the group working, remembering the key points of the skill. Analyse the reasons for errors. Decide on a correction procedure. Do not tell them they are doing it wrong, be positive and tell them how to improve. If necessary, stop any group and bring them in once again. Do not single out any one player. Correct faults positively. Demonstrate again if need be.
6   Group practice: improvement is a slow process; be patient, allow them to practise once more, do not talk too much. Observe and analyse, correct-ing individually. Be prepared to progress gradu-ally, advancing fundamental technique towards a game situation. Increase pressure gradually.

The game, twenty minutes

In an ideal situation, each session should include a game. Be certain that the game is constructive, encouraging the development of skill and the forma-tion of correct habits. The game must be enjoyable, but should enhance previous coaching, not destroy it. It is often advisable to condition the game in such a way that the children are encouraged and rewarded for performing the skill previously coached. Although Rugby League is played by teams of 13 players, and that must be the eventual aim, do not underestimate the value of games with fewer players.

During the game, the coach should still be actively involved in coaching.

Warm-down, five minutes

At the end of each session, allow the children to warm down in order that their body gradually returns to a normal state. This prevents stiffness, reduces tired-ness, and makes the individual better able to perform the next day.

Discussion, five minutes

At the end of each session it is often a good idea to talk to the squad for a few minutes (not too long), evaluating the work that has been done. The children may be praised as a group for their efforts and important points of the session re-emphasized.

Progression

There are many skills that the majority of children will be able to learn by the simple process of observation and practice. The coach must ensure that the demonstration is both clear and precise, and then perform the important duties of observation, analysis and correction during the practice.

Other skills will be too complex for this process to be entirely successful, and this may mean breaking a skill down. Once introduced, gradually progress until the skill can be performed in its entirety against opposition. This process can take weeks to develop.

For instance, when introducing passing and han-dling, a coach may have to follow this pattern:

1   Standing passing
2   Walking passing
3   Jogging passing
4   Running passing
5   Sprinting passing.

When the children can fully master the techniques of passing, the pressure of match conditions should be introduced gradually. It should always be remem-bered that the nature of Rugby League means that the skilful child has to perform techniques under the intense pressure of hard, physical contact. The next progression would be:

6 Sprinting and passing, attacking cones
7 Sprinting and passing, attacking stationary
   defenders
8 Sprinting and passing, attacking conditioned
   moving defenders
9 Match conditions.

In this way the build-up of pressure is both
gradual and logical, with high chances of success. It is
unreasonable to expect children to be able to progress
from stage 5 directly to match conditions with any
degree of success. The coach must realize that skills
are a means to an end, rather than an end in
themselves, and that games have to be played in
which the children are encouraged to use their skills.

Small-sided games in which pressure is controlled
are ideal stepping-stones to the 13-a-side game and
play a vital part in the child's development. Not only
do they have to use the skills, but also think and make
decisions on which skills to use: to pass, evade, or
kick; and how to use them: direction, angle, and
timing of run. The coach must encourage and guide
their thinking in these conditioned games, which
should be similar to the 13-a-side game.

Organizing and planning the season

At the beginning of each season, it is important to
write down the year's aims. Remember that each
season attracts different children and what worked
last season may not necessarily work this.

Write down the targets as general statements
which can be measured as the season progresses.
Break down how to teach those targets step by step –
the skills to be taught, and so on. List the skills and
constantly evaluate your progress. Make sure that
these skills are suitable for the age, maturation levels,
strength, co-ordination and previous experience of
the children.

Once the skills to be taught have been identified,
organize your method of instruction. Estimate how
much time it will take a child to learn, then practise a
specific skill. Schedule the season accordingly. Remember that an acceptable ratio of coaches to children is 1:10. Ensure that the skills are taught in a
logical sequence. Teach fundamentals first, and then
develop to more specialized skills. Be flexible in your
schedule.

Some children will be ready to progress before
others. Those that are not ready require the skills to
be broken down. The pattern of development of
learning is similar, but progression is varied. Always
consider streaming the abilities within the coaching
session. Because some children will learn quickly,
plan to teach a little more than you think.

Remember the practice time available to you and
understand that all the skills do not have to be taught
in one year. Some skills will need to be developed
through many sessions, and for them to become a
habit the children need to practise them constantly.
Understand that it is far better for children to learn a
few skills thoroughly than to be briefly introduced to
many, only to master none.

The learning process is also dependent upon
facilities and equipment. The latter is more easily
controlled and coaches should constantly attempt to
improve their resources. Clubs should consider
spending more money on equipment, and less on
trophies.

Coaching the youth player

1   MAJOR CONSIDERATIONS

The aim of the youth coach

The youth coach provides the vital link between the junior coach and senior coach, and so has an important role to play both in the development of the individual and in raising the playing standards of the game.

The youth coach should be fully aware of the work of the junior coach, to help him understand the previous development of his charges, and similarly be acquainted with the expectations of the senior coach because that is where they are heading. His major responsibility, therefore, is to the individual. His duty is to observe and analyse each of them, and to embark on a coaching programme aimed at developing the maximum potential of each.

The characteristics of the players

1   Communication. The players at this level (16+) are often physically mature but still unsure of themselves and their standing in the world. They are ready to find out, and can be inquisitive, aggressive, yet self-conscious and easily offended. Because of this they are often trying and frustrating to handle, so it is important that the coach should be able to communicate well.

2   Maturity. Though the majority in this age group (16+) will have matured physically, the late developers are still catching up. They are eager to prove their maturity and to adopt adult habits. Often they use trial and error, but they require firm advice and guidance, particularly as they are establishing habits which will determine their future lifestyle.

Players with ambitions in the game should

never smoke
drink alcohol only in moderation – or even better not at all
adopt correct eating habits
get enough sleep, particularly when involved in an intensive training programme.

The role of the coach cannot be exaggerated. In many cases he has an even greater influence than the parents.

3   Mental skills. It is important to develop each player's   confidence,   relaxation,   concentration, visualization, and ability to overcome anxiety.

4 Physical conditioning.   The growing process has been replaced by the need for physical development. A well-balanced physical conditioning programme is now essential.

5 Success.   Many youngsters are ready to play the game seriously. For some, success replaces enjoyment as the major driving force.

6 Social skills.   The youngsters are developing social skills. Personal discipline, comradeship, loyalty, understanding of others, the ability to be able to handle success and failure, and many similar social skills can be developed through the game.

2 THE ROLE OF THE YOUTH COACH

1 The individual and the team.   The success of the team is important to the players, who themselves now require intensive coaching in all the varied and complex team skills. Team preparation should therefore consume a greater percentage of training time. The youth coach must realise, however, that his major responsibility is to develop the maximum potential of each player.

2 Respect.   The majority of children will obey the coach for no other reason than that he is an adult and in charge. Youths are more discerning and the youth coach has to earn respect. Young men of this age respond to those who have time for them, are helpful and considerate, knowledgeable, patient and understanding. They also welcome discussion and have more respect for the coach who listens to their ideas than the one who merely instructs.

Youngsters tend to imitate and this gives the coach added responsibility. On the pitch, the players will copy his skills and the way he plays the game. Off the pitch, they will imitate his language, attitude and other social skills.

3 Enjoyment.   Being a member of the club and the team should be an enjoyable experience. Each player should be welcomed and made to feel at home. Team spirit and club spirit should be carefully nurtured and in this environment, club discipline and general attitude should be cultivated. All officials should be wary of making too much of the star performer, particularly at the expense of other members of the club.

4 Assessment.   A necessary and often difficult duty of the coach is to assess performance and predict development. Care must be taken not to make too stringent demands on those youngsters who have neither the ability nor desire to make it to the top, otherwise they may give up the game.

It is equally important that those with potential should be encouraged, advised and cajoled into extra effort. This applies particularly to physical preparation. All the players aiming for the top should be placed on individual training programmes as described in Section 6.

5 Skill.   All players, whatever their abilities and ambitions, need to perfect the game's fundamental skills. The majority of the players will have had extensive skills-coaching in the junior teams, but their education is incomplete. The coach should have a check list of his players with various skills at the side, and should tick off those that each can perform. In this way, he will be able to identify skills that each player still has to develop. Some players will need to spend a great deal of time on this aspect of their development; others will have mastered most but will need to concentrate on others. And it is necessary to emphasize again that all players need continuous skills revision to help them perform quickly in pressure situations.

The skills check-list used for the first month's work at the BARLA Under-19 centres of excellence in the summer of 1987 is set out on the opposite page.

6 Encourage players to think and make correct decisions.   Because teams are now playing in a more intense competition, there is a danger that some players will be discouraged from using their skills and will be turned into defensive machines or battering rams. This should never happen.

Name ....

SKILLS ASSESSMENT

	Tick/Cross	Comments
Passing		
To Right	☐	
To Left	☐	
Short Pass	☐	
Long Right	☐	
Long Left	☐	
From Ground	☐	
2 v. 1	☐	
3 v. 2 (middle)	☐	
3 v. 2 (end)	☐	
Run Around	☐	
Drop Off	☐	
Switches	☐	
Loop	☐	
Running		
Determination	☐	
Straight	☐	
Arc	☐	
Timing	☐	
Support	☐	
Play the Ball		
Technique	☐	
Duties:	☐	
Dummy Half	☐	
First/Second Receiver	☐	
Support	☐	
Decision-making		
Control	☐	
Support	☐	
Switches of Play	☐	
Reaction Time	☐	
Vision	☐	

7   Tactics and team organization.   Just as the junior coach concentrated on developing basic skills, the youth coach should concentrate on an understanding of team organization and tactics. Most of the players, by a process of trial and error accompanied by advice from the coach, will have already decided in which position to play. The youth coach will develop their understanding of the requirements of this position in the overall team strategy. They will be encouraged to combine with others, to think and to make the correct decisions.

The four major principles of play – control, support, defence and kicking – should be given priority.

8   Physical conditioning.   Physical conditioning is a major priority, so the coach should have a thorough understanding of the physical requirements of the game, and of ways to increase his players' fitness levels.

Assessment of his squad is important. Those with ability to progress towards the top require a specialist programme to develop stamina, suppleness, strength and speed. At the age of sixteen they should be placed on an individual programme involving sessions on non-club training days, with emphasis on strength acquisition during the close season. Others need to develop adequate fitness levels so they can enjoy this physically demanding contact sport.

9   Attitude.   The club, particularly the coach, has a duty to develop correct attitudes to both life and the game (see Section 1, Chapter 1).

Coaching the senior player

1   The aims of the coach
2   Organization of the senior coaching programme
3   The annual coaching programme
4   A typical week

1   THE AIMS OF THE COACH

Producing a winning team

A survey of the top 100 graded players in Sydney, New South Wales, in the issue of *Rugby League Week* of 21 May 1986, gave the following statistics in answer to the question: 'How many hours would you train for Rugby League each week?'

less than 8	8–10	10–12	12–15	15–18	more than 18
6%	6%	32%	40%	9%	7%

The majority of players in Sydney have other occupations outside Rugby League, so the clubs' training programmes are restricted to three sessions each week just as they are in Britain. It is obvious from the survey that most of them do additional training on their own.

Similar standards need to be established in Britain, certainly by all professionals but also by BARLA's more ambitious youth and senior players. This chapter is devoted to these top levels of senior rugby, and makes the following assumptions:

1   The players take responsibility for their own physical conditioning and train on non-club-training days

2   The additional training is monitored and controlled by the club coach

3   The players train or play on average six days a week for fifty weeks a year.

This sort of schedule, with only one rest day a week and allowing only two weeks holiday a year, demands absolute commitment to the game and an absolute determination to improve every facet of performance.

The aim of the senior coach is to produce a winning team. Once appointed he should be given the full support of the club and adequate time for any changes to become effective. He should concentrate on obtaining the best from each player, blending the players into a unit, and improving (a) the team and (b) the individual players in the team.

1   **Obtaining the best from each player.**   'The

players would not play for him,' is a statement often made about a departing coach who perhaps has lost the confidence of his players and the ability to motivate them.

Obtaining the best match-day performance from each of his players is certainly the coach's first aim. He must understand the importance of:

a) Communication. The coach should try to create a positive relationship with each of his players. The players will respond to his interest in them and the coach will be made aware of any personal problems which may be affecting any of them.

b) Respect. The coach should earn the respect of the players. It is often an advantage if he has been an outstanding player himself, but essentially he should be respected because of his abilities as a coach, and for his character as a man. Fairness, honesty, diligence, enthusiasm, consistency, humour and compassion are qualities to which the players will respond.

c) Motivation. This is an essential coaching skill based on an appreciation of each player's determination and self-confidence. It is fully discussed both in Chapter 2 of Section 7, and in the appendix.

2   Blending the players into a unit. Once the players have been motivated to produce their best, the coach has to blend them into a cohesive unit. Team spirit, organization, a game plan and discipline are the four most important factors.

a) Team spirit. The coach must try to produce a happy, united club atmosphere, hungry for success. This will be influenced by good facilities, helpful club officials, and feelings of trust and unity.

The playing staff should be treated in the best way possible and made to feel important. Medical facilities, equipment, kit, pitch and training areas, changing-rooms, showers and bath facilities, clubhouse, travel arrangements, and so on should be seen to be the best available.

Club officials should be respected by the playing staff, but it is equally important for them to respect the players. Particular care should be taken in the timing of any criticism of a player's performance. Unity between players and coach is strengthened if the coach refrains from criticizing the players in public, particularly in the press. It is far better for him to do this man-to-man. Similarly, players demoted to substitute or the reserves should be told directly by the man who has made the decision.

The coach should be slightly distant from the players, but always approachable. A too-close relationship can be as detrimental as aloofness – a middle way is needed. Coaches with strong forceful characters should be wary of dominating the players; instead they must try to develop each player's ego and self-confidence.

There is nothing so detrimental to team spirit as a squad divided into small groups, particularly if one is critical of the other. The coach must make sure that this does not occur. Unity among the players is promoted by regular team meetings, particularly if the players are encouraged to air all criticisms at the meetings and nowhere else. These meetings, in addition to individual player discussions, give the coach the opportunity to foster team spirit.

b) Team organization. Success will be elusive unless the coach blends the team into a cohesive unit, gives it organization, and develops a pattern of play. To do this he must analyse the strengths of his playing staff and organize a pattern of play which makes best use of those strengths. Organization with the ball in each quarter of the field should be considered, so too when attacking close to a play-the-ball, midfield, blind and on the far side of the pitch. Each player should be fully aware of his duties in each attack, and those not being used directly should be encouraged to adopt positions of support. Moves from tap-plays, scrums, and set pieces should be included in the general organization. Similarly, the organization when defending, kicking and receiving kicks should be made clear to all.

c) Game plan. The overall success rate will be improved if teams capable of playing to instructions have a game plan which has been devised after a careful study of the opposition's play. The game plan should make full use of the team's strengths, while trying to exploit the weaknesses of the opposition.

d) Discipline. Rugby League is one of the hardest and most demanding of team sports, requiring sacrifices of both time and effort in preparation, and the ability to compete in conditions of severe pressure. Only those with high levels of personal discipline have any hope of realizing their potential. It is the coach's duty to establish these levels and to insist that the players meet them.

3 Improvement. Once the coach is satisfied that players are performing to the best of their ability, and he has blended them into a unit, he must try to improve their performance. Obviously those coaching professional teams may enter the transfer market to buy and sell players. The skill of buying and selling is important, but is a quality of management. Coaching involves the improvement, not replacement, of individual players.

a) Team improvement. The coach should never stop learning. It is essential that he continue to analyse, modify, improve and update his team preparation. During his time in control, he will quite naturally progress and gradually be able to extend his team's ability. He should also be open minded, aware, and hungry for personal improvement. He may be able to learn from rivals, from those in another country, or even from another sport. Above all he should always be ready to update and extend his own innovations.

b) Individual improvement. The personal qualities needed for success in Rugby League are attitude, mental toughness, physical conditioning, skill, awareness, decision-making and tactical knowledge. By observation, analysis and correction the coach must try to improve each of these quantities in all his players.

This is the most demanding and time-consuming of all his responsibilities, and those who find it too difficult can never really answer to the title of coach.

2 ORGANIZATION OF THE SENIOR COACHING PROGRAMME

The emphasis in this chapter is on the well-organized professional club, and senior coaches at other levels may have to modify the methods to suit their particular situations.

Physical conditioning. The last chapter established the principle that ambitious players should take a greater responsibility towards physical conditioning and train most days of the year. Full details are contained in Section 6.

Training diaries. Players need advice, and the coach should motivate and monitor their progress. Individual training diaries, periodically checked, enable him constantly to update their training (see Section 6, Chapter 7).

Coaching diary. The coach should himself keep a diary – a simple record – of every training session. This has the following advantages:

1 Innovation. The coach has more knowledge of his team and their abilities than anyone else, and will occasionally have a brilliant idea in training. A record prevents these ideas being forgotten.

2 Fewer mistakes. A coach will make mistakes and a record will reduce the chance of them being repeated.

3 Variety. Training often becomes repetitive, particularly in mid-season. A coach who is able to read through previous seasons' coaching diaries has more chance of maintaining variety.

Video, and match statistics. Clubs should video-record all games and compile statistics to assist the coach to improve team and individual performance (see Section 7, Chapter 2).

Team meetings. Regular meetings (to discuss the previous game) between the coach and his playing staff help to clarify thoughts and identify correction procedures. If, in these meetings, the players are encouraged to make a positive input, understanding between the coach and the players will improve and so too will team spirit.

Medical. The medical staff make an important contribution to team morale. They should be made to feel part of the team, and encouraged to log all injuries and treatment. An additional duty could be to assist in the testing and measurement of the players' physical conditioning.

3   THE ANNUAL COACHING PROGRAMME

The suggested annual coaching programme should be run in conjunction with the annual conditioning programme (see Section 6, Chapter 7).

April – May: the end of season

Summary of conditioning

1   Clubs involved in important end-of-season games will organize training in an attempt to reach peak performance.
2   Others may slightly intensify endurance levels.
3   Before the end of the season, all players should be weighed.
4   The club should have individual fitness records for all the players, completed during the new year. These levels should be improved during the close season.

The coach should

1   Plan the close season's physical conditioning programme, providing each player with a training diary. In fact, it may be an advantage for the conditioning programme to be planned by someone other than the head coach, particularly if the club is involved in important and hectic end-of-season fixtures.
2   Explain to the players the importance of the conditioning programme, and motivate them into action.
3   Analyse the season, writing down major points

which will form the basis for next season's plan of action.

End of May: off season

Training at the club stops, but it is important for the players to maintain levels of fitness.

The coach

Rests and recharges his batteries.

The players

1   *Diet*: those who have not been placed on a specialized diet should take care not to increase weight.
2   *Aerobic endurance*: should increase fitness levels by completing three long runs each week.
3   *Muscular endurance*: should increase levels and prepare a foundation for strength training; two sessions per week.

Players with high levels of endurance can immediately progress to a heavy strength-training programme.

June – mid-July: conditioning foundation period

Although formal club training has yet to start, this period is the most important in the players' annual physical preparation. Players who work hard will attain levels of fitness out of reach of those who do not.

The coach

1   Rest period continues.
2   Mid-July: the plan for next season should be finalized. Reference is made to the previous year's coaching diary and the notes completed at the end of the season.
3   Players' profiles are reconsidered and individual faults identified to be improved during the skills foundation period.

The players

1 The players have a mental break; training takes place away from the club.
2 Emphasis is placed on strength, stamina, and suppleness.
3 A record of all training is kept in training diaries.

Mid-July – mid-August: skills foundation period

Organized club training begins. The players are tested so that the physical improvement made during the conditioning foundation period is known.

Players continue to train on non-club training days.

The coach

1 First priority: individual player improvement, particularly in skills (see Section 2), games awareness and decision-making (see Section 3) and tactical appreciation (see Section 7).
2 Second priority: improvements of the four principles of play (see Section 5) – control of the ball, defence, support play, tactical kicking.
3 Conditioning programme is maintained: training diaries are checked, and from the results of the physical tests each player's individual conditioning programme is modified.

   Interval training, muscular endurance, and speed are incorporated into the club session, and made specific to the game wherever possible, for example, defence circuits, interval runs, passing a ball, and so on.

The players

1 Strength acquisition and aerobic endurance levels are improved on non-training days, with emphasis on
Suppleness
Strength
Stamina
Speed
2 Individual fitness tests are completed during the first few club training sessions.

Mid-August – late August: pre-season

The coach

1 First priority: to develop the team's tactical ability, particularly planned moves, and patterns of play
2 Second priority: to revise strategy and individual skills
3 Conditioning: to monitor each player's progress with emphasis on speed.

The players

1 Players continue to train on non-club training days.
2 Strength training is reduced by half to three sessions in two weeks.
3 Major emphasis: speed.
4 Levels maintained: suppleness
                              stamina
                              strength.
5 Final pre-season conditioning tests completed before team selection for the first game.

September – May: the season

The season's training will be subdivided according to cup and other important fixtures, the performance of the team, and so on.

The coach

Major priority is to achieve a winning team. Important considerations are:

Obtaining the best from each player
Blending the players into a unit
Improvement of the team and players.

The players

1 High levels of fitness maintained; continue to train on non-club training days.
2 Training diaries checked, with periodic fitness testing at the club.

4   A TYPICAL WEEK

Sunday: match day

1   The game is videoed
2   Statistics are compiled
3   Injuries: all injuries are reported to the medical staff; the badly injured are taken to hospital. Treatment begins immediately with ice available in the dressing-room.

Monday: non-club training

The coach prepares

1   Video analysis of the game
2   A detailed report on team and individual performances

The analysis is made from video evidence, statistics and observations throughout the game (see Section 7, Chapter 2).

3   The week's coaching programme is considered
4   Receives a report on next week's opponents

The players

1   Those injured report to the club
2   All others complete a long run away from the club in home environment.

Medical staff

Treat the injured at the club.

Tuesday: club training

6.00   *Coaching staff meeting*: discussion of game; coaching programme for the week is finalized.
6.30   *Players report.*
6.45   *Team meeting*: all players attend, including those unfit to train, for a discussion of the game, analysis of team performance, and analysis of individual performance.
    The video is available, with action marked with numbers to guarantee immediate viewing.
7.15   *Practical training.*

Objectives: physical – anaerobic endurance at speed;
tactical – support play and improved communication.
Organization: all teams together in groups of six.

7.20   *Warm-up.*
1   Angled runs at 60% effort (see page 66)
2   Flexibility (see Section 6, Chapter 3)
3   Single file at 90% effort (see page 54)

7.40   *Speed, support and communication.*
1   Following the ball and moving it wide:

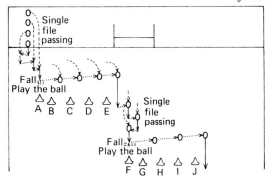

Diagram 2

Start at in-goal with single-file passing to the half-way line; all players must handle the ball. Player reaching cone A falls down, quickly regains his feet and plays the ball. The ball is moved across field wide of cone E with quick passing; all players must handle.
Immediately, when wide of the cones, players revert to single-file passing; all players handle the ball before the next line of cones. Player reaching cone F falls down, quickly regains his feet and plays the ball. The ball is moved across the field wide of cone J with all players handling quickly to the end man who bursts on to the ball and scores (as in diagram 2).

Every player handles the ball on four occasions.

Each group is timed, and competition introduced with four runs per group.

2   Follow-the-ball intervals:
A group moves into the centre of the pitch and forms a circle, interpassing. On a command the

player with the ball sprints towards either goal-line or touch-line. The rest follow, catch up, and call for the ball. The ball carrier, maintaining maximum speed, passes to the support. The player receiving the pass changes the direction of his run while the rest support.

The group runs continuously for thirty seconds.

3   Organization:
Each group makes four thirty-second runs at maximum speed; then rests between runs for two and a half minutes.

8.15 *Supporting the ball in the tackle*
   1 Hitting the defensive line and keeping the ball alive   (see page 200)
   2 Corridor football   (see page 201)

8.40 *Defence: line and hits*
   Pairs: shield practice.   (see page 189)

8.50 *Training ends*

9.00 *Coaches – team selection*

Wednesday: non-club training

The coach

1   Has a night free of rugby; or
2   Studies video of week-end's opposition; or
3   Runs a coaching clinic for individuals or groups of players.

The players

Flexibility work, and
heavy-weights programme.

Thursday: club training

6.30 *Players report*
6.45 *Team meeting*:
   1 Teams for week-end announced.
   2 Each squad with its own coach.
   3 Discussion on week-end's game plan.
   4 Players talk through the moves to be used.
7.10 *Practical Training*
   Objectives
   Physical: speed
   Tactical: improvement of kicking game and

   revision of team organization
   Organization: each team with own coach.
7.15 *Warm-up and defence*
   1 Defensive line (see page 188)
   2 Defensive line and drift (see page 189)
   3 Flexibility exercises (see Section 6, Chapter 3).
7.45 *Speed training*
   1 Bounding (see page 252)
   2 Sprinting with full recovery: 3×30 metres, 3×60, 2×80, 2×100, and 1×150.
8.05 *Kicking game*
   Revision and improvement of the kicking game, particularly on controlling the area in which the game is played (see Section 5, Chapter 4); performed as a semi-opposed practice.
8.25–8.45 *Unopposed*
   The team goes through the tactics to be used in the coming game in an unopposed drill. They cover:
   1 Team moves
   2 Offence: combination of six plays from kick-off returns (sticks, 22, half-way)
       scrums
       taps
       turnovers
       opposition's handling errors
   3 Defence as above
   4 Offence and defence in each quarter of the field.
8.45 *Training ends.*

Friday: rest day

Saturday

8.45 *Players report*
9.00 *Warm-up and flexibility*
9.20 *Unopposed and conditioned opposition*: an extension of the training which concluded Thursday's session with squad members providing conditioned opposition
10.00 *Training ends.*

Coaching the less ambitious

1   COACHING THE LESS AMBITIOUS

Many amateur Rugby League teams are professional in both organization and preparation, and will be more than capable of adopting the methods previously discussed.

Others do not aim quite so high and are motivated by sheer enjoyment, accepting that they have neither the talents nor the ambition to reach the top. Coaches at these levels must adopt different approaches. These are suggested guidelines:

1   Enjoyment

Make the training enjoyable. All the players are involved because they enjoy playing Rugby League, otherwise they would not be there. Use this enjoyment by making most of the training game-related.

2   Physical conditioning

Rugby League is a physically demanding sport which involves physical preparation. It is unacceptable, even dangerous, to play the game to keep fit; players must be fit before they play the game. The essential ingredients are:

Suppleness

A warm-up and flexibility programme should precede all training.

Stamina

a) Aerobic endurance: encourage all players to complete every week at least one twenty-minute run in their own time on non-club training nights.
b) Anaerobic endurance: one interval-training session each week at the club. Make the runs game-related: use the ball, emphasizing technique, support play and so on; introduce competition.
c) Muscular endurance: encourage the players, particularly the front row, to do a home circuit each week. This involves no more than fifteen minutes' commitment. If this is beyond them, include some exercises in the club programme. Make circuits game-related. Use shields, tackle bags,

inner tubes wherever possible. Ensure that the three major muscle groups – upper body, stomach and legs – are exercised (see Section 6, Chapter 4).

Skill

Make the club training game-related.

Strength and speed will improve performance but are not essential requirements.

3   Organization and planning

Ensure that time is not wasted because the clubhouse has not been opened, equipment is not available, balls have not been blown up, the training programme not decided, and so on. Plan each session carefully.

4   Competition

All Rugby League players are competitive, and respond to challenges. Introduce competition into training. Have the players competing with themselves, one another, and in groups.

5   Discipline

This is important at every club, whatever the sport, whatever the standard. Introduce rules which are necessary and fair. The players may help in establishing them.

6   Relationships

Create a relationship with each individual. Be pleasant, approachable and helpful.

7   Facilities

Make every attempt to improve the club and training conditions.

A world-class player, such as Ellery Hanley (Wigan and Great Britain), needs to have all-round attributes: speed, stamina, strength, courage, determination, discipline, tactical knowledge and the ability to make the correct decisions under intense pressure on the field. But all this is of little account if the player has not complete mastery of the game's basic skills.

Section 2

THE BASIC SKILLS

INTRODUCTION

Players of all age groups and abilities require to practise regularly the various skills of the game. Coaches should have a check-list of teaching points for all such skills, which they can refer to when there is a breakdown in performance.

Coaching juniors

Skills training will provide the backbone of each coaching session, but consideration must be given to the age of the children and their maximum attention span (see pages 22–26.)

Coaching youth and open-age players

Although priorities have changed, skills coaching should still play a very important part in the coaching programme. Each player should be assessed, those skills identified which need attention, and specialist coaching given. It is important also for all players to receive continuous skills revision to help them perform quickly in pressure situations.

Young children learning the game need to be encouraged to run forward with the ball.

Running with the ball

Though the player who carries the ball too far when a pass would be more appropriate, is a problem in senior rugby, young children learning the game need to be encouraged to run forward with the ball. Many are reluctant to run at the opposition and tend to throw the ball away rather than be tackled. Others become disheartened with the problems of passing and playing within the confines of the laws of the game. They can quickly become confused and lose their initial enthusiasm, which must be nurtured. It is often a good idea to organize a game in the first training session. Encourage beginners to have fun, and to run with the ball.

The first game of Rugby League football

Do not explain too many rules, and keep the game simple. Children should spend as much time playing and as little time listening as possible.

Quickly explain to them that the idea is to run forward carrying the ball and to place it over the goal-line. The opposition at this stage have to stop them by tigging them below the level of the shorts with both hands. If possible, work in grids with small groups of no more than five-a-side. The coach stands in the middle of the two teams and throws the ball to one of the players, who then sets off running and tries to score. If he is tigged by the opposition the ball is returned to the coach who then throws it to a member of the opposing team. Eventually the ball should be thrown to each child and if any has difficulty in catching it, the ball should be handed to him. The aim is to encourage the children to run with the ball and to give them an early opportunity of scoring a try.

Coaching points

1 Run with the ball
2 Hold the ball firmly
3 Run straight (i.e. attack the goal-line and not the touchline)
4 Run with determination.

At this stage it does not matter whether the ball is held in two hands or one, as long as it is held firmly. Praise is of paramount importance, and in the early sessions the coach should strongly encourage and praise all his group. He should also try to manipulate

7 Joe Lydon (Wigan and Great Britain) sprints seventy metres to score a great try against Australia in the first Test at Old Trafford in 1986. Henderson Gill (Wigan and Great Britain) is in support.

8 A child who goes home after his first coaching session to tell his parents that he has scored a try may well become an enthusiast for life.

the game so that all the children experience success. If possible, he should create situations in which each scores a try. A child who goes home after his first coaching session and tells his parents that he has not only played Rugby League, but has scored a try, will be eagerly awaiting his next game.

However, do not spend too long on this game; simply whet the appetite and use it at the beginning and end of early coaching sessions. It is important that children learning the game do not become bored by too many skills practices. Most of the time at the rugby club should be spent playing enjoyable small-sided games with only around fifteen minutes each session devoted to skills practice.

Catching and passing

Children need to become adept at the techniques of passing and handling very early in their development. Rugby League is basically a handling game. All players, whatever their eventual playing position, need to become proficient at the techniques of catching and passing before developing ball sense, games awareness and timing.

The coach should be aware that many right-handed people experience difficulty passing to the right, and left-handers to the left. It is often a good idea to introduce a skill or drill through passing to the left which the majority of players will find easier, but then to progress and concentrate on the more difficult pass to the right. It is essential for all players to master fully the technique of passing well in both directions.

Work on the techniques of catching and passing should be included in every coaching session, whatever the age or ability of the group. Perfecting the skills is an on-going task; progression and revision are most important to its development.

1   HOLDING THE BALL

Coaching points

1   A cradle is made with the hands, fingers outspread under the ball with the palms facing inwards. The thumbs are placed on the upper part of the ball to hold it in position.

2   Arms should be relaxed with elbows slightly bent and close to the side.

Practices

1   The player stands with the ball cradled in both hands, with fingers splayed underneath and thumbs on either side. The player should move and rotate the ball with his wrists whilst the coach checks the position and indicates the need for relaxed, bent arms and loose supple wrists.

2   It is important for players to develop a 'feel' for the ball so that eventually they are able to perform more advanced handling skills.

9 & 10   A young player stands with the ball cradled in both hands, with fingers splayed underneath and thumbs on either side. It is important for young players to develop a 'feel' for the ball as a preparation for more advanced handling skills.

Young players using a ball of the correct size will enjoy practising:

1 Throwing the ball into the air and catching it
2 Moving the ball from one hand to the other
3 Moving the ball around the upper body
4 Moving the ball around one leg and then the other.

Similar drills can be devised all of which will encourage youngsters to play on their own with a rugby ball.

2   PASSING THE BALL

Coaching points

1 Hold the ball correctly
2 Keep eyes on the target – in advance of the receiver and between his lower chest and waist (the bread-basket)
3 The trunk should be twisted at the hips so that the shoulders are square to the receiver
4 The arms take the ball well back at the side of the hips
5 The ball is aimed at the target (bread-basket) in front of the receiver
6 The ball is passed with a straight trajectory, and not lobbed
7 The distance in front depends on the speed of the receiver
8 The ball is directed by the fingers and wrists
9 There is a follow-through with the arms so that finally they are fully extended towards the receiver with fingers pointing at the target.

It is most important, even at the first coaching session, for players to practise passing to both left and right.

11   Harry Pinner (Leigh, formerly St Helens, and Great Britain) shows how the ball should be held.

3   CATCHING THE BALL

Coaching points

1   Keep eyes on the ball, all the way from the passer's hands
2   Prepare to receive the ball with arms and fingers extended
3   Twist the trunk to face the passer
4   Use both hands whenever possible
5   Bring the ball into the bread-basket to make sure of possession, but then hold it in the hands ready to pass: do not cuddle it
6   Be prepared to adjust the position of the body to receive a badly directed pass
7   Be prepared for an unexpected pass as this is often the one that leads to a try
8   Concentration is important
9   Do not slacken speed when catching the ball.

Practices

1   Stationary passing in pairs

In pairs, the players should pass to one another. Vary the distances they are apart, ensuring that all passes are weighted correctly and that the trajectory of each pass is flat.

2   Stationary passing in fours

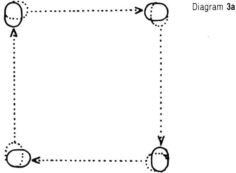

Diagram **3a**

Place the players in groups of four in small squares within easy passing distance, facing inwards. Encourage them to pass around the square, first to the left and then to the right, bringing out the previously mentioned teaching points (see diagram 3a).

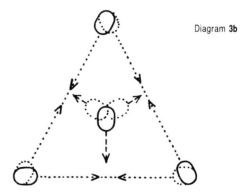

Diagram **3b**

Pressure and fun may be introduced by making the practices competitive, each group trying to make the most number of passes (a) before dropping the ball, and (b) in a given time.

3   Three against one

Progress by bringing one of the group into the middle to try to intercept the passes. The other three now have to combine and may move within the limits of a confined space to make as many successful passes as possible (see diagram 3b).

The major teaching point is to keep possession. It should be instilled in players at an early age that if there is any doubt about making a successful pass, they should keep hold of the ball and wait for support. With absolute beginners it may be necessary to have four or even five players interpassing against one opponent. As they become more successful the numbers can be reduced.

4   Four against four

Increase the pressure and the enjoyment by introducing a competitive game: combine the groups and play four against four in grids, with no body contact allowed. All the players can move except the one holding the ball. The aim is for the team in possession to make as many passes as possible, and at this stage they can pass in any direction.

Coaching points

1   Maintain possession
2   Give an accurate pass
3   Support the ball
4   Call for the ball when in an open space
5   If in doubt – keep hold of the ball.

4   PASSING BACKWARDS

The players are now ready to be introduced to the major rule of Rugby League: *the ball must not be passed forward.*

Warm-up activities should encourage the players to handle the ball rather than kick it. Organize them in pairs and encourage them upon arriving at each coaching session to lap the pitch, passing the ball. Teach them always to pass correctly, which now means passing backwards.

Practices

Line out the players in groups of four within comfortable passing distance and facing up the pitch. Each player should be wide of, and behind, whomsoever is to pass to him. Pass accurately along the line.

When the ball has been passed all along the line the players should turn about so that the ball is passed in the opposite direction, as in diagram 4, ensuring that each pass is made backwards.

It is important, at all times, to stress mobility at the waist. Below the waist the legs and feet should be pointing directly down field. Above the waist the body moves to face the passer, presenting him with the fullest target area of bread-basket and chest. On receiving the ball, the upper body turns to face the receiver. The head, and particularly the eyes, should lead the movement; at this stage it is not advisable to catch and pass without first making a visual check.

Progress this practice to:

walking
jogging, and then
running.

Encourage the groups to progress upfield in the same direction. When the ball has been passed to the end of the line, the players should be encouraged automatically to adjust their speed and position so that the ball can be passed back along the line.

Coaching points

1   Run straight – attack the goal-line, not the touch-line

Diagram 4

2 Mobilize the upper body
3 Pass accurately
4 Look at the target area
5 Direct the ball a suitable distance in front of the receiver
6 Develop the ball carrier's awareness of the position of the support player.

As the practice develops, the coach should encourage the players to give and take a pass without slowing down, and gradually introduce them to timing their run, so they can handle the ball at speed. Make them aware that it is speed on to the ball that matters. These practices are important. Use them frequently.

Diagram **5**

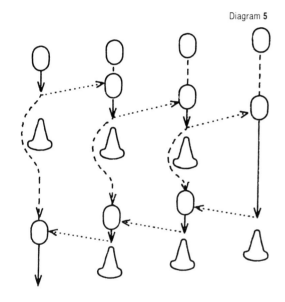

The next development is to introduce pressure in the form of opposition:

1 Cones should be placed in a slanting line, as in diagram 5. At first they should be around ten paces deep, but as the young players become more proficient they should be moved closer together. Each player jogs towards a cone and passes to the receiver without stopping.
   The ball carrier should check early to ensure where his support is positioned. He will then jog forward, aware of the cones but moving his eyes

to concentrate on the bread-basket of the receiver fractionally before passing.
2 As soon as the passers are proficient the cones are replaced by players. Initially they should be stationary, but are later allowed to move their arms, and finally jog forward.

Encourage the players to run straight: the passer should drift slightly away from the pass to the opposite side of the cone from where the pass is made. The movement should not be exaggerated, however, for in a game the passer will more often than not be encouraged to support by following the ball.

5 PASSING FROM THE GROUND

This is a skill similar to the pass from the waist, but the ball should be passed directly from the ground. It is used in most play-the-ball movements, and also from the base of the scrum. Unless the acting half-back is going to run with the ball, he should not pick it up as this wastes time and allows the defence to come closer. Thus, 'passing from the ground' is the springboard of most attacks and correct technique is essential. Particular care is needed to ensure that each pass is correctly weighted and executed in the shortest possible time.

Coaching points

1 Be aware of the speed of the receiver, the position of the target and the weight of the pass required
2 Bend over the ball
3 Hold the ball firmly in both hands, and be prepared to pass from the ground
4 Turn the head and upper body towards the target
5 Pass from the ground without lifting the ball up and without straightening the back
6 As the pass is made the nearest foot will be in front of the body, pointing at the receiver
7 The ball is aimed to the bread-basket in front of the receiver, the distance in front depending on the speed of the receiver
8 The ball is directed by the fingers and wrists

9 There is a follow-through with the arms, so that finally they are fully extended towards the receiver with fingers pointing at the target.

Practices

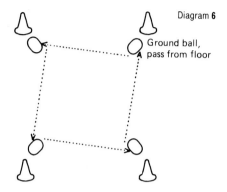

Diagram **6**

Ground ball, pass from floor

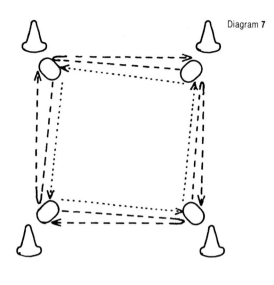

Diagram 7

In diagram 6, four players stand in each corner of a grid passing the ball around it. After catching the ball, each player should place it on the ground before making the pass. Diagram 7 shows an identical practice, but after each pass the player should run after the ball to the next corner before returning to his position. This teaches players to support the ball.

Advanced handling skills

1   The long pass
2   The short pass
3   The quick pass
4   The loop round
5   The run around
6   The switch pass
7   The drop off
8   The spin pass
9   The pass in the tackle
10   Unopposed practices
11   Opposed practices

12   Mike Ford (Oldham, formerly Leigh and Wigan) weights a pass with pin-point accuracy.

The beauty of Rugby League is that it encourages all players to be good handlers of the ball. They should be given every opportunity to improve their handling abilities and enough rugby balls should be available at every practice session to make this possible.

Children, from the very beginning, should develop a feel for the ball and be able to develop the ability to deliver a pass at the correct speed. This 'weighting' of the pass is dependent upon finger-tip control and use of the wrists. It is generally accepted, in both rugby codes, that British Rugby League players are the best handlers in the world. Coaches of all age groups must maintain this tradition, emphasizing quality all the time. Players cannot practise handling skills enough. All available time should be used for handling the ball, whether running to the training area or as part of the warm-up. Insist on perfection. A good training rule is that no rugby ball should be thrown on the ground. Care should be taken that every pass goes to hand, and when not in use balls should be placed in a corner safely out of the way.

1   THE LONG PASS

The long pass gives width to an attack and often splits a defence, particularly when a player is missed out. In this case the ball carrier passes to the next-but-one player in the attacking line.

Coaching points

The same as for the orthodox pass with the following exceptions:

1   The arms are taken further back
2   The follow-through is more pronounced, as is the flick of the wrists
3   The upper body should turn so that the shoulders are square and facing the receiver.

Unopposed practice

1   Each player passes as far as he can. The receivers make decisions as to their positioning, deciding how far each ball carrier can pass, and whether he can pass as far to the right as to the left.

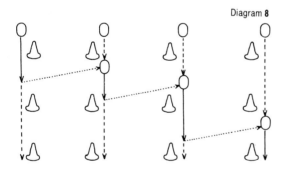

Diagram **8**

Players can be encouraged to pass long by marking out lines with cones, and insisting that they move on the outside of the cones, as in diagram 8.
2   Iain MacCorquodale, the former Workington Town and Fulham player, developed a drill using a rugby ball split and filled with sand. Iain discovered that players' passing ability improved after working with the heavy ball.

Opposed practice

A long cut-out pass against opposition. Practice three against two, with the ball carrier at the end (see page 119.)

2   THE SHORT PASS

The short pass is given to a support player who is moving close, and usually at speed. It is imperative that the ball is 'softly' directed by the wrists and fingertips to be easily caught. Correct weighting is the key coaching point.

Coaching points

1   The ball should be held close to the body with arms bent and elbows in
2   The ball should be guided with an upward flick of the wrists. The arms do not follow through
3   The player should read the situation. At times the ball carrier can hand the ball to the receiver, at others the ball has to be flicked into the air enabling the support player to run on to it.

Unopposed practice

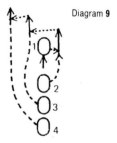

Diagram **9**

Single file: As in diagram 9, have the group move forward in single file with the ball carrier at the front. The next player in line sprints through close to the ball carrier who gives a short pass; he then readjusts and rejoins the group at the back. Encourage the players to pass and support.

Communication and understanding can also be developed during this drill. The support player should be encouraged to shout for the ball at all times, thereby conveying his message to the ball carrier. The shout must be short, but quite a lot of information can be passed on: for example, 'short, right!' not only says the support is there, but also where it is.

The ball carrier must realize at all times that he is responsible for the ball and if any pass is intercepted it is his fault. The golden rules to follow are: (a) the *support player* should communicate his availability to the ball carrier, giving as much information as possible in a few words; (b) the *ball carrier* has total responsibility for the ball, and should not pass to the shout without first looking to make sure that his pass will go directly to a team-mate with no danger of being intercepted.

Unopposed combination of long and short passes

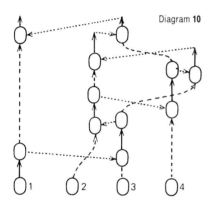

Diagram **10**

1   Alternate long and short passing in groups of four (diagram 10).   Player 1 starts with the ball and sends a long pass across player 2 to player 3, who carries the ball forward. Player 2 readjusts and comes on the inside of player 3, receiving a short pass. Player 2 carries the ball forward, giving the players time to readjust, then sends a long pass to 4 across 3. 3 loops round and receives a return pass on the outside of 4. The ball is then passed back using the same sequence.

The players are encouraged to communicate with

one another. A pass which goes in front of a player to another is termed a 'face pass'.

2   Long and short passing in two groups of four (diagram 11).   Group 1 start with the ball, with

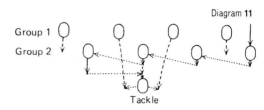

Diagram **11**

group 2 behind. Group 1 space themselves out for long passes, and group 2 are ready at the back to offer close support. Group 1 move down field interpassing with group 2 behind them.

On a given command, the player from group 1 in possession simulates being tackled and either stops or falls. The two players from group 2 immediately behind him come through close at each side and the pass is made to either one of them. Group 2 then continue down field making long passes with group 1 ready to support from behind.

3   Single file and wide passing (diagram 12).   The

Diagram **12**

group move down field passing, in single file. On reaching a given position, or on a command, the group fan out and make normal lateral passes, each player looping round so that the sequence can continue. On the second command the group revert to single-file passing again.

Opposed practice (diagram 13)

Diagram **13**

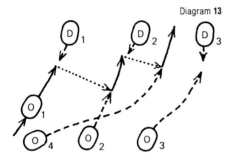

Four players in possession attack three defenders: Three of the attackers (O1, O2, O3) are closely marked by the three defenders (D1, D2, D3) who have maintained a defensive line. The extra player, O4, is introduced after a crossfield run.

Ball carrier O1 must:

1   draw D1, but pass early enough to give time for O2 to perform the skill
2   support O2 on the left otherwise D1 will be able to move in to tackle him.

Ball carrier O2 must:

1   carry the ball into D2, and commit him to the tackle
2   pass immediately prior to being tackled
3   drift back away from the gap, towards D1, before releasing the ball; this can be a side-step and should cause D2 also to move away from the gap
4   weight the pass softly using fingertips and wrists
5   look directly at D2, thereby helping to commit him
6   glance at the last second at O4
7   if in doubt (a) that the ball will not go safely to player O4, or (b) that D2 has not been committed,

keep hold of the ball in two hands and attempt to break the tackle.

Support player O3 must:

1   move away from the ball carrier, thereby widening the gap between D2 and D3
2   when O4 receives the ball, give support
3   be prepared for the unexpected pass from O2. If D3 is drawn towards O4, the support player O3 could be in the gap.

Support player O4:

1   should leave his move late so there is less chance of the opposition marking him; but arrive on time
2   run in an arc, first of all across the field to move into position, but then straighten up
3   receive the ball close to the ball carrier O2
4   run straight
5   hold the ball in two hands
6   communicate; feed information to the ball carrier.

3   THE QUICK PASS

An essential advanced skill is to be able to pass in the shortest time possible. Advantages include: (a) when moving the ball across field, a quick passing action enables the runner to receive the ball before the defence moves up; (b) a quick passing action often enables a player under pressure to make a successful pass before being tackled.

Players making quick passes should catch and pass in one movement.

(a)   When moving the ball across field

1   Reach out the hands to catch the ball early, then immediately swing the arms in front of the body and release the ball in one movement.
2   When running at speed and passing to the right, try to catch the ball as the right foot touches the ground and complete the pass before the left foot connects.
3   When passing to a receiver who is to make a quick pass, the target is in front of his hands.

(b)   When passing under pressure

1   Catch the ball close to the body and release with a quick flick of the wrist, concentrating on the position of the support player and the opposition.
2   Do not pass if there is doubt concerning:
    (a)   the position of the receiver
    (b)   the angle of the receiver's run
    (c)   a possible interception, or
    (d)   the receiver being tackled immediately he receives the ball.

Unopposed practice

1   Circles. A group of four or five players pass the ball quickly around the circle. It is important to pass in both directions.
2   Line passing. A group of four or five players run upfield passing quickly. It is again important to pass in both directions.

Unopposed practice with pressure

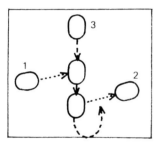

Diagram **14**

1   Grid practice. Have three players in a grid, as in diagram 14. Players 1 and 2 are stationary at each side. Player 3 runs across the grid, receiving the ball from 1 and making a quick pass to 2. Immediately on crossing the grid player 3 turns and sprints back again, this time taking the pass from 2 and quickly passing to 1. This practice is continuous.
2   Corridor practice. Use groups of four players, as in diagram 15. They sprint in line up a corridor, receiving passes from feeders 1, 2 and 3, who are here shown on the left. On receiving a pass from 1, A passes to B, and immediately receives a pass from 2, then from 3.

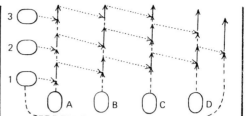

Diagram **15**

A, B and C pass the ball to D. Player 1, on passing the ball to A, supports and receives a pass outside D. The next group sprint along the corridor receiving passes from the right-hand side.

Opposed practice

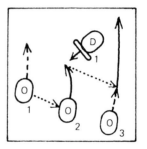

Diagram **16**

Have four players in a grid, as in diagram 16. D1 holds a shield putting pressure on O2 who attempts to receive a pass from O1, and then makes a quick pass to O3.

4   THE LOOP ROUND

A player passes to another then runs round his back to receive a return pass. This skill encourages players to pass and follow, and is important in establishing the principles of support play.

Initially the pivot should turn in such a way that the player on the loop is always in vision, and the receiver can always see the ball.

Because both players are always in vision, there is no danger of the pass being made if the support player stumbles, or if a member of the opposition positions himself for a possible interception.

An alternative is for a player to loop round while supporting a player running with the ball. This is most effective if the ball carrier faces forward all the time, relying on peripheral vision and communication.

The line should move downfield and not across. The receiver must therefore run across field, in an arc, to get into position, then straighten up before receiving the pass.

Coaching points

1   Immediately after passing, follow the ball
2   Loop round, but come on to the ball running straight and attacking the goal-line.

In vision

3   The receiver turns towards the support player, keeping him in sight, while the support player can see the ball
4   The pass may be made early, the ball carrier executing the pass at speed, by merely turning his upper body from the waist. Otherwise he must execute a full turn and will be almost stationary when the pass is executed.

Out of vision

5   The pass is made late when the player on the loop has passed completely round the back of the ball carrier
6   Communication is important, with the player on the loop conveying his intentions to the ball carrier
7   The support player needs to arc sharply, arriving close beside the ball carrier
8   There is more chance of creating a gap for the receiver to run through, if the passer drifts away from the direction of the pass and tries to pull the defence with him
9   The pass should not be made blind: the ball carrier should see the support player before the pass is made (peripheral vision is important)
10   The movement may be executed at speed.

Unopposed practices (in groups of four or five)

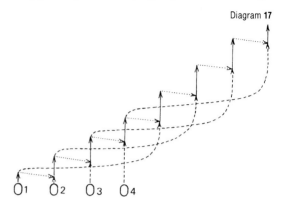

Diagram **17**

1   First man to end of line (diagram 17). The player starting with the ball passes and sprints round to join the end of the line. Each player in turn receives, passes, and follows him. It is imperative for the group to move down field and not across, so each receiver must make a conscious effort to straighten the line.

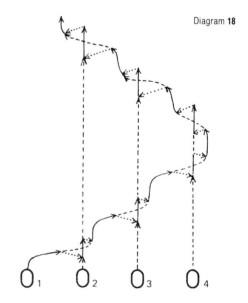

Diagram **18**

2   Continuous loops (diagram 18). The player starting with the ball loops round each player in the line, first passing to the man next to him, looping round, receiving the pass, and then passing to the next one. Upon reaching the end the drill can be extended by the same player bringing the ball back in the same way.

The above drills can incorporate both the turn and non-turn methods of passing.

Opposed practices

Opposition should be introduced gradually, and defenders holding shields are of value. It is important that the ball carrier is able to execute the pass under pressure while concentrating on running and decision-making. This is particularly relevant to the pass out of vision; on no account must the ball carrier pass to a player about to be tackled.

Another practice has player O1 coming round O2 for the return pass, as in diagram 19.

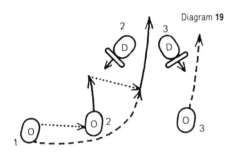

Diagram **19**

Ball carrier O1

1 passes to O2
2 loops round and receives the pass
3 runs in an arc, straightening up to attack the goal-line when he receives the ball, and
4 communicates with O2.

Ball carrier O2

1 receives the pass and carries the ball into D2,
2 he commits D2 to the tackle, then
3 drifts to the left when passing to the right, pulling D2 with him

4 he watches D2 – if he is not committed, the pass must not be made
5 he checks other defenders, particularly D3. If a gap for O1 to run through has not been created, the pass must not be made
6 he sees O1 at the final second before the pass is made.

Ball carrier O3

angles away from O2, pulling D3 with him and opening up a gap for O1 to run into.

5   THE RUN AROUND

The loop more often than not is executed wide out from the play-the-ball, and usually by the three-quarters. The run around is a similar play usually executed close to the play-the-ball and close to the defence. The aim of the run around is to create a hole in the defence which either:

1 the player on the run-around goes through, or
2 another player goes through.

The run around, therefore, has two versions:

Run Around 1 (diagram 20)

Ball carrier O1

1 runs across the field towards the pivot O2
2 weights an accurate pass so that it can be controlled easily
3 passes early thereby giving the pivot O2 time to turn
4 moves behind O2 and receives a softly weighted pass, or even takes the ball from O2's hands
5 upon receiving the ball immediately straightens and arcs through the gap, close to O2

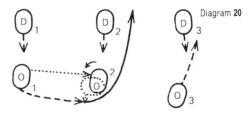

Diagram **20**

6   this play should be executed close to the opposition.

Pivot O2

1   receives the ball in a flat position
2   moves forward one or two paces towards the opposition, otherwise O1 will have to run back towards his own posts
3   he should be on top of the defence, thereby fully committing them
4   while moving forward he turns inwards so that O1 is always in vision, and can see the ball all the time
5   once fully turned he takes a step towards D1. D2 should follow, thereby increasing the hole in the defensive wall
6   he bends at the waist for protection, thrusting the buttocks towards the opposition
7   the pass should be soft, weighted with wrist and fingertips. An alternative is to hand the ball to the receiver.

Attacker O3

1   moves outwards, thus taking D3 away from D2 and creating a wider hole
2   stays ready to support.

Run Around 1 – variation (diagram 21)

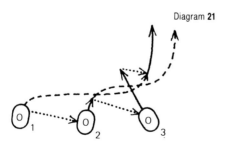

Diagram **21**

A variation from the above with O1 and O2 passing and then running round pivot O3.

Pivot O3

1   receives the ball from O2, and then

2   immediately angles his run into the opposition to prevent the defence drifting over.

Ball carrier O2

1   after passing to O3, runs round on a wide arc acting as a decoy.

Ball carrier O1

1   passes and follows
2   times his run to arrive around O3 slightly after O2
3   arcs in between O3 and O2, receiving the pass from O3
4   straightens up, taking the ball to attack the goal-line.

Run Around 2 (diagram 22)

Ball carrier O1

Runs as in Run Around 1 but without straightening up.
1   On receiving the ball, he angles across the field thereby creating an extra man on the outside and causing D3 and D4 to react
2   depending on their reaction, passes to the player in the gap.

Diagram **22**

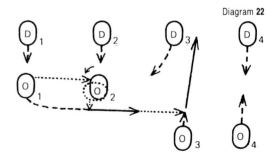

Pivot O2

As in Run Around 1.

Attacker O3

1   delays his run allowing O1 to draw D3
2   times his run to receive the ball and penetrate.

Variations

Variations can be developed, particularly by introducing extra attackers running off either O2 or O1. Example:

Pivot O2

In diagram 23, the pivot O2 has the two passing options of either giving the ball to O1 as he completes the run around or passing to O3 who has run from deep. The last option is most effective if the pivot side-steps away from the pass, and the runner goes directly through his original position.

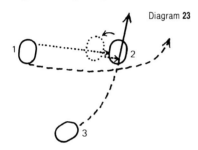

Diagram **23**

Attacker O1

Two runners O3 and O4 come inside and outside of O1 as he completes the run around as in diagram 24, thereby giving him at least two passing options.

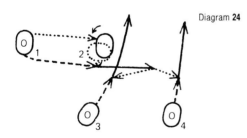

Diagram **24**

Unopposed practices

These establish: timing, angle of run, and execution of pass.

Opposed practices

As described in diagrams 20–22.

6   THE SWITCH PASS

The ball carrier angles across the playing area passing to a support player, who is either running straight or angling slightly inside the path of the passer. The support player originally positioned on the outside of the ball carrier receives the pass on the inside.

Coaching points

1   The ball carrier arcs towards the outside
2   The ball carrier has his support in vision on the outside
3   On a signal from the ball carrier the support player changes the angle of his run and comes inside
4   The pass is made as the paths of the two players cross
5   The ball carrier should execute the pass turning outwards so that the support player is always in vision, and the support player can always see the ball
6   The closer the players are when the pass is made the better
7   The pass should be gentle and executed with the wrists and finger tips
8   Timing is essential.

An advanced variation is for the ball carrier to make a one-handed flick pass to the support player. This is dependent upon the two players having a full knowledge of each other's play. It is not recommended for beginners, but can be an effective advanced skill.

Unopposed practices

In pairs, concentrating on

execution
timing
angle of run.

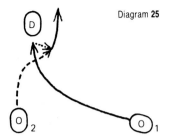

Diagram **25**

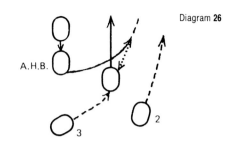

Diagram **26**

Opposed practices (diagram 25)

The ball carrier O1 commits the defender D1 before the pass is executed:

Ball carrier O1

1   runs in an arc initially across field, then straightens up towards D1
2   D2 must be committed to the tackle
3   O1 calls O2 inside.

Ball carrier O2

1   runs straight and waits for O1 to commit the defender D1
2   when instructed, he accelerates inside on to the ball.

7   THE DROP-OFF

A skill similar to the switch pass, but usually executed closer to the play-the-ball. The ball carrier moves across the field, crossing the path of the runner, and gives a close pass on the inside.

In diagram 26, the drop-off is executed by the acting half-back at the play-the-ball. He picks the

ball up and moves quickly across the field giving an inside pass to O3.

The acting half-back

1   picks the ball up then moves quickly across the field
2   crosses the path of the runner O3
3   gives the pass immediately – a gentle inside pass into the bread-basket
4   turns his upper body to face O3
5   O3 is kept in sight all the time.

The ball carrier

1   attacks the goal-line, running straight
2   timing is important

Practices

Unopposed – as above, then gradually introduce opposition.

8   THE SPIN-PASS (diagram 27)

A spin-pass propels the ball quickly a long way. When used wisely it can give great width to the attack, causing the opposition either to be out-

Diagram **27**

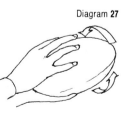

flanked, or to spread, thereby creating gaps between players.

It is an advanced skill which should not be introduced to players unless they have thoroughly mastered all the other handling skills.

Some young players become too dependent on the spin-pass, losing the ability to weight a pass correctly. It is usually given when the player is almost station- ary and, more often than not, is delivered at great speed. It is important to coach players to spin-pass both to the left and to the right.

Coaching points

1   Hold the ball as for the normal pass
2   The back hand becomes dominant and propels the ball by moving forward and over it.

Practices

1   Pairs face one another, gradually moving further apart. The pass is given without moving
2   Pairs move forward and pass sideways. Right-handed players have more success when passing to the left, but should practice the skill passing in both directions. Left-handed players should do likewise.

9   THE PASS IN THE TACKLE

The ability to pass the ball while being tackled is a most valuable skill to develop. It falls into two major categories: driving through the tackle and passing, or turning in the tackle and passing.

13   Kevin Ward (Castleford and Great Britain) driving through the tackle and passing to Andy Gregory (Wigan and Great Britain) during the Great Britain v Papua New Guinea Test in 1987. Gregory then passed to Shaun Edwards who scored.

Driving through the tackle and passing

The ball carrier drives with determination into the tackler, holds the ball firmly, and passes around the back of the tackler.

The advantage of this is that despite the ball carrier being tackled, the ball is passed to a support player who has already penetrated the defensive line.

Coaching points

1 Hold the ball firmly, preferably in two hands
2 Drive with determination into the tackle, lifting the torso up and forward
3 Thrust the ball forward behind the tackler and be prepared to make a quick accurate pass to the support player
4 Make a visual check and pass only to an unmarked player
5 If support is not immediately available, bring the ball into the chest in order to prevent the opposition having the opportunity of stealing it.

Practices

1 *Unopposed.* Players move forward passing in line, concentrating on thrusting the upper body forward before the pass is made.
2 *Passive opposition.* Two defenders close together and kneeling. The ball carrier jogs into them, concentrating on thrusting his upper body upwards and forwards over the two defenders. The pass is made to a player in close support.
3 *Shield opposition* (see page 73 for a description of shields). The shields are held by two defenders standing close together but lower than usual, at lower chest height. The ball carrier runs in between the shields and thrusts his upper body upwards and forwards through the shields, passing to a player in close support.

   Decision-making should now be introduced. As the ball carrier thrusts his body through into space he should hold the ball out and look for support. If there is any doubt whether a successful pass will be made, the ball should be brought back into the chest and made safe using both hands.

Turning in the tackle and passing

The ball carrier attempts to break, but if unsuccessful turns in the tackle to face his own in-goal area, and makes the ball available.

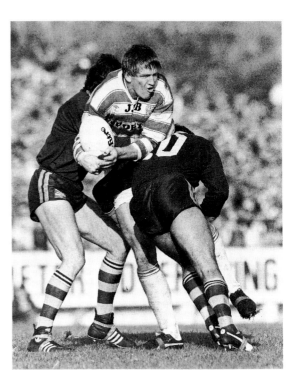

14   Graeme West (Wigan), the former New Zealand captain, turns in the tackle and makes the ball available in Wigan's match against the Australians in 1986.

Coaching points

1 The ball carrier holds the ball firmly, preferably in two hands
2 Drives with determination into the tackle, and attempts to break through
3 If unsuccessful, he turns towards his in-goal area, putting his body between the tackler and the ball
4 Passes if an unmarked player is available.

Unopposed practices

1   Single file. Players move forward, turning and then passing. This is a skill similar to the single file practice on page 54, but with the ball carrier turning fully round.
2   Line. Players move forward but pass one handed, turning towards the receiver and using the back hand, the one furthest away from the opposition.

Opposed practices

1   Shield opposition, players working in threes. The ball carrier runs into the shield holder, turns and passes to support at the rear. He practises both two-handed and one-handed passes.
2   Continuous banks of shields. On receiving the ball, the ball carrier runs into a shield, turns and offloads. Additional practices can be found in Chapter 6 of this section.

10   UNOPPOSED PRACTICES

Many practices can be devised which develop all the combinations discussed. Some examples are:

Groups of five players

1   Long and short passing
2   Single-file passing
3   Single-file and wide passing
4   First man to end of line
5   Continuous loops

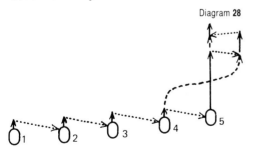

Diagram **28**

Quick pass and loop (diagram 28)

Players 1, 2, and 3 handle quickly, then 4 passes to 5

and loops round for the return. The ball is passed back using a similar sequence.

Quick pass, long pass, loop and short pass (diagram 29)

Players 1 and 2 handle quickly
3 passes long to 5 in front of 4 (face pass)
3 loops round and takes return pass outside 5
4 readjusts and receives a short pass from 3 on the inside, and the ball is passed quickly back along the line.

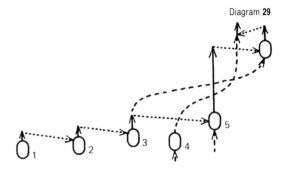

Diagram **29**

Run around, short pass and switch (diagram 30)

Player 1 passes to 2 and receives a run-around return pass 1 gives a short pass to 3 who is running hard and straight
3 passes to 4 who runs outside and executes a switch with 5, and the ball is returned along the line by quick passes.

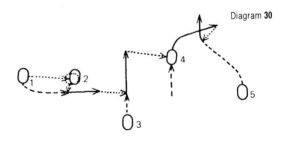

Diagram **30**

Spin-pass and drop-off (diagram 31)

Player 1 spin-passes to 2, who spin-passes to 3
3 runs across away from the direction of the pass

Diagram **31**

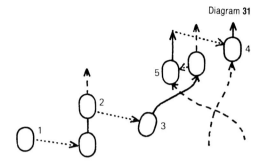

4 follows 3
5 angles in field and receives a drop-off from 3
5 straightens up and passes to 4.

Combinations

These drills and similar ones can be combined to enable the groups to move down the field.

Angled runs

A major objective of the ball carrier in match play is to pull the defenders out of position, thereby creating a hole in the defensive line for a support player to run through.

The angle of run can be in field or across field, and on each occasion the hole created could be inside or outside depending on how the defence reacts.

Once the players are proficient handlers, a useful unopposed practice is for groups of players to move downfield interpassing and concentrating upon the angle of their run.

Communication and the timing of the support are equally important.

Points to remember

1   Insist on perfect passing.
2   Encourage other important skills, for example, support play, pass and follow.
3   Increase physical conditioning. Many of the drills are excellent conditioning practice, and when performed at speed can give the same benefits as interval training.
4   Once the players have mastered the techniques of the various skills it is important to introduce gradually the pressure of opposition.

11   OPPOSED PRACTICES

As above

Identical drills can be performed against a fairly passive opposition.

Pass in the tackle

An extension is for a couple of the opposition to hold shields. The drills are performed incorporating both the passes in the tackle, and are described more fully in Chapter 6 of this Section.

Tackling

1   Side tackle
2   Rear tackle
3   Front tackle
4   Smother tackle
5   Practices
6   Tackling equipment

15   Brian Niebling, Brett Kenny and Peter Sterling (from left to right) execute a perfect tackle on Great Britain's Andy Goodway in the second Test against Australia in 1986 and demonstrate the benefit of attack through defence.

Tackling is one of the most important individual skills in the game, and players of all age groups and abilities should include tackling practice as part of their weekly programme.

Defence will be discussed later and the question of attitude fully explored. Suffice it to say that the senior player is required to adopt a positive attitude to tackling. 'Attack through defence' should be the approach, and the aim of most tackles should be not merely to stop the other side's progress, but to go forward and attempt to gain possession by forcing the ball carrier into handling errors.

How early this mental attitude should be encouraged in a player's development is open to debate. Certainly a youngster first of all should become proficient in the techniques of all the various tackles, and needs to be coached in such a way that he finds the game enjoyable. This obviously means being free of any pressure. Even so, the junior coach might consider slightly changing the emphasis on defence even with this tender age group.

Rather than suggesting that players go forward when they have the ball, with the implication that they lose ground when the opposition is in possession, it may be worth encouraging players to think 'go forward' all the time, whether in possession of the ball or not.

Another point is also worth considering: many British coaches have emphasized the importance of tackling the ball. Thus, they have tended to concentrate on the smother tackle, resulting in too many players tackling around the shoulders and chest. Such high tackles can be broken by the ball carrier far more easily than a determined tackle around the thighs and legs.

Coaches should accept this fact and concentrate on developing players capable of executing low, determined tackles. In team play the ball is more efficiently stopped by the first man tackling hard and low, and the second man stopping the ball.

Children should be taught the techniques of all the tackles early in their development. Coaching needs to be positive at all times and emphasis should be placed on the pleasure that can be obtained from executing a full-blooded tackle, rather than mentioning the possibility of injury or fear. Children enjoy tackling as long as:

the ground and weather conditions are suitable
they are in groups of similar age and size
the practice is relatively short.

16   Barry Ledger (St Helens and Great Britain) about to side tackle Michael O'Connor in the second Test against Australia in 1986.

1   SIDE TACKLE

The side tackle is the easiest to execute and for this reason should be introduced first.

Coaching points

1   Tackle with determination
2   Keep eyes on the target, the thigh
3   The head of the tackler should be behind the ball carrier at all times
4   The shoulder should make contact and drive powerfully into the target
5   The arms should strongly encircle the thighs and grip tight
6   The tackler should hold the ball carrier until he is well and truly tackled and on the ground
7   The tackler should finish on top of the ball carrier.

17 Garry Schofield (Leeds, formerly Hull, and Great Britain) halted by a determined tackle from the rear during a Hull v Hull KR derby.

2 REAR TACKLE

Coaching points

1 Tackle with determination
2 Keep eyes on the target, the thigh
3 The head of the tackler should always be to the side of the ball carrier
4 The shoulder should make contact and drive powerfully into the target.
5 The arms should strongly encircle the thighs and grip tight
6 The arms may then slide down the ball carrier's legs
7 The tackler should finish on top of the ball carrier

3 FRONT TACKLE

Tackling head-on is vital to team play. Coaches should ensure that all their players are introduced to the techniques of the front tackle, and then encouraged to practise. A player who is reluctant to tackle head-on is always suspect when playing against faster opposition, and will cause untold problems in team play if he persistently manoeuvres the ball carrier into position before he performs a side tackle.

 There are two types of head-on tackle:

1 *Passive* – when the tackler uses the body weight of the ball carrier
2 *The blockbuster* – when the tackler forcefully knocks the ball carrier backwards.

1 Passive, using the ball carrier's momentum

This is easier to execute than the blockbuster. It is used most often when the ball carrier is larger than the tackler and is approaching at speed. The aim is to encircle his legs quickly and use his momentum to bring him down.

Coaching points

1 Keep eyes on the target, the thigh
2 Position the body so that the head and neck are to the side of the ball carrier
3 Use the ball carrier's own weight and momentum to make the tackle
4 The tackler should block the thighs of the ball carrier with his shoulder
5 The arms should powerfully encircle the legs and grip tight
6 The ball carrier should be rolled on to his side
7 The tackler should finish on top of the tackled player.

18 The blockbuster: a youngster shows perfect technique.

2   The blockbuster

With the blockbuster the tackler must move quickly into position, and contact is usually made before the ball carrier has had time to build up momentum. By driving and lifting, the opponent is forcefully knocked over backwards. The target area for this tackle is slightly below the waist, and timing is the key to success. When coaching the blockbuster it is advisable to have a crash mat available. The tackler hits and drives the ball carrier on to the mat.

Coaching points

1   Determination: the shoulder should drive powerfully into the target area with the utmost determination
2   Keep eyes on the target, the waist
3   Quickly move forward into position
4   The head of the tackler should be to the side of the ball carrier
5   The arms should powerfully encircle the ball carrier below the centre of gravity, that is, below the buttocks, and grip tightly
6   Drive powerfully with the legs

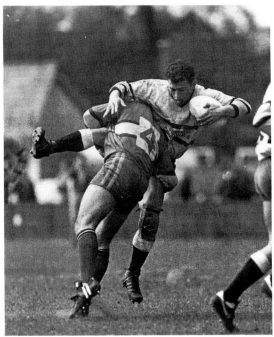

19 The blockbuster: Puni Jordan (South London ARLFC) executes a successful blockbuster on Kevin Durr (London Colonials) during the London Amateur League Cup final in 1987.

7   Pull and lift with the arms and shoulder
8   Drive the ball carrier upwards and then backwards
9   Finish on top of the ball carrier, with the shoulder buried into the target area
10   Timing is the key to success.

4   THE SMOTHER TACKLE

The smother tackle should only be introduced to youngsters when they are fully proficient at tackling hard and low, and team players who develop the habit of persistently tackling high should be quickly discouraged.

The second player into the tackle should be encouraged to smother the ball.

Occasionally, however, a smother tackle can be most effective, especially when the tackler is left facing a ball carrier who has support. A quick tackle, smothering the ball, will prevent a pass.

20   A successful smother-tackle: Lee Crooks smothers the ball in the third Great Britain v Australia Test in 1986.

Coaching points

1 Tackle with determination
2 Keep eyes on the target, the player and ball
3 It is important that the coach does not emphasize that the ball is the target even though with this tackle it is the ball we are trying to smother. If the coach does stress that the ball is the target area, the would-be tackler could be deceived by a dummy pass
4 Move forward into position quickly
5 Pin the ball between the body of the tackler and the ball carrier
6 The arms should be powerfully wrapped round the upper part of the ball carrier's body
7 The arms of the ball carrier must be trapped to his sides
8 The ball carrier should be forced to the ground whenever possible

9 Timing is of the utmost importance.

The most effective smother tackle is the one in which the tackler approaches the ball carrier from the outside. The tackler is thus able to see the player he is about to tackle, as well as the progress of the ball along the line towards him. He should try to time this tackle so that the ball carrier is tackled at the exact moment he receives the ball. Again the emphasis is on power, determination and timing.

5   PRACTICES – ALL TACKLES

Pairs

1   Introductory practice

In pairs, using the natural progression, and checking all the coaching points.

1 Tackler kneeling, ball carrier stationary.
2 Tackler kneeling, ball carrier walking.
3 Tackler crouching, ball carrier walking.
4 Tackler standing, ball carrier walking.
5 Tackler standing, ball carrier jogging.

2   Consecutive tackle drill

In pairs, with players facing one another two metres apart. 1 tackles 2. Both regain their feet quickly and the practice continues with 1 trying to make a maximum number of tackles in a given time (perhaps thirty seconds).
After sufficient rest the players alternate.

3   Confidence and timing

In pairs, with players facing one another two metres apart. On a command from the coach, 1 runs backwards, 2 chases and executes a determined tackle making contact on the thighs, head to the side.

Relays

1   Technique drill

Players form two lines at right-angles, as shown in

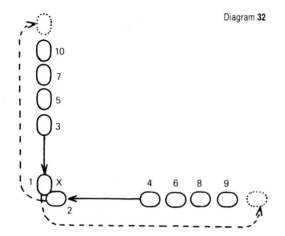

Diagram **32**

diagram 32. The players in one line are to be tackled; the others are the tacklers. 1 moves forward. 2, judging his run, comes in and tackles 1 at X. After the tackle 1 runs behind 9 and 2 runs behind 10. The other players repeat the process in progression. The tackles should be practised from both right and left and each group takes turn at tackling and being tackled. This practice can be used, with some variation, for all methods of tackling.

2   Competitive drill

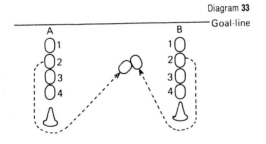

Diagram **33**

Players in lines A and B have corresponding numbers. The coach calls a number from 1 to 4 and both players run round the cones, then back towards the goal-line as shown in diagram 33. The player running in line A must attempt to tackle the player running in line B before he reaches the goal-line.

After the players in line A have tackled, the players in line B tackle.

3   Consecutive tackling

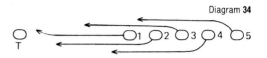

Diagram **34**

T, the player tackling, faces a line of five attackers, as in diagram 34. On a command, 1 runs forward to be tackled by T. Immediately the tackle has been completed T regains his feet. As T regains his feet, 2 runs forward to be tackled. The relay continues.

The tempo can be increased as soon as the players become proficient.

Grid tackling

1   Controlled pressure

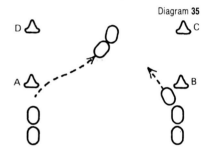

Diagram **35**

The tackler stands in the middle of four cones, which have been placed in a square about five metres apart, as in diagram 35.

Three players line up behind cone A, and their aim is to cross the square to reach point C. Three players line up on cone B, and their aim is to cross the square to cone D. The first player from cone A moves across the square and is forcefully tackled. As soon as the tackler has regained his feet, the first player from cone B sets off. The practice continues alternately.

2   Continuous pressure

With groups of four or five for each ten-metre grid, one player has to tackle the others as quickly as possible. Movement within the grid is allowed.

Channel running

The tackler is placed at the far end of a narrow channel. The rest of the group run through the channel one at a time. Each carries a ball and may use any method of evasion within the laws of the game, but is not allowed to move outside the channel.

The width of the channel may be controlled, being narrow to begin with to give the tackler success, then gradually being widened to make his task more difficult.

British bulldog

Place a player in the middle of a grid facing colleagues lined up along one side. On a command, they quickly move across the grid to the other side and the player in the middle has to tackle one of them. On being tackled, the player joins the one in the middle and the game continues until they have all been tackled.

Defence from the rear: one on two

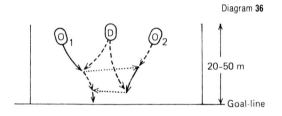

Diagram **36**

20-50 m

Goal-line

The defending player D starts in line with the attacking players O1 and O2. O1 starts to run with the ball, while D attempts to defend against O1 and O2 to prevent them scoring, as in diagram 36.

Small-sided games

See Section 3, Chapter 4.

6 TACKLING EQUIPMENT

It is vital that all players include tackling practice each week as part of their training programme. It is important, therefore, to try to build up a supply of tackling equipment which helps confidence, assists with technique and timing, and generally encourages players to become more aware and involved with defensive duties.

Tackle shields

Tackle shields originated in the USA and have been part of the training equipment for grid-iron football for decades. They were introduced into Australia by Rugby League coaches who studied grid-iron techniques in the 1970s, and are now essential training aids at every club. They were first introduced into Britain by Frank Stanton, the coach of the 1982 Kangaroos.

The shields are similar to the cushion of an armchair with two straps at the back. They are approximately 70 cm × 50 cm (31 in. × 20 in.), and 15 cm (6 in.) thick, and usually made from strong top quality foam, covered with a tough polyester cloth and reinforced by a waterproof cover. These shields cushion the impact of two players colliding and provide protection when tackling.

Players should be introduced to shields gradually, and must be made aware of the possible dangers of incorrect use, which are:

1 Whiplash: players involved in continuous head-on collision run the risk of whiplash, unless the body is braced upon impact.

2 Head clash: all collision drills can result in a clash of heads. At all times players involved should have their eyes open and be ready to move their heads to one side on the point of impact.

3 Being knocked over backwards: this can occur if either player should take both feet off the ground at the point of impact.

The chance of injury is slight if the shields are used correctly, and they provide such a valuable training aid that all clubs should use them.

Practice

Introduction: the squad should divide into pairs with each pair using a shield.

Every player with a shield should place both arms through the two straps at the back, and hold the shield in front of the chest and abdomen. The shield should not be held one-handed. The player not using the shield should stand opposite the shield holder and approximately five metres away.

They should both jog towards one another. Immediately prior to impact the player without the shield should place both arms round the shield and the shield carrier while forcing his upper body into the shield. The shield carrier must hold the shield firmly.

Both players on the point of impact must:

1 Brace their entire body
2 Have both feet firmly on the ground
3 Lean forcefully into the opposition
4 Watch their partner at all times
5 Move the head to one side on the point of impact.

The tempo should be increased gradually from a slow jog until the players are forcefully colliding with each other, as rigorously as in a match.

Tackling practices: all tackles can be practised with the player to be tackled holding the shield in front of the point of impact.

Tackle bags

Large free-standing bags, constructed of heavy-duty double-sided PVC-coated nylon, and filled with foam, provide ideal tackling aids though they are expensive to buy. Tacklers can develop skill and confidence by executing tackles with maximum determination completely free from the risk of injury.

Once the tacklers are proficient, the intensity of the collisions can be increased, by encouraging the

21 a & b Tackle shields and tackle bags: Ian Potter (Wigan and Great Britain) and Brian Case (Wigan and Great Britain) take part in tackle drills during a Great Britain squad preparation in the summer of 1987.

players to dive into the tackle so that at the point of impact their bodies are horizontal to the floor. The hit must be made with the shoulder, not with the upper arm. Once in the air the tackler should have his arms by his sides, and concentrate on forcing his shoulder into the target. Once in the air he should hold his chin firmly against his chest to eliminate the possibility of flinching prior to impact.

Inner tubes

Large heavy-duty tractor or lorry inner tubes can usually be obtained from garages at a minimal cost.

Because of their cheapness and value as a tackling aid it is worth encouraging every player to have his own inner tube, and every club to build up a supply of tubes to enable two players to work together at training sessions.

Safety

It is necessary for inner tubes to be made totally safe before use, so the metallic valve must be adequately covered. Thick foam placed over the valve, and then covered with carpet, is one recommended method. The tubes should always be checked before use.

Practices

All the tackles can be developed by a series of tube drills, of which a few are included as examples:

Blockbuster drill

The coach should instruct the tacklers to move up quickly for the tackle and aim to hit the tubes with their shoulders in the centre above the ground. They should continue to drive with their legs as they wrap their arms around the tubes and force them buckling up and backwards. If the tackles are made too high on

the tubes the players will roll up and over and hit the ground hard. When the tackles are executed correctly the tubes will cushion the players' fall to the ground.

In the blockbuster tube-tackling illustrated in diagram 37, 2 rolls the tube direct at 1 who moves quickly to carry out a diving tackle. When his shoulder hits the tube 3 begins to count from one to eight (approximately four seconds) and immediately rolls the tube straight at 1 who should have regained his feet swiftly for his second tackle.

Tackling from the rear

The practice starts with 2 rolling his tube downfield and the coach signalling for 1 to make his first diving tackle, as in diagram 38.

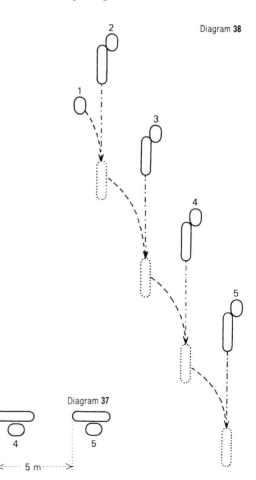

Diagram **38**

Diagram **37**

1 ○- - ->   <- - - ⊂==⊃   ⊂==⊃   ⊂==⊃   ⊂==⊃
                      ○   ○   ○   ○
                      2   3   4   5

|<········ 10 m ········>|<···· 5 m ····>|<···· 5 m ····>|<···· 5 m ····>|

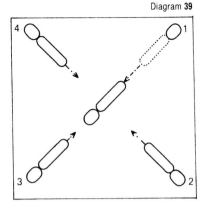

Diagram **39**

3, 4 and 5 should immediately move forward keeping five metres apart with their tubes.

3 positions his tube directly opposite to the point where 1 has completed the first tackle; then, as he regains his feet, 3 rolls the tube and the practice continues.

It is possible to time each player as he completes the four tackles.

Tackling in grids

Four players each with a tube are at the corners of a ten-metre grid. The player in the middle tackles the tubes as they are rolled to him in succession from 1 to 4, as in diagram 39.

The practice may continue for any length of time. Additional pressure can be added by reducing the time between the roll of each tube.

The play-the-ball

1   Explanation
2   Practices
3   Advanced play-the-ball practices

22   David Watkinson (Hull KR and Great Britain) at acting half-back gives out a quick pass following a play-the-ball from Lee Crooks during the third Test against Australia in 1986.

The play-the-ball movement restarts play after a tackle; a quick, efficient play-the-ball enables the team in possession to launch sustained attacks. On average there are more than 300 play-the-ball movements in a game of Rugby League, so it is an important technique to learn.

Diagram **40**

Players must realize that a ball which is brought back into play slowly allows the defence time to retreat the required five metres and to regroup. A fast play-the-ball is likely to catch the defence bunched up and moving backwards, and will not allow them time to regroup in a good defensive pattern. Obviously an unprepared defence is far easier to attack, so the importance of the following cannot be overemphasized:

Regain one's feet quickly
Heel smoothly
Give a pass from the ground.

1 EXPLANATION

The play-the-ball movement is similar to a scrum, inasmuch as opposing players take part in it. The tackled player, having retained possession, regains his feet as quickly as possible, bringing the ball up with him. Facing the opponent's goal-line, he drops or places the ball in front of his foremost foot, between himself and the player marking him. Neither may touch, push or interfere with the other.

After the ball has touched the ground, either player may play it with his foot in any direction, after which it is in play.

Although a player may drop the ball, ideally he should place it on the ground so that control is certain. Every player should strive to play-the-ball back as smoothly as possible, giving the acting half-back every chance of passing quickly from the ground. It is also within the laws of the game for a player to play the ball to himself, by placing the

ball on the ground and releasing it before touching it with his foot.

Speed at all times is essential, as long as the ball is played correctly.

Coaching points

1 The tackled player should regain his feet as quickly as possible, lifting the ball clear of the ground facing the opponent's goal-line.
2 While regaining his feet, he should hold the ball in both hands, though adults can often control a ball adequately with one hand.
3 While bending the body well over the ball, he places it in front of and by the inside of his front foot longways on, and releases it.
4 Simultaneously he places the sole of his other foot on top of the ball.
5 He rolls the ball back with full control, as in diagram 40.
6 The acting half-back should pass from the ground (see page 51).

2 PRACTICES

In pairs

One player plays the ball, the other acts as acting half-back. The practice begins with the ball carrier lying on the ground as if tackled. He regains his feet as quickly as possible and plays the ball as previously explained.

Diagram **41**

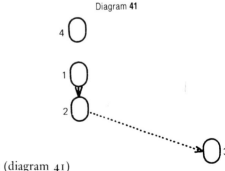

In fours (diagram 41)

1 plays the ball, 2 is acting half-back, 3 receives the pass, 4 is the marker. The marker should put pressure on the ball carrier, who ensures that the ball

is played in such a way that the opposition cannot gain possession. The acting half-back should pass from the ground. The position of the players should be rotated after each one has practised each position adequately. 3 must be five metres behind the play-the-ball to comply with the laws of the game.

In sixes (diagram 42)

1 is on the ground. On a command, he regains his feet and quickly plays the ball to 2. 2 passes from the ground to 3, who falls on the ground and then regains his feet, and plays the ball properly to 4. 4 passes to 5 who plays the ball to 6.

When 6 receives the ball, all players about turn and the ball is worked back along the line in the same way until 1 regains possession. This practice can take the form of a competition against other groups of six.

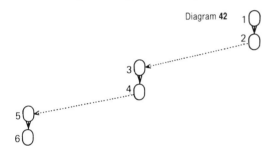

Diagram **42**

Small-sided games

See Section 3, Chapter 4.

3 ADVANCED PLAY-THE-BALL PRACTICES

It is an advantage if the acting half-back has advanced handling skills and is capable of creating play from the play-the-ball. Understanding and skills can be developed by groups working down ten-metre channels, as follows:

Groups of two (diagram 43)

1 plays the ball, then 2, the acting half-back, moves forward quickly as if penetrating the defence, then passes to 1, who has supported.

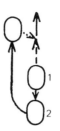

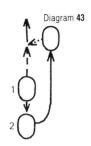

Diagram **43**

Groups of three (diagram 44)

Pass to a runner

(a) Going straight:
  1 plays the ball, then 2, the acting half-back, passes to 3, who is running forward on a straight path. The pass must be correctly weighted. It is an advantage if the pass is almost level, allowing 3 to reach the goal-line as soon as possible. 1 and 2 support 3.

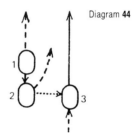

Diagram **44**

(b) Switch of play (diagram 45)
  1 plays the ball
  2 is the acting half-back
  3 stands on the right-hand side of the play-the-ball, but runs in an arc to the left and receives the ball. The pass must be correctly weighted, and the acting half-back should turn to keep 3 always in sight. 1 links up with 3 and takes the pass.

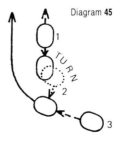

Diagram **45**

Run around (diagram 46)

1 plays the ball, then 2, the acting half-back, passes to 3, and receives a run-around pass.

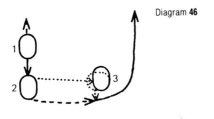

Diagram **46**

Drop-off (diagram 47)

1 plays the ball, then 2, the acting half-back, turns at an angle and drops-off 3. 1 links up with 3

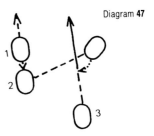

Diagram **47**

Evading and breaking a tackle

1 Side-step
2 Change of pace
3 Swerve
4 Dummy pass
5 Breaking the tackle
6 Bumping off
7 Hit-and-spin
8 Hand-off

A player who is elusive and difficult to tackle is not only a great crowd pleaser, but also an important weapon in the attacking armoury of the team.

It is necessary for players to develop and practise various methods of evasion, and coaches who devote time to developing these important skills will earn lasting gratitude from the players.

23 a & b   Henderson Gill (Wigan and Great Britain), faced in the left-hand picture with the defending Wally Lewis (no 6), side-steps and, in the right-hand picture, accelerates away in the first Test against Australia in 1986.

1   SIDE-STEP

The side-step is a sudden, quick change of direction followed by an immediate straightening up. Players who find this difficult will develop a side-step with adequate practice. For those who perform this skill naturally, practice will perfect it.

Coaching points (diagram 48)

1   Run at the defender at speed
2   Either encourage the defender to position himself in anticipation of making a tackle, or if at all possible wrong-foot him
3   When two to five metres from the defender, drive the toes of either foot powerfully into the ground and thrust off in the other direction
4   Accelerate into the gap and straighten up
5   The skill should be performed without shortening the stride and at maximum speed.

Diagram **48**

Practices

Demonstration

Many youngsters will be able to perform this skill naturally after seeing a good demonstration.

Cones

Players can practise the side-step with cones placed in line, but at a slight angle.

Tyre tubes

The use of car tyres in this side-stepping drill teaches players to lift their knees high and retain balance as they step in and out of the tyres. When practising side-stepping to the right, players should plant their left foot in the tyre and spring off it on to their right foot which is lifted and planted in the second tyre before accelerating away.

Players should start the drill by running straight for ten metres with the ball in both hands. They should then move inwards at an angle to practise beating a defender by drawing him inside.

As they side-step away from left to right, the ball is moved to the right side so the left hand can be used for a hand-off.

Off the field

Encourage players to practise side-stepping on the way to school or work.

Combinations

Encourage players to combine the side-step with a dummy pass.

2   CHANGE OF PACE

The change of pace is sudden acceleration of the ball carrier causing the would-be tackler to mistime his tackle.

Coaching points

1   Be aware of the speed and direction of the would-be tackler.
2   Slow down slightly, forcing the would-be tackler to alter his positioning and timing.
3   Suddenly accelerate sharply away.
4   Concentrate on a high knee lift.

Practices

1   Players have to develop the ability to accelerate sharply, which is best done by sprint training.

Encourage the players to slow down, and then by vigorous arm movements and short, high strides to accelerate quickly. This practice should also be performed with the player carrying the ball.

2 In pairs with a defender and attacker, simulating match conditions.

3 SWERVE

This technique takes the ball carrier in a wide arc round his opponent or round the cover defence. It should be executed at maximum speed.

Coaching points (diagram 49)

1 Change direction round the would-be tackler
2 The change of direction is sudden but not as extreme as the side-step
3 The path of the ball carrier is an arc, away from the defender
4 The hips should also sway away from the tackler
5 Balance is most important.

Diagram **49**

Practices (diagram 50)

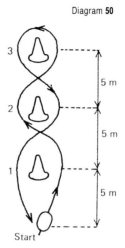

Diagram **50**

1 Stakes, cones or players are set out in staggered lines about five metres apart. Players in turn, carrying the ball with both hands, swerve in alternate directions, moving their shoulders around each obstacle as if it were an imaginary opponent
2 A practice which players can do in an open area on their own
3 In pairs with the tackler coming from the side: swerve round him
4 Combinations: the swerve is particularly effective when combined with a change of pace.

4 THE DUMMY PASS

The ball carrier makes a passing motion but retains possession of the ball, thus encouraging the defence to switch its attention from the ball carrier to the support player.

Coaching points

1 Look at the would-be receiver
2 Take the arms back and make as if to execute a pass, perhaps even exaggerate the motion
3 Follow through with the arms
4 Retain possession.

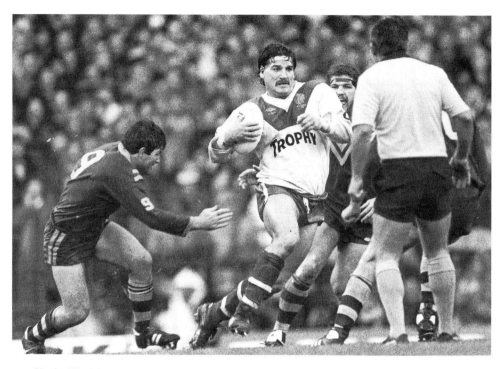

24 Kevin Ward breaks through the attempted tackles of the Australians Greg Dowling and Royce Simmons in the second Test against Australia in 1986.

Practices

This skill can be practised individually.

5   BREAKING THE TACKLE

There are few skills more satisfying than breaking through the opposition defence. To do so requires a combination of technique, determination and self-confidence.

Coaching points

1 Run with determination
2 Hold the ball firmly, using both hands
3 Accelerate at the gap
4 Brace the body
5 Hit the would-be tackler with the chest or shoulders

6 Have one foot on the ground at the point of impact
7 Keep the eyes open

Practices

1 Breaking the tackle

Players 1 and 2, holding shields, stand a metre apart with the shields slanting inwards, as in diagram 51. Player 3 starts the practice by running with the ball and bursting through the shields. He then turns and sends a pass to player 4 before rejoining the back of the line. Player 4 then follows suit.

The shield holders should allow the players to

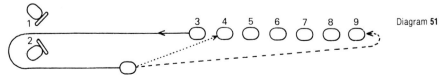

Diagram **51**

burst through successfully at first, but gradually they can introduce more pressure. The coach can also increase pressure by introducing more shield carriers behind players 1 and 2.

This drill can be developed to incorporate receiving the ball immediately prior to impact (diagram 52) and later to passing the ball prior to impact (diagram 53).

2   Receiving the ball, then breaking the tackle

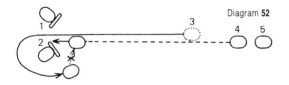

Diagram **52**

This drill increases the pressure on the ball carrier, as he now receives the ball immediately prior to impact.

The practice is identical to the one mentioned before, but the ball carrier, after breaking through, goes to point X, as in diagram 52, and becomes the feeder for the next runner, who sprints towards the shield and is given a pass immediately in front of them.

All the major coaching points should be emphasized, but particularly keeping the eye on the ball.

3   Receiving the ball and giving a pass under pressure

In this extension of the previous drill, the player is placed under pressure when giving and receiving a pass.

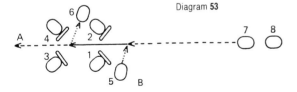

Diagram **53**

In diagram 53, player 7 runs hard at the shields. He receives a pass from player 5 prior to breaking through the shields held by 1 and 2. As soon as these shields have been broken, and immediately prior to

breaking through the additional shields held by 3 and 4, he passes to player 6.

In order for the practice to continue, 6 moves to point B, 7 replaces 6, and 5 joins the end of the line.

Coaching points:

1   Receive the pass with eye on the ball
2   Give the pass with eye on the receiver.

The drills are particularly useful for children when being introduced to the game. It is often too great a step to move from unopposed skills practices to the intensity of competition. Contact drills bridge this gap.

Once the players are competent at these drills they should begin to work in groups developing the skill and incorporating support play.

A recommended development, as in diagram 54, is for two players to approach the shields. Once the ball carrier has broken through he should pass to his partner. The impact will cause the ball carrier to slow down, so it is essential that the support player times his run perfectly. This drill will be explored more fully in Section 5, Chapter 3.

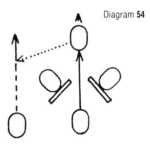

Diagram **54**

6   BUMPING OFF

Players should be encouraged to practise contact skills from an early age, for practice not only encourages the player to break tackles, but develops sufficient self-confidence to run into tackles with determination. The ball carrier should use the hard part of his body, particularly the shoulder or hip, to

25 Paul Rose (Hull) prepares to bump-off a would-be tackler in a Hull v Bradford Northern match.

bump off the opponent. When using the chest the player should be encouraged to fold his arms over the ball, hands upwards and elbows downwards, and take the brunt of the collision on the forearm.

Coaching points

1 Size up the would-be tackler
2 Run with determination
3 At the correct moment, with full power thrust the shoulders, hip or chest into the would-be tackler
4 Drive the legs, ensuring that one foot is in contact with the ground at the moment of impact.

Practices

The ball carrier, with support, runs at a player holding a shield. The ball carrier must be determined, while the shield holder needs to set himself and present strong resistance.

The ball carrier should hit the shield forcibly, bounce off, and be prepared immediately to off-load to his support. Again the timing of the support player's run is an important coaching point.

7 HIT AND SPIN

The hit and spin is an evasive tactic which originated in American football. On the point of impact the ball carrier spins off the defender and either offloads the ball or makes ground.

Coaching points

1 Hold the ball firmly
2 Take short steps
3 Pump legs quickly throughout the entire operation
4 When moving to the right, hit with the right shoulder and spin, turning to the left with the back into the tackle, keeping the ball available
5 Dip the shoulder on the point of impact.

Practices

1   Shoulder hit and spin (diagram 55)

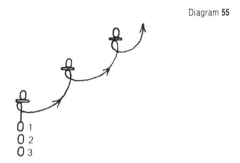

Diagram **55**

Player 1 'attacks' and hits the first shield with his right shoulder, spinning towards the right and into the next shield. The practice is continuous.

It is important for players to develop a spin to both right and left.

2   Hand-off and spin (diagram 56)

Player 1 runs 'the gauntlet' handing off and spinning at each shield (see also below, the hand-off).

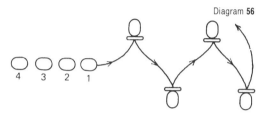

Diagram **56**

3   Reverse-spin (diagram 57)

Player 1 rebounds continuously off 2 and 3, practising the technique of hitting and reversing direction.

4   Hit, spin and pass (diagram 58)

Practise in pairs at half pace, building up speed gradually. To pass to the left, hit with left shoulder by dipping it, rotate to the right, and pass.

To pass to the right, hit with the right shoulder by dipping it, rotate to the left, and pass.

Feet should keep moving with a fast pumping action.

Spin in the opposite direction on the way back.

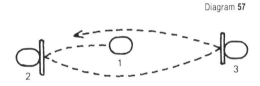

Diagram **57**

8   HAND-OFF

The hand-off is a forceful thrust of the arm, open palm outwards, into the head, chest, or shoulder of the would-be tackler. The ball carrier either forcefully pushes the tackler away or uses the tackler's own weight to push himself out of the way.

Youngsters should be made to realize that the hand-off is a stabbing motion, and should not be encouraged to run with an arm out. Timing is essential.

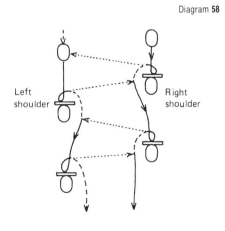

Diagram **58**

Left shoulder

Right shoulder

Coaching points

1   Size up the would-be tackler
2   Timing is important

26 Tony Myler (Widnes and Great Britain) successfully hands-off Clayton Friend in the third Test against New Zealand in 1985.

3 At the correct moment the ball carrier thrusts his arm, open palm outwards, into the head, chest or shoulder of the would-be tackler

4 The arm should be bent when contact is made and then immediately straightened.

Practices

1 In pairs with one player carrying the ball and the other a shield; then the ball carrier runs at his partner and hands off the shield which is held at chest height

2 Similar to the above, but incorporating a hand-off and side-step

3 The ball carrier in a winger's position against a covering full-back. The full-back has to touch the ball carrier's shorts with two hands; to do this he must stretch forward, encouraging a hand-off to the top of the head and an outside swerve.

Combination drills

Practices should be designed to encourage players to select the methods of evasion and breaking a tackle which are best suited to a particular situation.

Grid game

In a ten-metre square grid one player has to tackle as many as possible of the four other players in thirty seconds. The four ball carriers can use any method of evasion to stay 'alive' for the allocated time.

Channel rugby

One player defends in the middle of a narrow channel. The others, running one at a time, have to evade the would-be tackler and score a try. The width of the channel, wide at first, may be made narrower as the runners improve their evasive skills.

British bulldog with shields

A wider channel than above with two players in the middle holding shields. On a command, the rest of the group run through the channel to the other side as the players with shields attempt to stop them. Players eliminated collect the shields and join in the centre.

Scrummaging

1   Description
2   Rule governing scrum formation and put-in
3   The importance of possession
4   Major principles of scrummaging
5   Practices

27   The scrummage: the Great Britain and New Zealand packs about to scrum down in the third Test in 1985.

1   DESCRIPTION

The scrum is a formation unique to rugby, creating a situation in which both teams have an opportunity of gaining possession. As possession is a vital factor of Rugby League, the art of scrummaging should be practised constantly.

A scrum in Rugby League usually consists of six players packing in a 3-2-1 formation as in diagram 59.

Diagram **59**

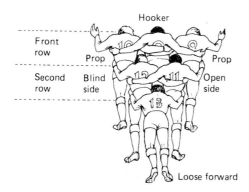

The pack consists of three players in the front row, who by interlocking their arms and heads with their opponents form a clear tunnel at right-angles to the touchline. The open-side prop forward should stand at the side of the scrum which is next to the referee as this is where the ball will be put in. The man in the middle is the hooker, who is supported on each side by the prop forwards; it is his task to heel the ball backwards. Two second-row forwards pack down behind the front row and are bound together by their arms entwining each other's body, and their heads being placed in the two gaps between the hooker and the props. The loose forward packs down behind the second-row forwards with his head in between them. The bodies of all the forwards should be horizontal to the ground.

When the scrummage has been correctly formed, the forwards are allowed to push. The scrum-half puts the ball into the centre of the tunnel, by rolling it along the ground, and the hooker is allowed to strike the ball with either foot once it has made contact with the ground in the centre of the tunnel. A good strike

from the hooker accompanied by a forceful push from the entire pack will ensure that the ball emerges from between the inner feet of the second-row forwards, allowing the side in possession to launch an attack.

The team winning possession should consider launching an immediate attack by its three-quarters so long as a good clean heel has been achieved.

2   RULE GOVERNING SCRUM FORMATION AND PUT-IN

The non-offending team have both the loose head and put-in, except when the ball is kicked into touch with a bounce before the fifth tackle. In this case the attacking team have the loose head but the defending team have the put-in.

3   THE IMPORTANCE OF POSSESSION

Scrummaging is an important contributory factor to possession, and possession in Rugby League football is probably more important than in any other team game. Statistics suggest that the team which has most possession in a game invariably wins.

Under the guidance of Joe Manley, the referees' assessor, the Rugby Football League conducted a survey of the scrums in all the professional first-team fixtures during the 1984–85 season. The law then stated that for every scrum the team having the loose head also had the put-in. The survey concluded that on average there were:

19.4   scrums per game, with
9.1   scrums won with the head,
2.4   scrums won against the head, and
7.9   scrum penalties.

Coaches studying these facts may conclude that a team should:

win every scrum when they have the head;
aim to win at least three per game against the head; and
reduce the number of scrum penalties conceded.

To achieve these objectives a team needs to develop the skill of efficient scrummaging within the laws of the game.

4 MAJOR PRINCIPLES OF SCRUMMAGING

Aim: to win possession at the scrum.

The major factors influencing this are:

1 The ability to push the hooker closer to the ball than the opposition's hooker
2 To create a good striking position, while at the same time making difficulties for the opposition
3 To push over the ball, and push the opposition off it.

On occasions when playing against a good scrummaging pack who have the head and put-in, it may be worth accepting that their hooker is going to strike the ball, and therefore concentrate on a six-man drive in an attempt to push them off it.

The major principles of scrummaging are, therefore, scrum formation, a quick strike for the ball, and a strong co-ordinated push.

A Formation of the scrum

Coaching points

All forwards:

1 The hooker should try to be the first to arrive at the mark of the scrum
2 The rest of the pack should follow quickly and form up before the opposition.

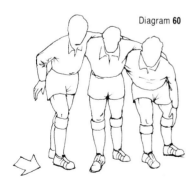

Diagram **60**

Front row (diagram 60)

1 The props position themselves beside the hooker, with the open-side prop standing at the side of the referee

2 To assist the hooker it is an advantage if the open-side prop is taller than the blind-side prop. The position is made easier if the blind-side prop packs in a lower position than the open-side prop. By doing this the hooker is naturally turned towards the put-in, and has a better view of the ball coming in

3 The heads and bodies of the three front-row forwards should be close together

4 The open-side prop should place his inside shoulder behind that of his hooker

Diagram **61**

5 He should grasp either: (a) the shirt of the blind-side prop firmly under the shoulder, commonly used if the hooker is strongly built as in diagram 61, or (b) the hip of the hooker and help to pull him over the ball, particularly if the hooker is slightly built, as in diagram 62.

Diagram **62**

6   The blind-side prop has his inside shoulder pushing into the armpit of his hooker, and grasps the shirt of the open-side prop firmly under the armpit. This binding gives the blind-side prop the longest possible extension of his arm, to assist in pushing his hooker over the ball

7   The hooker binds over the shoulders of the two prop forwards

8   The front row should on no account go down into the scrum until the second row is securely in position.

Diagram **63**

Second row (diagram 63)

1   The two second-row forwards bind firmly together before entering the scrum

2   The open-side second-row forward should bind over the arm of the blind-side second row, who should have his arm under the arm of the open-side second row

3   The second-row forwards should not disturb the front row, and must move into position low down with their heads going into the gaps between the hooker and props

4   The second-row's shoulders should be moved up so that they rest underneath the natural bulge of the prop's buttocks

5   Both second-row's backs should be straight and parallel to the ground. To ensure a flat back the head is kept up, locking the back in a strong, straight, safe position

6   The second-row forwards should help bind the front row tight.

Diagram **64**

Loose forward (diagram 64)

1   The loose forward should place his head between the two second-row forwards

2   The loose forward's shoulders should rest underneath the natural bulge of the second-row's buttocks

3   The loose forward's back should be straight and parallel to the ground in a strong, safe pushing position

4   The loose forward's arms should encircle the two second-row forwards and bind them securely together

5   The loose forward should be in position before the scrum is set.

B   Striking for the ball

1   The formation of the scrum should take into

account the individual preferences of the hooker, holding him in a position which enables him to strike quickly

2   The formation of the scrum should also push the hooker as close as possible to the point of entry of the ball

3   It is an advantage for the hooker to strike for the ball with the near foot because that is closest to the ball, and children, particularly those with ambitions in the game, should be encouraged to use this method.

There are two actions:

the near foot, and have to rake the ball back with a swinging action.

(a)   Advantages of far-foot hooking (diagram 67): (i) children will often have more control over the ball; (ii) when being beaten for the ball by a faster striking hooker, the far-foot can be used to go in behind the opposition's legs to trap the ball. He would then have to call for the full weight of his scrum so that his pack can push over the ball to win it back.

(b)   Disadvantages of far-foot hooking: (i) the hooker immediately loses any advantage of

Diagram 65

Diagram 67

Diagram 66

(a)   Raking action (diagram 65): the hooker bends his knee closest to the put-in and reaches over the ball, raking it back with his heel. The action is similar to riding a bicycle

(b)   Striking action (diagram 66): a faster action in which the hooker strikes straight ahead, hitting the ground with his heel and immediately turning the foot outwards round the ball. With practice the ball will be directed through the scrum in a straight line.

4   Hookers using the far foot have their weight on

having the head, and is at an even greater disadvantage when the opposition has it; (ii) he has to turn his body to face out towards the ball and runs the risk of being penalized for not packing square.

5   Hookers should be discouraged from squatting as this will slow their hooking action, particularly when pinned down by the weight of the opposition's front row.

C   The push

1   The pack should attempt to form up before the opposition, but they should not form the scrum until all their forwards are in position.

2   All the forwards should be aware of their duties, and should concentrate on them. Possession is important and the scrum is no place to have a rest!

3   The pack should attempt to push the hooker over the ball at the earliest legal moment. The push should be a single force towards the opposing front row. In order to achieve this concerted force, attention must be paid to the following:

(a)   The forwards must be parallel. Any forward out of line is wasting his effort, and is unable to transmit in the right direction the force applied by the players behind him.

(b)   The upper bodies of the pack must be as near horizontal as possible, with their backs flat and parallel with the ground.

(c)   A forward pushing with a rounded back is not only in a weak position, but will also hinder the pushing of the other forwards.

(d)   All the forwards must push at the same time.

4   There is no doubt that the strongest pushing position is achieved with the outside arms of the second row extended between the legs of the props, hands gripping the tops of the props' shorts. Because many props find this position too restrictive, the most common method to bind is with the second row placing their outside arms around the props' hips.

5   The second row should push the hooker towards the ball. It helps if the taller of the two second-row forwards packs down behind the open-side prop forward, and places his arm over that of the blind-side second row.

6   The blind-side second row, with his arm under the open-side second row, is able to place his inside shoulder under the hooker's buttocks and push him over the ball.

7   The position of the feet is very important (diagram 68): *the open-side prop forward* should have his nearest foot forward to keep his hooker on side. His furthest foot, the pushing foot, is placed slightly behind the front. *The hooker* should

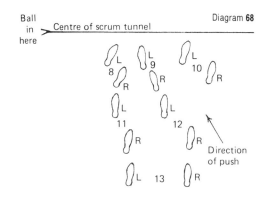

Diagram **68**

position himself so that his striking foot is slightly forward. *The blind-side prop forward* should have his non-pushing foot next to the hooker, forward and touching the centre of the scrum. His furthest, pushing, foot is placed to the side and back, in line with the heel of his inside foot. In this way the prop's near-side hip is able to give strong support to the hooker.

8   The second rows should push with their furthest legs back.

9   The loose forward's feet are spread for pushing and balance.

5   PRACTICES

1   General conditioning

It is necessary for all forwards, but particularly the front row, to develop their all-round strength and pay particular attention to the muscles of the neck, shoulders and upper body.

General strengthening exercises will be discussed in Section 6, Chapter 5 but it is valuable for the forwards to perform regular exercises to strengthen the neck. For example (diagram 69):

(a)   Static neck-muscle exercises (no movement, just an equal and opposite force from head and hands). Press the head forward, backward, left and right, tensing each time for ten seconds. Perform ten repetitions for each direction.

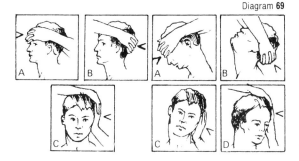

Diagram **69**

(b)   Dynamic neck-muscle exercises (the head slowly moves against the pressure of the hands). Use the same movement and repetitions as above.

2   *Partner exercises*

Competitive practices involving partners pushing and pulling one another provide excellent introductory and warm-up games before scrummaging is introduced:

(a)   Pulling and pushing (diagram 70): partners grip each other's jerseys, and either pull or push. Children should be with those of a similar size.

Diagram **70**

(b)   Two-man scrum: two players in a safe and strong scrummaging position compete against one another. They have chins lifted and backs flat, with feet spread out, and each grips his partner's jersey at the shoulders while endeavouring to pull or push him off balance.

3   *Hooker and scrum-half*

The hooker faces forward, with the scrum-half to his side. The scrum-half is holding the ball and facing the hooker.

The scrum-half:

(a)   Bends down holding the ball, point to point, close to the ground

(b)   The ball is rolled along the ground, in front of the hooker

(c)   The scrum-half quickly retires behind the hooker

(d)   As the ball appears, the scrum-half quickly picks it up and moves forward.

The hooker:

(a)   Bends forward, with head turned to concentrate upon the ball

(b)   Strikes for the ball with the near foot

(c)   The foot should be cocked so that contact is made with the outside of the near foot

(d)   The ball should be diverted backwards.

The ball should be put in from both sides so that the hooker becomes skilled at using both feet.

4   *Front row and scrum-half*

Two sets of front rows pack down against one another. With young children care should be taken that all six are evenly matched physically, and the opportunity used to make them fully aware of the rules relative to the head and the put-in.

The practice should progress to the scrum-half putting the ball in. At this stage the two packs should set with their feet back. The ball should be put in from the right and left.

5   *Pack and scrum-half*

Two sets of forwards pack down together. Care should be taken with the positions they take up. Once the ball has been put in, the back three should channel it back so that it comes out between the loose forward's feet.

If the back three have problems they can be taken out of the practice and placed in a pushing position against a wall. In this way they can practice controlling the passage of the ball out of the scrum.

Gaining possession

1 Falling on a stationary ball
2 Picking up a stationary ball
3 Controlling a moving ball
4 Catching a high ball
5 Practices for gaining possession

The importance of possession in Rugby League football cannot be overemphasized. The team in possession controls the game, and is always likely to score points. The team in opposition can only defend, unable to launch a counter-attack until it has the ball. The various techniques of gaining possession are therefore essential for winning rugby.

Most of the techniques are simple, but even international footballers need to practise them continuously in order to react quickly in pressure situations.

1   FALLING ON A STATIONARY BALL

Because possession is so important, a player under pressure should always be encouraged to play safe and quickly drop on any loose ball.

Coaching points

1 Move quickly to the ball
2 Keep the eye on the ball
3 The player should fall quickly and decisively next to the ball and place his body between the ball and the opposition, thus shielding it

4 He should hold the ball safely in his midriff and curl his body round it

2   PICKING UP A STATIONARY BALL

If a player is certain that he can pick up a stationary ball safely, he should do so because this will enable him to launch a counter-attack, which can be productive especially if the ball has been picked up in open play. It should be stressed, however, that if there is any doubt in the player's mind of his ability to pick up the ball cleanly, he should play safe and drop on it.

Coaching points

1 Move quickly to the ball
2 Keep the eye on the ball. On approaching the ball, the player should adjust his feet so that they are correctly positioned
3 Run at the side of the ball
4 Straddle the ball so that the inner leg is at the back of the ball
5 Lean the body down close to the ground

6   If the ball is lengthways across, scoop it with the rear hand going underneath the ball and the other at the front, thus preventing a knock-on

7   If the ball is lying with the point facing the player he should scoop up the ball by placing the hands at each side of the ball.

3   CONTROLLING A MOVING BALL

A moving rugby ball bounces and wobbles, and is often difficult to pick up cleanly. Players of all ages and abilities must be able to control the ball because possession is vital. More often than not a player should be encouraged to fall on to a moving ball and immediately gain possesion. The coaching points for this skill are no different from those already listed above.

If time allows, a player can control the ball with his feet, soccer fashion, before picking it up. It is also possible for a player to judge the bounce of the ball and collect it as it bounces into the air. This skill needs thorough training.

28   Steve Hampson (Wigan and Great Britain) catches perfectly a high ball under pressure in a Wigan v St Helens match in 1984. On the left, John Pendlebury offers protection.

Coaching points

1   Move quickly to the ball
2   Keep the eye on the ball
3   On approaching the ball, readjust the feet
4   Lean the body close to the ground
5   Extend the hands
6   Be prepared to catch the ball as it bounces up
7   Timing is important

Because possession is so vital the golden rule is: if in doubt fall on it.

4   CATCHING A HIGH BALL

Because kicking is an important tactic in Rugby League all players must be able to catch a ball that has been kicked high into the air.

Coaching points

1   Concentrate on the ball – resist the temptation to glance at oncoming opponents
2   Judge the flight of the ball

3   Move into position quickly
4   Keep the eye on the ball
5   Hold the arms out and up in a searching attitude, with the fingers spread
6   Allow the ball to land in a cradle formed by the hands, forearms and chest
7   Trap the ball with hand and forearm as high as possible on the chest
8   On catching the ball, round the shoulders
9   Keep the elbows close to the body and close together: bend the knees
10 The player should turn his side into the opponents, thus giving himself protection, and ensuring the ball cannot be jolted out of his arms in the tackle. By doing this he will ensure that any dropped ball goes back towards his own posts and is not a knock-on.

Progression

As soon as players are proficient catchers, they should

be encouraged to perform this skill while leaping high into the air. This requires them to move to the ball, and timing is important. This advanced skill will be fully explored later (see Section 5, Chapter 4).

5 PRACTICES FOR GAINING POSSESSION

Individuals

Players of all age groups should practise the skills of the game individually both in their own time and as part of the club coaching session. This requires them each to have a ball, and it may be worth considering encouraging children to bring their own ball with them to every coaching session.

Initially children should practise these techniques slowly and without pressure. Gradually, as they become more proficient, the tempo should be increased, and eventually opposition introduced. At first the opposition's movements should be monitored by the coach then gradually match conditions should be simulated.

Pairs

Two players working together, with one feeding the ball while the other safely gains possession. Pressure can then be developed by the feeder following the ball in and offering some form of opposition. The opposition needs to be controlled, being almost passive at first, but gradually increased as the receiver becomes more proficient.

Groups

Picking up a stationary ball (diagram 71):   The group stand in a line at point X with the ball lying on the floor fifteen metres in front of them, at point Y. At a given command the first player sprints forward, quickly picks the ball up at point Y, runs to point Z, and then returns placing the ball at point Y on his way back. When he arrives at point X, the second runner continues the practice.

Picking up a moving ball

1   From the side (diagram 72): 1 rolls the ball forward towards point X then runs to the end of the file. 2 runs forward and picks up the ball at X. He runs on to point Z then changes direction to take his place at Y. He rolls the ball towards X then runs to the end of the file as 3 goes forward to pick up. Each player completes this procedure. This can be repeated with the ball being rolled from the other side.

2   A ball moving towards the player: as above, but the ball is rolled towards the player from point Z.

3   A ball moving away from the player: as above but the ball is rolled from X away from the player, who sprints, picks it up, and continues to point Z before returning to X and starting the practice again.

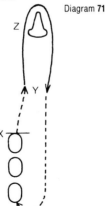

Diagram 71

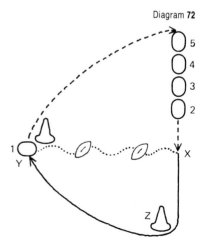

Diagram 72

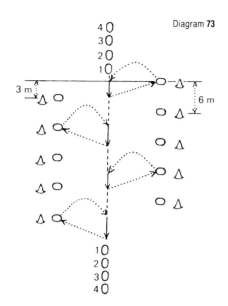

Diagram **73**

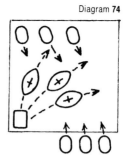

Diagram **74**

Catching a high ball. The cones are placed approximately twelve metres apart and staggered as in diagram 73.

Using three groups of players, two groups stand inside and opposite a cone, six metres apart, each holding a rugby ball. In turn, the third group of players move quickly down the centre of the two groups.

The players holding the rugby balls should take turns at throwing up a high ball for the runner, then as each runner catches the high ball he should quickly pass it to the thrower.

The runners may complete this drill three to four times as they move down the centre; the procedure should then be reversed back to the start.

All groups take a turn.

4 Games

(a) Three against three. Two teams of three, in a ten × ten metre grid. Team A lines up outside one end of the grid while the second team, B, groups at the other end. Three balls are placed at the coach's feet as shown in diagram 74.

On a signal the coach kicks the three balls about the grid. The A team sets off to gather the balls, one each, and they then run with them to 'score' at the other end of the grid. The ball is held in *both* hands while running. The B team may harass the A team but not 'grab' them. The winner is the team which takes less time for *all* players to 'score'.

(b) Catch and pass. Two teams, four against four, in a ten × ten metre grid. The players act as catchers (see diagram 75).

Diagram **75**

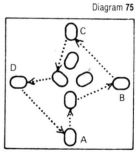

A throws in first; the ball is caught and passed to B. B passes to C who throws it in: it is caught and passed to D. D passes to A and the exercise is repeated.

The catchers' positions may vary, while A, B, C, and D may rotate their positions. A three against three situation may also be used: in this drop D, and have the catchers pass to B only.

(c) Kicking tennis. Two teams, four against

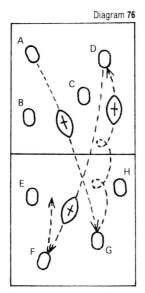

Diagram **76**

four, in a forty × twenty metres area, with one team in each half, as in diagram 76.

A starts the game by either throwing or kicking (depending on the level of skill) the ball into the other half, but if the ball goes out of bounds without a bounce the servers lose a point.

The receivers have to control the ball quickly. All punts must be caught cleanly before the ball touches the ground, while grubber kicks should be controlled immediately. The kickers receive one point if the receivers knock on, or if the ball bounces before going out of the grid. The ball is either kicked or thrown back, and the game continues.

(d) The chase. Players compete in pairs within the channels A, B and C as in diagram 77. These drills are controlled by the coach.

On the initial command each pair moves down the channels interpassing. On the second command they react quickly with the ball carrier in A kicking a bomb, in B a grubber, and in C a kick-over. Immediately the kick has been executed the partners compete in chasing and making the ball safe.

Diagram **77**

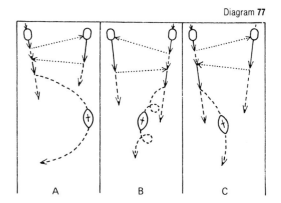

A   B   C

Kicking

1 Punt
2 Drop-kick
3 Place-kick
4 Bomb
5 Grubber
6 Push-through
7 Kick-over

Although Rugby League is essentially a handling game, kicking is a skill which also plays an important part in its scoring and tactics. All players should become proficient kickers.

1 PUNT

The punt is kicking a ball from the hand, and is used to:

(a) *Gain ground from a penalty kick.* From a penalty kick the ball may be kicked directly out of play over the touchline without bouncing.

(b) *Gain touch directly from play.* In order to gain ground the ball must first of all bounce in the field of play before crossing the touchline.

(c) *Take play downfield.* In this case the kicking team are content to give away possession in order to gain territorial advantage. It is important for the chasers to comply with the laws of the game before completing the tackle.

Coaching points

There are two forms of punt. The *torpedo* is used

29 Deryck Fox (Featherstone Rovers and Great Britain) punts downfield in the second Test against Australia in 1986.

when the aim is to gain a great deal of distance, or height, and the ball spins through the air. The *orthodox* method is easier to execute and is used to kick accurately over a short distance.

The correct execution of both types of punt depends greatly upon:

1 The way the ball is held
2 The way the ball is guided to contact with the foot
3 Positioning of the foot at the point of contact
4 Follow-through.

Because the orthodox punt is more easily executed it should be introduced before the torpedo.

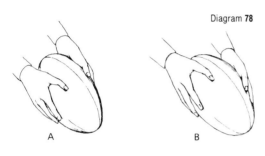

Diagram **78**

The orthodox punt (diagram 78, drawing A)

1 Hold the ball as for passing. Since the kick is often used as a snap tactic in general play it is an advantage not to change the position of the hands on the ball
2 Line up with the target so that the shoulders are square
3 The head should be down and the eyes kept on the ball until it has been kicked
4 The ball should be held a comfortable distance away from the body, and guided down to the point of contact with the foot
5 The round of the ball should fit into the round of the foot
6 The toes are straightened by being forced downwards from the ankle
7 Drive through the ball and follow through towards the target
8 Head and eyes are still down.

The torpedo punt (diagram 78, drawing B)

The coaching points are identical to those for the orthodox punt except that:

1 The right hand should be placed slightly under and to the rear of the right-hand side of the ball, and the left hand placed in a similar manner underneath and to the front of the left-hand side (vice versa for left-footed kickers)
2 The ball should feel comfortable in the hands and should be pointing slightly inwards
3 The kicking foot should be twisted slightly inwards as it meets the ball.

Practices

Individual practice

Players should be encouraged to practise the various techniques of kicking on their own. Because the ball is kicked over increasing distances it is often more practicable to work out with a partner.

Pairs

Practices in which partners kick to one another should concentrate on technique, accuracy and then distance.

1 Accuracy in kicking the ball:
   (a) to a partner who should not have to move to catch the ball
   (b) between the posts
   (c) into a grid or area of the pitch
   (d) bouncing into touch
2 Distance, attempting to force a partner back. Start an equal distance from a line and then try to finish closer to the line than the partner.

Group games

(1) *Forcing back.* Teams of equal numbers each try to force the opposition downfield. This enjoyable game can be played with any number of players from two upwards.
(2) *Game of catch* (diagram 79). A group of players

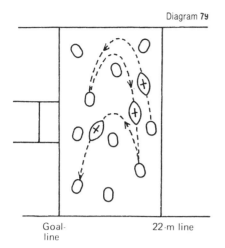

Diagram **79**

Goal-line   22-m line

is spread in an area approximately one-quarter of the playing field. Each player is given a number. One player kicks the ball high and calls a number. The player whose number is called must run and catch the kick. He immediately kicks the ball high and calls another number. Each player has a number of lives and they lose one life

(a)   for each kick which lands out of bounds, and

(b)   for each dropped ball.

2   DROP-KICK

The drop-kick is made:

(a)   To restart the game from a dead-ball situation

(b)   To score a point from the field of play.

Coaching points

The drop-kick is based on the same principles as the orthodox punt. The only variation is the timing of the release of the ball, which must be such that the foot meets the ball just as it touches the ground:

1   To start with, look where the kick is to be directed and aim the ball, but then the eyes must concentrate on the area where the foot will connect with the ball

2   The head should be down and the eyes kept on the ball until the ball has been kicked

3   Hold the ball away from the body: the action should not be cramped by holding the ball too close

4   Hold the ball as for a pass and then adjust to an angle from the ground

5   Guide the ball to the ground at the same angle and without any tilt so that it will hit the ground beside the toes of the non-kicking foot

6   With the toe pointing to the ground at approximately the same angle as the ball, kick the ball with the lower part of the instep, not the toe-cap.

Practices

Individuals

Individual practice, kicking over the posts for accuracy. As the players become proficient the angle and distance are increased. Confidence is important and kickers of all age groups and abilities should practise from positions where they are competent.

Pairs

Drop-kicking to each other so that the partner does not have to move to catch the ball.

Group practices

To improve the ability to drop a goal during play, practices must incorporate a pass and, later, opposition:

1   *In pairs, one passing the other kicking*: the pass may be from the ground if the kicker is likely to be kicking from first receiver.

2   *Opposition moving into the kicker*: as always the opposition should be instructed to move in very slowly to start with, and match conditions should be introduced only when the kicker is proficient.

It is worth mentioning that some coaches have been successful in teaching the drop-kick with soccer balls. This eliminates the irregular bounce which young children find difficult to control.

3   PLACE-KICK

A place-kick is used to start and restart the game and to kick for goal. A successful goal kick gives the team two points and is thus an important part of the game.

Two methods can be adopted:

1   round-the-corner, and
2   toe-end.

Round-the-corner

With this method the ball is kicked soccer fashion with the instep or inside of the foot. The advantages are that the kicker gains more mobility in the thigh and is able to kick powerfully using the commonly-worn lightweight football boots.

The problem is that the trajectory of the ball is often curved, which makes accuracy for the right-footed kicker, kicking from the right-hand side of the pitch, difficult.

Coaching points

1   On no account must the ball be buried into the ground, but should be in an elevated position with the point clearly visible to the kicker. It should be teed up in the same way that a golfer tees up a golf ball, as in diagram 80. The tee can be made by digging the toe into the ground in four places, and thus elevating a small piece of turf on which the ball can be securely placed. An alternative is to use a small mound of sand
2   Aim a seam at the target while placing the ball
3   The kicker, ball and target should be in a straight line
4   The kicker should stand directly behind the ball and place his non-kicking foot level with it
5   His body should be directly over the ball; a visual check should be made to ensure the seam is pointing at the target

30 a & b   David Stephenson (Leeds, formerly Wigan, and Great Britain) kicked seven goals out of seven attempts in the Test match against Papua New Guinea in 1987. In the left-hand picture Stephenson lines up the ball before one of those successful goal-kicks; in the right-hand picture he kicks and follows through.

Diagram **80**

6   The head should be bent with eyes looking down at the spot of the ball (about $2\frac{1}{2}$ cm or 1 in. from the bottom)

7   Maintaining good balance, the kicker should take the required number of steps backwards and to the side

8   The kicker should maintain deep concentration as he takes a final visual check of the target

9   The approach to the ball should be along a curved arc, the final two strides being straight, keeping his eye on the ball all the time

10   The ball should be kicked with the instep or the side of the foot

11   The non-kicking foot should be slightly further away from the ball than for the toe-end method, allowing greater mobility of the hip

12   The body should lean over the ball with head bent

13   The foot should follow through powerfully in a direct line through the ball and towards the target

14   The shoulder should be level and the arms out to aid balance.

It is important to note that if the last two strides are directly in line with the ball and the target, and the follow-through goes straight through the ball in a line directly towards the target, then the trajectory of the ball will be straight.

The importance of concentration and confidence cannot be overemphasized.

Toe-end

The advantage of this method is that target, ball and kicker are in a straight line throughout, so accuracy is more easily obtained.

It is important for the toe of the kicking foot to connect exactly on the 'the spot' of the ball, which will otherwise deviate from the target. Because the point of the toe makes contact with the ball, it is usual for the goal kicker to have a kicking boot which has a hard, square toe and more often than not a reinforced sole.

There are two methods of placing the ball for the toe-end method of kicking:

(a)   Upright. The ball should be placed in an upright position with a seam pointing at the posts. The spot of the ball should be clearly visible.

It is usual for the ball to be placed in a small dent in the ground which may be made by the heel of the boot. This dent should allow the spot to be visible.

Some kickers build a tee similar to that described for the round-the corner method. It is important that the ball is not teed too high otherwise the boot will go directly under the ball and power will be lost.

(b)   Bullet style. The ball is placed in an elevated position (again sand may be used) on the ground, lengthways with a seam pointing directly at goal, and at an angle, as in diagram 81. The kicker must take great pains to line up the ball with the target; body, ball and target should always be in a straight line:

1   Tee up the ball so that the point of impact is clearly visible: this is the 'spot'

2   Aim a seam at the target while bending over the ball

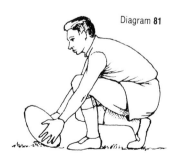

Diagram **81**

3   The kicker, ball and target should be in a straight line
4   The kicker should stand directly behind the ball with his non-kicking foot level and close to the ball, and his kicking foot directly behind it, as in diagram 82
5   His body should be directly over the ball. A visual check should be made to ensure the seam is pointing at the target, and the kicker, ball and target are directly in line
6   The head should be bent and with eyes looking down at the spot of the ball
7   Maintaining good balance, the kicker should take the required number of steps backwards
8   The kicker should maintain deep concentration as he takes a final visual check of the target
9   The kicker moves slowly forward in a rhythmic movement keeping his eye on the ball
10 The non-kicking foot should be placed next to the ball
11 The body should be over the ball with head bent
12 The toe should make contact with the spot of the ball
13 The foot should follow through powerfully in a direct line through the ball and towards the target
14 The shoulders should be level and the arms out to aid balance. Again confidence and concentration are important.

Practice

It is important that the coach recognizes the importance of both methods of goal kicking, and introduces his players to each so that they can choose the method which suits them best.

Confidence is the most important factor in successful goal-kicking. Before each goal-kicking practice it is important to:

1   Warm-up
2   Use the correct equipment: the rugby balls should be inflated to the correct poundage, boots studded and well laced
3   Concentration is important: concentrate as keenly as on match days

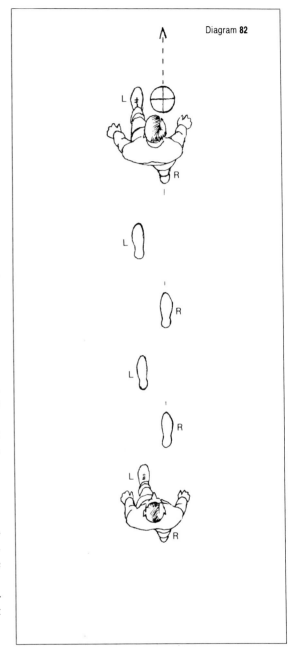

Diagram 82

4   Be positive: each kick is going to be successful. Talk to the ball and tell it to go between the posts
5   Visualize a successful kick: before placing the ball imagine the kick going between the posts.

When practising kicks there are two major areas:

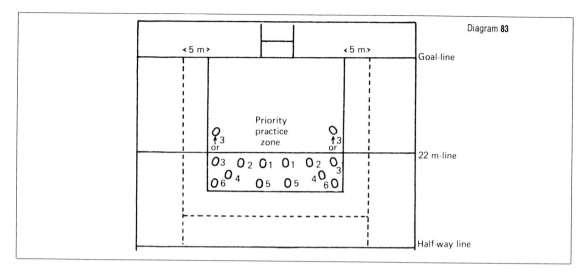

Diagram **83**

(a) *Priority area* (diagram 83). This is the area from which shots at goal should always be successful. It obviously varies for each individual, depending on both age and ability. The diagram below is the suggested priority area for an above-average adult goal kicker.

Have three shots from each of the twelve positions marked in diagram 83. This should take twelve to eighteen minutes. Take stock and note the success/failure rate. Aim for 95% – thirty-four successes out of thirty-six. Any difficulties should be overcome before the session is completed.

(b) *Area of difficulty* (diagram 84). Successful attempts from this area are often considered a bonus. The chances of failure are relatively high and the kicker should be aware of this. Do not worry about missed kicks, but praise success.

Before starting work in this session warm up thoroughly, and then take one shot from each position in the priority area. Aim for a 95% success rate or ten out of twelve. Then take three shots from each of the positions shown.

Work at this range over five or six weeks. Keep a success/failure record, and aim to improve it.

Organization of practice

Initially the goal kicker is trying to make himself consistent with all kicks in the priority area. He should concentrate upon this until he achieves the required consistency. When this is achieved the kicker must try to improve his consistency in the area of difficulty. This should not, however, be at the expense of losing consistency in the priority area.

An ideal time to work on the more difficult kicks is during the close season, or early in the week, but kicks immediately prior to the game should be from the priority area. This is the time to revise and boost confidence.

Kicking analysis

During each practice session and after each game the coach should analyse the performance of his kicker, with awareness of the success/failure percentage. Faults should be analysed and steps taken to eradicate them before the next game.

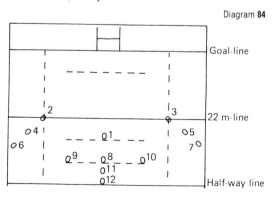

Diagram **84**

Mental rehearsal

Place-kicking is one of the few closed skills in rugby football. It is not affected by the opposition. Recognized kickers should spend time each day visualizing successful kicks at goal. The imagery should incorporate the sense of the surroundings, the smell of the pitch, the sound from the terraces, and the feel of the ball. Imagine placing the ball, the walk back, the approach. Visualize the action of the kick, and above all the ball going successfully between the posts.

This procedure should be followed before each shot at goal during the game. Not only does this boost confidence, but it also assists concentration.

Flexibility exercises

Kickers should perform flexibility exercises regularly (see Section 6, Chapter 3).

4   BOMB

The bomb or 'up and under' is a punt which is directed high into the air. The intention of this tactical kick is to enable the kicking side to arrive underneath the ball from an onside position, thereby putting the catcher under extreme pressure.

Coaching points

As for the punt, but:

1 The body leans backwards
2 The foot makes contact directly under the ball
3 The drive of the foot is upwards
4 The point of contact of the ball with the foot is usually vertical to the punt.

There can be minor variations:

1 The inexperienced kicker may have success holding the ball point to point, giving him a large surface on the ball on which to make contact, as in diagram 85.
2 An experienced kicker will often make contact directly on the point of the ball, as in diagram 86, in an attempt to increase height and accuracy.

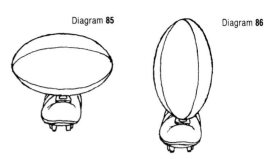

Diagram **85**   Diagram **86**

The foot must make contact at the precise point to guarantee success.

Practices

This is a specialist skill and the kicker will experience most success by working on his own, aiming for height and accuracy. It is often an advantage to mark out a target area with cones, or if on a pitch to aim for each kick to land just before the in-goal area.

Often the kicking practice can be combined with catching practice, working in pairs as described in the section on catching.

When working with a team it is necessary to set up the kick from a play-the-ball situation with a determined chase from an onside position. This will be explored fully in the section on tactical kicking (see Section 5, Chapter 4).

5   GRUBBER-KICK

A grubber-kick projects the ball along the ground, making it roll point over point and eventually causing it to bounce up into the air. This is a particularly useful device to breach a defence that has been tackling well. The aim is to kick the ball along the ground between two opposing players, allowing a team-mate who is onside to run through, regain possession and to advance the attack.

Coaching points

1 Hold the ball as if for passing but slightly lower than for the punt
2 Keep the eye on the ball
3 Strike the top of the ball just before it makes contact with the ground, as in diagram 87

4   Kick with knee bent, and head over the ball
5   The instep should be stretched down
6   The foot drives the ball into the ground.

Diagram **87**

Practices

1   Roll the ball, end over end, to a partner thereby demonstrating the aim of the skill
2   Also with a partner, practise grubber-kicking to one another
3   Kicking relay: squads of four or more should be used, arranged as in diagram 88. On the coach's command, 1 grubber-kicks the ball past the marker cone (at fifteen metres), regathers it and

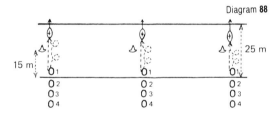

Diagram **88**

touches down over the 25-metre line. He then either kicks the ball to 2, or runs back passing him the ball. The relay continues with all team members
4   Team drills with opposition: two teams, four against four, for example. As the opposition is approached, the ball carrier grubber-kicks the ball between any two of them for a team-mate to run and regather.

6   PUSH-THROUGH

This is similar to the grubber, but the ball is side-footed. The disadvantage is that the ball when kicked

in this way will not stand up. However, it has the advantages of being:

1   Easier to execute
2   Can be performed at speed
3   The distance at which the ball stops can be more easily controlled.

Coaching points

1   Hold the ball as if for passing
2   Keep the eye on the ball
3   Strike the ball with the side of the foot immediately it makes contact with the ground
4   The foot follows through with the weight of the kick being closely controlled
5   Contact with the ball should be made when the body is over the ball.

Practices

1   Individually or with a partner, practising the technique and paying particular attention to the weighting of the kick
2   Relay, as for the grubber
3   Team drills with opposition close to the goal-line. As the opposition is approached, the ball carrier 'pushes' the ball through a gap, weighting it so that it stops in the in-goal area. A team-mate chases from an onside position.

7   KICK-OVER

A similar play to both the grubber-kick and the push-through, with the identical aim of breaching a well-organized defence. In this case the ball is kicked over the heads of the opposition for the kicker or a team-mate to run through and regather.

Coaching points

Identical to the punt except that the foot is slightly cocked, and does not follow through.

The foot lifts the ball over a short distance. Correct weighting of the ball is exceptionally important and the kicker should be able to perform this skill at speed.

Practices

1   *Individual*: the ball is kicked, followed and caught before it touches the ground. Gradually speed should be increased so that eventually the skill can be performed at full speed.
2   *Pairs, with partner acting as opposition*: the ball carrier approaches at speed. When close to his partner the ball is kicked over and caught before it bounces.
3   *Relay*: a similar relay as for the grubber.

Practices for the bomb, the grubber-kick, the push-through and kick-over (diagram 89)

From a play-the-ball fifteen metres from the goal-line, the acting half-back passes to the first receiver who kicks into the in-goal area. The rest of the

players chase and the ball must be secured. Any of the above kicks may be practised in this way.

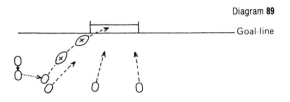

Diagram **89**

Goal-line

Haphazard kicking practices should be discouraged, particularly those that take place prior to training and before an adequate warm-up.

It is necessary for the coach to discipline the players to begin every training session with a well structured warm-up which should involve an easy paced run with the players passing the ball, or incorporating practise of some skill. Time should later be allocated to practising and perfecting kicking techniques.

THINKING AND DECISION-MAKING

Andy Gregory, very much the 'general' of the side, is outstanding in his decision-making on the field.

The skilled performer

1   WHO IS A SKILFUL PLAYER?

The many skills of Rugby League football were discussed in the previous chapter. Drills and practices were suggested for the players, and relevant teaching points for the coaches. It is now appropriate to ask the question, 'Who is a skilful player?'

Is he simply someone who can perform successfully these skills in a training environment, or is there more to it than that? Certain individuals can perform the skills perfectly when there is no opposition, but as soon as they are faced with opponents intent on knocking them to the ground with determined tackling, their skills leave them. Are these players skilful? The answer is – not yet.

First, we have to determine why their skills break down. Unfortunately, certain individuals do not have the 'heart' to play Rugby League at a high level. No matter how hard they try they cannot overcome the fear of hard physical contact, and because of this they will never be successful at the sport. Others, however, have the 'heart' but need time to progress from performing their skills unopposed, to performing them against full-blooded opposition.

The coach must realize that it is far easier to catch a high ball without opposition, than to catch one which has (a) been kicked as high as the floodlights, (b) is coming down close to the goal-posts, and (c) is being followed by players who are onside and will arrive at the same time as the ball. A player who can do the former requires progressive practices to prepare him to become competent at the latter. The coach must recognize these facts, and structure subsequent drills accordingly.

Perhaps we are now getting closer to our definition. Is a skilled performer one who can perform the skills against determined opposition? Well, almost. Consider the example already referred to on page 7 of the centre with an unmarked winger outside him, running towards the touchline and switching the winger into the covering loose forward. Assuming that the switch pass was executed perfectly, is the centre a skilled performer? Obviously again the answer must be no. Why? Because the player performed the incorrect skill.

Skill must therefore be linked to thinking and the making of correct decisions.

A skilful performer is one who can (a) perform the techniques perfectly, (b) perform those techniques against opposition, and (c) decide correctly at any given moment which technique to perform.

2   DECISION-MAKING

Successful decision-making can best be described as the ability to think when on the rugby field, to arrive at the correct decision, to have the skill to execute the action, and to have the time in which to achieve it. Thinking must be encouraged at every stage of a player's development, and falls into two broad catagories:

1   *Skill*

Ability to apply the correct skills, which all players need to develop.

2   *Tactical ability*

Ability to choose the correct tactics to control the game.

3   TIME

The speed at which players are able to make decisions and put them into practice determines their effectiveness. The game's tactics and skills are similar at every level, but the time available to make decisions is reduced the higher the standard of competition. This has two implications:

1   *Preparation of the team*

Ensure that time is taken into consideration. Once the players have demonstrated their ability to make decisions, increase the pressure by reducing the time they have available.

2   *Game plan*

Attempt to pressurize the opposition into error by reducing the time they have to think; in other words, increase the speed of the defensive line.

Decision-making: use of skills

1   Games awareness
2   Knowledge of specific principles of play:
 a)   using the extra man
 b)   creating the extra man
3   Attacking a defence with an equal number of players
4   Principal factors
5   Previous experience

Correct decision-making applies to the four major categories of running and handling, tackling, gaining possession and kicking.

It is dependent on:

1   Games awareness
2   Knowledge of specific principles of play
3   Previous experience.

The examples in this chapter apply to running and handling.

1   GAMES AWARENESS

Players have to be aware of the changing situation around them, particularly the position and movement of team-mates, the position and movement of the opposition, and the creation of space. Games awareness depends on:

1   *Skill*:   once the players become so proficient in the game's basic skills that they are performed by reflex action, they are able to become more alert to the changing situation around them.
2   *Scanning*:   the ability to look quickly around the pitch in the middle of the action, and understand what is happening.

3   *Peripheral vision*:   the ability to observe the action directly at the front, yet at the same time to understand the images which appear outside the central vision.

Practices

1   Skill: players of all ages and abilities need to practise continuously the skills of the game so that they can be performed as reflex actions. Pressure in the form of opposition should also be introduced.
2   Scanning: correct decisions can only be made by the player who is aware of the positions of his own players in relation to the opposition. This involves scanning the playing area, and should be developed by performing in game-like situations which involve the making of decisions (see the numerous small-sided games listed towards the end of this Section).
3   Peripheral vision:
 (a)   *Grid passing*: divide the group into pairs each with a ball. The pairs move about passing the ball in a confined area. Suppose there is a squad of twenty players, in ten

pairs. Interpass in four grids, then two grids and finally one. The ball must not be dropped. The players concentrate on giving and catching the ball, but have to be aware of the other players in the grid(s).

(b)   *Union jack*: take eight players in one grid. They pair up as in diagram 90, A with B, C with D, E with F and G with H. A and B each hold a ball. On a command, the balls are passed to the left around the outside of the grid. Each player, after passing the ball, sprints across the grid and interchanges position with his partner. The drill is continuous. Each player should:

(i)   Communicate, asking for the ball
(ii)   Catch
(iii)   Watch the person he is going to pass to
(iv)   Pass, and
(v)   Sprint across the grid into position.

The players must be aware of all the images appearing out of central vision.

Diagram **90**

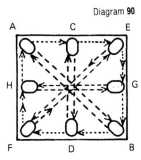

(c)   *Channel drill*: divide the squad into threes, working in a narrow channel or corridor, as in diagram 91. Each group has a ball, and on a command they move down the grid interpassing towards the end C–D. Upon reaching C–D, they immediately turn round and move in the other direction towards A–B. Once the drill is underway each group will have to pass the ball as the others approach to go past them moving in the opposite direction.

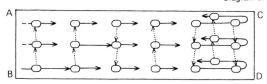

Diagram **91**

This drill develops scanning as all the players not only have to watch the ball but must also be aware of the other group's approach.

2   KNOWLEDGE OF SPECIFIC PRINCIPLES OF PLAY

The major objective of successful Rugby League is to create situations in which a team has more players around the ball than the opposition, and then when in possession to convert that overload into points. This depends on:

(a)   Using the extra man
(b)   Creating the extra man.

a)   Using the extra man

It helps in making decisions to be able to predict the movements of the opposition.

A good team will soon recognize that they are outnumbered, and will quickly bring more players into the area. Numerical superiority will not last long, therefore, so speed of execution is vitally important.

The major principles are simply:

1   run straight,
2   run quickly, and
3   force the defence to react, then pass to the unmarked player.

Practices

1   Two against one

In the confines of a grid, have two players attack one defender. At first have the defender standing directly in front of the attacker and condition him to attempt to tackle the ball carrier.

31   Two against one: Noel Cleal (Australia) draws Joe Lydon (Great Britain) and then passes to his full-back, Gary Jack, in the second Great Britain v Australia Test in 1986.

Coaching points

The ball carrier must:

1   Run at speed
2   Be aware of the position of the support player, and of the defender
3   Run at the opposite shoulder of the defender to where the support is, causing the defender to turn away from his support, as in diagram 92.

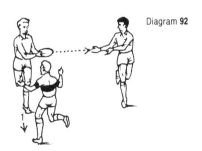

Diagram **92**

4   Immediately prior to the pass, and during it, look at the receiver. The defender will be visible from the corner of the eye (peripheral vision)
5   If in doubt whether the pass will go directly to the support player because he is too flat, too deep, too far away, or because he is not looking at the ball carrier, then hold on to the ball firmly with two hands.

The support players must:

1   Keep behind the ball carrier at all times. It is an advantage to lie further back than normal if faster than the ball carrier, in order to accelerate on to the pass, but remember that the ball carrier will be moving at speed
2   Run straight, keep it simple
3   Be aware of the position and movements of the defender, but look at the ball carrier

4 Immediately you realize the defender cannot tackle you, shout clearly for the ball.

Thinking

1 It is important for the ball carriers not to plan their actions beforehand. Concentrate on forcing the defence to react, then select the option which will out-manoeuvre them.
2 The ball carrier controls the situation. He selects the option which is to commit the defence.
3 Communication is vital. If, for instance, the ball carrier is in broken play, and approaching the full-back, he may be unaware of the position of his support. It is the duty of the other players to support the ball and to inform the ball carrier when they are in position.
4 The support player can help the ball carrier to decide when to pass by calling for the ball.

Development

As the attackers become more confident, allow the defenders to play as they would in a match. Remember to make the drill realistic. Few coaches would encourage a defender to go for an interception, the majority quite rightly encouraging him to try to tackle the ball carrier. Progress then to placing the defender in a winger's position, still encouraging the ball carrier to run straight and fast. As the defender comes in, the man 'in space' should call for the ball.

A more difficult progression is for the defender to adopt the position of a covering full-back. The ball carrier now has three options:

1 To give an early ball to the winger and then support him on the inside

2 To arc infield towards the defender, slowing down his progress before making the pass
3 To commit the defender, then pass in the tackle.

These three options depend on the skills of the attackers and each situation as it arises. Practising all the variations under the analytical eye of the coach will help the players to understand the principles of two against one, and assist them with decision-making.

During all handling practices the players should be encouraged to stay 'alive' when making a pass, and support the ball carrier. A worthwhile progression is to place a ten-metre channel down the field with defenders at intervals of fifteen to twenty metres. The two players have to combine several times. Each in turn acts as the ball carrier, and at all times they have to stay 'alive' and in support, as in diagram 93.

2   Three against two (ball carrier in the middle)

In the confines of a channel twenty × ten metres, three players attack two defenders, as in diagram 94. Condition the defenders to stay in line, with one to take the ball carrier.

Coaching points

The ball carrier must

1 Run at speed
2 Run straight, with no crossfield running
3 Be aware of the position of both support players and defenders
4 Run hard between the two defenders, forcing them to react: one or both will move to tackle the ball carrier, leaving an unmarked player

Diagram **93**

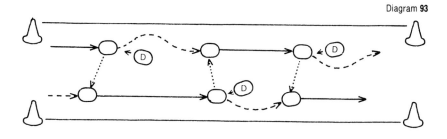

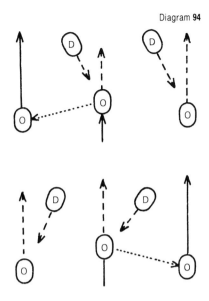

Diagram **94**

5 Immediately look at the unmarked player, and prepare to pass

6 If in any doubt whether the pass will go directly to the support player, keep hold of the ball in two hands and attempt to break the tackle.

Support players must

1 Keep behind the ball carrier at all times. It is an advantage to lie further back than normal if faster than the ball carrier, in order to accelerate on to the pass, but remember that the ball carrier will be moving at speed

2 Be aware of the position and movements of the defenders, but look at the ball carrier

3 Immediately you realize the defenders have been drawn away, shout clearly for the ball.

Thinking

1 Again, the ball carriers must not plan their actions beforehand. Concentrate on forcing the defence to react, and then select the option which will out-manoeuvre them.

2 The ball carrier initially controls the situation, deciding on the angle of run to commit the defence. He is also aware of the position of the

defence, and when drawn is immediately aware that a pass is possible.

3 This process of thinking can be helped by communication from the support players, particularly when the support finds himself in space.

4 Control of the ball is vital. If in doubt, hold the ball in two hands and try to break the tackle.

Progression

Allow the defence to adopt match-like conditions, insisting that:

1 They operate in line

2 They set themselves as if attempting to make a tackle on a determined ball carrier, and

3 One of them takes the man with the ball.

3   Three against two (ball carrier at the end)

An identical drill to the one above, except that the end man carries the ball. Encourage the players to solve the problem themselves. They will quickly work out that the ball carrier has three options:

(a)   Quick passing. All three players handle the ball, trying to move it quickly to the end man in space. The ball carrier must attract a defender, but pass early enough to the middle man to allow him time to catch and pass before being tackled.

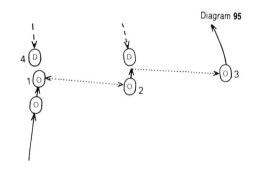

Diagram **95**

Coaching points

The ball carrier O1 (diagram 95) must

1 Run at speed

2 Run at the opposite shoulder of the defender D4

to where the support is, causing the defender to move that way

3   Immediately the attention of defender D4 has been attracted, prepare to pass
4   Check visually on the support from O2: can a pass be made allowing O2 enough time to catch and pass the ball before being tackled by D5?
5   If so – pass to O2's hands
6   If not – either pass directly to O3, or try to break D4's tackle.

The support player O2 must

1   Support ball carrier O1
2   Be aware of the position of O3 and the defenders
3   Hold hands out presenting a target to O1
4   As O1 passes, decide if an immediate pass to O3 will be successful
5   If the decision is yes, catch and pass the ball in one movement. Then support
6   If there is any doubt about (a) the position of O3, or (b) the position of D5, keep hold of the ball and make ground.

The support player O3 must

1   Be prepared to receive a pass from either O1 or O2
2   Keep eyes inwards on O1 and O2, but be aware of the position of the defenders
3   When in space, shout for the ball.

(b)   Early pass: An early pass by O1 to O2, who carries the ball forward and commits the defence, thus reverting to the three against two practice (ball carrier in the middle) previously described.

(c)   Pass to player in space: Run at the opposition committing the two defenders, then pass to whichever player is in space.

Coaching points

The ball carrier must

1   Run at speed
2   Run straight
3   Be aware of the positions of the support players and defence
4   As the defenders react, pass directly to the unmarked player. This will be either:
    (a)   a pass to the player in the middle, or
    (b)   a pass in front of the player in the middle to the one at the end
5   If in any doubt hold the ball firmly in both hands, and try to break the tackle.

The support players must

1   Run straight
2   Keep behind the ball carrier at all times – indeed the end player will need to be even further back to allow the ball carrier the chance of making a wide pass
3   Be aware of the movements of the defender but look at the ball carrier
4   Immediately upon realizing that you are unmarked shout clearly.
5   Timing is important; accelerate on to the ball.

32   Three against two: the ball carrier in the middle passes towards the player in space during a Great Britain squad training session at the Lilleshall National Sports Centre in the summer of 1986. Joe Lydon, blocked by Ronnie Duane, passes to the man in the middle, Shaun Wane, with Andy Gregory wide. The other defender is Shaun Edwards. Bob Beardmore observes.

Thinking

1   The ball carriers must not plan their strategy. Keep it simple and attack the goal-line. Concentrate on making the defence react, reading their actions, then out-manoeuvring them.
2   The ball carrier controls the situation, and decides on the angle of run to commit the defence. He is also aware of the movements of the defence and when drawn is immediately aware that a pass is on.
3   This process of thinking can be helped by communication from the support players, particularly when the support finds himself in space.
4   Control of the ball is vital. If in doubt, hold the ball in two hands and try to break the tackle.

Progression

Initially, condition the defence to take the ball carrier and outside man, and later the ball carrier and the inside man. When the ball carrier is proficient at making both the normal and long pass, allow the defence to select their strategy.

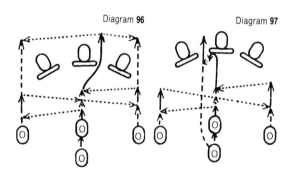

Diagram **96**   Diagram **97**

4   Four against three (with tackle shields)

Three players in line attack three defenders holding tackle shields. The ball carriers have an extra player behind them.

The three attackers interpass, with one of them carrying the ball strongly into the defence. The ball carrier is determined and tries to break through the tackle. If he is successful he should immediately pass

to the support, who will be at either side, as in diagram 96. If the ball carrier is prevented from making the break he should turn in the tackle and offload to the player at the back, as in diagram 97.

Be aware at all times of the positions of the support players and the defenders.

Coaching points

The ball carrier must

1   Run at speed
2   Run straight
3   Be aware of the position of the support players and the defenders
4   If more than one defender is drawn in, be prepared to pass to the player in space
5   If not, run into the opposition with determination, carrying the ball in both hands
6   Try to break the tackle: if successful, carry the ball through, off-load to your support, and then give support yourself
7   If unable to break the tackle, hit and turn, trying to offload to the support player at the back
8   If in any doubt whether the pass will go directly to the support player, keep hold of the ball with both hands.

The support players – to the side

Should position themselves as in previous practices, but lie deeper. If the ball carrier breaks the line, be quick to readjust positions to support him. Similarly, if the ball carrier offloads to the support at the back, readjust and support.

The support player – behind

1   Stay behind the front three
2   Read the situation
3   If the ball carrier breaks the line, support and communicate
4   If the ball carrier is stopped by the defence, watch which way he turns, and time your run to receive the ball; this will often mean that you start your run later than you first thought
5   On receiving the ball check what support you have.

Read the game

It is important in all these practices for the players to read the game and not to plan what they are going to do beforehand. Simply:

1 Run straight,
2 Run fast, and
3 The ball carrier should pass to the unmarked player.

(b) Creating the extra man

Players must be taught how best to make use of numerical superiority. First, they need to be made aware of the ways in which they can move around the pitch, and more important, around the ball. The junior coach lays the foundation with the advanced handling skills explained in the last Section, paying particular attention to the teaching points of the loop and run-around.

Similarly, coaches of all age groups should encourage the players to increase their involvement in the game. Commands such as 'Quickly on your feet!', 'Pass and follow!', and 'Support the ball!' will condition the players to become involved. The various drills explained under the heading 'Support play' in Section 5, Chapter 3 extend the process.

During the game, the coach should adopt tactics

which create the extra man, and encourage players to move across field to where the ball is.

At open-age level, patterns of play should be introduced. These enable players to anticipate the movement of the ball and to adopt positions of support. Ellery Hanley and Garry Schofield are masters of this art. During training sessions they make themselves aware of all the team moves, particularly those executed by the forwards, so they can adopt positions of support. Their timing and angle of run are superb.

Extra involvement, particularly at open-age level, is often controlled by fitness levels, another factor in the argument for improved conditioning.

3   ATTACKING A DEFENCE WHICH HAS AN EQUAL NUMBER OF PLAYERS

It is not always possible to gain numerical superiority, and players need to be aware that there are certain principles to be adopted when attacking a defence with an equal number of players.

The example used is of a centre and wing partnership, but the same principles apply wherever an attack is launched. The first aim of the ball carrier, in this case the centre, is to draw both defenders to him and to pass to the wing in the gap created. The success of the ploy is entirely dependent upon the ability of the two defenders: how they react will determine the development of the attacking play.

A   The ball carrier O4 tries to run outside his opposite number, causing the defensive winger D2 to be drawn infield and creating space on the outside for O5 to run through as in diagram 98.

33 Garry Schofield, up in support of his forwards, scores another fine try in the first Test against Australia in 1986.

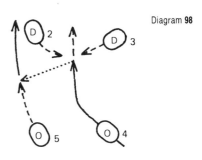

Diagram **98**

Coaching points

The ball carrier O4 must

1   Run at speed
2   Take an outside arc, initially angling towards the touch-line to get outside D3, but then immediately straightening and punching into the space between D3 and D2
3   This encourages D2 to leave his touchline, and commits him to the tackle
4   Be aware of supporting winger O5 out of the corner of his eye (peripheral vision)
5   Time the pass as soon as D2 has been drawn in
6   If in any doubt, keep hold of the ball in two hands and try to break the tackle.

The support player O5 must

1   Be guided by the ball carrier O4
2   Look directly at O4, but be aware of the defender's movements (using peripheral vision)
3   Time the run to comply with O4's thinking
4   Stay on the outside, and attack up the touchline
5   Shout for the ball when D2 has been drawn.

As the centre angles across, the winger will want to come for the inside ball. This urge must be resisted.

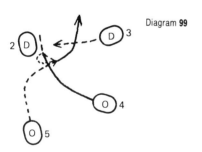

Diagram **99**

B   An identical situation with the ball carrier attempting to perform the same skill (diagram 99). However, the defence stands firm: defender D3 does not allow the ball carrier to outmanoeuvre him, and D2 stays wide. On realizing this the ball carrier, unable to straighten, angles into the defensive winger D2. Still controlling the action, he calls winger O5 inside at the last second. His intention is again to commit both defenders to him, but in this case it is centre D3 who is drawn out of position, and the gap is therefore on the inside. Winger O5 is turned inside at the last second, when both defenders have been committed.

Coaching points

The ball carrier O4 must

1   Run at speed
2   Adopt the same running arc as before, but on realizing that the centre D3 is not beaten, head directly at winger D2
3   Encourage winger D2 to tackle him
4   Directly before being tackled by D2, call the winger inside
5   Turn outwards so the winger is always in vision, and the winger can always see the ball
6   Weight the ball using wrist and finger-tip control
7   If in any doubt, hold the ball firmly in two hands and take the tackle.

The support player O5 must

1   Be guided by the ball carrier O4
2   Look directly at O4, but to be aware of the defenders' movements (using peripheral vision)
3   Time the run to comply with O4's thinking
4   Stay on the outside and attack up the touchline
5   Change direction sharply infield when 'called in' by O4
6   Shout for the ball when aware that the defence has been drawn.

The winger will have an urge to come for the inside ball early. This must be resisted until O4 calls him in.

C   The ball carrier O4 controls the combination, but he is angling towards the touchline and his eyes will be directed that way. Winger O5, however, is looking at O4 and will therefore be aware of positions infield. So it will be the winger who will see any gap in the defence infield from D3. If he spots a weakness here he should call for the ball.

A good idea, therefore, is for winger O5 to have a key call which O4 understands. This call tells centre O4 that winger O5 has now taken over responsibility and wants the ball immediately (diagram 100).

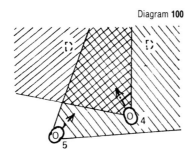

Diagram **100**

Coaching points

The ball carrier O4 acts entirely as before until he hears the 'key word' from winger O5, then he must:

1 Concentrate on O5, and read his actions
2 Pass to O5 as he comes inside
3 Turn outwards, so the winger is always in vision and can always see the ball
4 Weight the ball using wrist and finger-tip control
5 Keep possession if in any doubt.

The support player O5 must:

1 Be guided by the ball carrier O4
2 Look directly at O4 but be aware of the defenders' movements (using peripheral vision)
3 Upon seeing a weakness in the defence infield, must take control of the combination by calling the key word, then
4 Angle infield, close to ball carrier O4, and attack the defensive weakness. On taking control, O5 must act quickly with O4 making a quick response to the call.

Players combining together need to develop understanding. This should be developed during training sessions and is well worth the time and effort. Successful player combinations are not only entertaining but break down even the most well organized defences.

4   PRINCIPAL FACTORS

The majority of combinations are simple and can be

performed by most players. The skill is in making them work to prise open and penetrate the tightest of defences. Skilled performance, correct decision-making and successful player combination can be developed by well-structured practices accompanied by knowledgeable and intelligent coaching.

It is important, however, for the players to understand fully these factors:

1   Possession

The responsibility for possession is the ball carrier's. He should be fully aware of his support and react to their talking, but understand that every pass he makes must go into the hands of a team-mate. If in doubt keep hold of the ball!

2   Communication

Players need to convey information to one another. Talking should be encouraged.

3   Overload

Players should realize immediately they have an overload. As soon as they have more players around the ball than the opposition, quick decisive action is essential.

4   Space (diagram 101)

The team in possession controls to a large extent the movements of the opposition. Space can be created by players in line moving in opposite directions. When a runner from deep is brought into the line, his chances of penetration will be assisted by the passer moving away from the pass and the next player in line moving in the opposite direction.

Diagram **101**

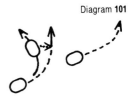

5   Arcs

Players running from deep have more chance of penetration when they run in arcs. If the player stands opposite the gap he is going to run into it is usual for a defender to pick him up. When possible a runner should stand opposite one gap but run through another.

In diagram 102 runner O5 is standing as if to run between ball carrier O1 and O2. The defence is likely to be aware of the danger and drifts across, D2 then taking O5, D3 taking O2, and so on. There is far more chance of penetration if O5 times his run correctly and runs across field to come, for example, between O2 and O3, as in diagram 103.

If, after receiving the ball, O5 maintains his direction he is likely to run directly into defender D3, as in diagram 104.

The gap has been created, but O5 will penetrate only if he straightens up and runs in an arc.

6   Timing

It is important for the runner to arrive at the correct second. If he times his run too late the chance will be lost, while an early run will cause him to overshoot the ball.

7   Depth

Timing can be affected by the distance the support stands behind the ball carrier. A common fault in junior rugby is for players to stand too flat, so coaches should encourage depth of support from an early age.

8   Width

It is usual for the defenders to mark closely the team in possession. The wider apart they stand, the wider apart the defenders will stand, thereby creating more space in between for the second line to attack.

9   Cover

It is important that every attack launched has a defensive cover in case possession is lost. It is usual for the full-back to adopt this role, but when he joins the attacking line another player should adopt covering duties. The blind-side winger is an ideal choice.

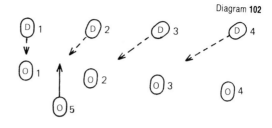

Diagram **102**

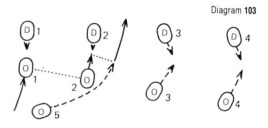

Diagram **103**

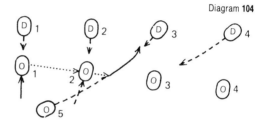

Diagram **104**

6   PREVIOUS EXPERIENCE

Players learn predominantly by trial and error, so improvement to a great extent depends on previous experience.

The learning process improves if the experience coincides with intelligent coaching. The coach who has the ability to analyse, diagnose errors of judgement, discuss his findings with the players concerned, and then structure specific practices to rectify the errors, is of great value.

Junior coaching

Young children will develop a greater understanding of the game if it is scaled down to their size. Small-sided games are invaluable. At every training session, therefore, children should

(a)   learn the skills, and
(b)   play small-sided games.

It is in these small-sided games that children not only put their skills into practice, but begin to learn decision-making. The ball carrier, for instance, has to decide whether to

(a)   make a determined run for the try-line,
(b)   pass, or
(c)   kick.

If he selects the first option he then has to decide

(a)   the direction of his run, and
(b)   which methods of evasion to use.

If he decides to pass he has even more decisions to make:

(a)   the angle and direction of run
(b)   which support player to pass to
(c)   timing of the pass
(d)   weighting of the pass.

The player has to go through a similar process of decision-making when kicking, defending, or supporting the ball carrier. The ability to select the correct option quickly depends on previous experience.

The benefits of small-sided games for young children are numerous, but in particular they are

(a)   enjoyable, and
(b)   create a situation where all the players are around the ball, and therefore directly involved in making decisions.

It is valuable to play these games in confined areas, or grids, which should be ten metres square for youngsters and fifteen metres square for youths and adults. The grids should be marked out in the training area, as in diagram 105. Games of three against three or even four against four can then be played by combining grids A with B, C with D, E with F, and G with H to provide four games, and cater for as many as thirty-two players. A mini-league structure can be devised by moving teams from one

Diagram **105**

Training grid

grid to another. (A full list of small-sided games is contained in Chapter 4 of this section.)

Although it is important for the games to progress, the coach is still active and in a position to make valuable coaching points. The Australian Rugby League, influenced by Peter Corcoran, their Director of Coaching, have replaced the 13-a-side game with an 8-a-side game for Under-10s (mini-footy) and a 10-a-side game for Under-13s (modified league). This is a brave and commendable step forward, aimed at improving awareness, decision-making and understanding among Australia's young players.

Youth and senior coaching

It is important that youth and senior coaches should continue to observe and analyse each player's performance in all matches, and help them to improve their thinking and decision-making.

A perfect example of this occurred during the Test matches with Australia in 1986. In the second Test at Elland Road, with the score 0–2, Britain launched an attack from deep in their own half. Kevin Ward and Barry Ledger combined to enable Harry Pinner to put Widnes's stand-off, Tony Myler, into a gap. Garry Schofield had read the situation brilliantly and was joining Tony Marchant in a position of support,

34   Tony Myler (Widnes and Great Britain) breaks down-field, with Garry Schofield in support, in the second Test against Australia in 1986. Sadly, Myler elected to kick and a try was lost. However, two weeks later, in the third Test, a similar situation arose and this time Myler passed to Schofield who scored the first of his two tries.

when Myler elected to kick over full-back Gary Jack's head. Unfortunately the ball went dead so a try chance was lost, and Australia went on to score a resounding victory.

In the third Test, two weeks later at Central Park, a virtually identical situation arose with Pinner again putting Myler in the clear. Schofield supported the break, and this time Myler selected the right option, drew Jack and passed. Schofield scored under the posts. Myler's decision was based on his previous experience in the second Test, discussions in camp with Schofield and the Great Britain coaching team, and structured training drills.

The process of improved decision-making is therefore dependent upon:

1   Analysis and diagnosis: careful observation by the coach during the game is helped considerably by video analysis.

2   Player/coach discussion: a process which assists players to clarify their thinking.

3   Structured drills   which allow the players to develop their thinking in readiness for the next game.

Further details are included in Section 7, Chapter 2.

Decision-making: choice of tactics

Tactical decision-making is an extension of the thinking process. It is necessary to have an advanced level of individual skill, combined with thorough understanding of the rules and tactics of the game.

Here again the numbers game cannot be overemphasized. A tactician who can constantly create situations in which his team has more men around the ball than the opposition is bound to be successful, particularly if he also has the personal skills to exploit the situation. An understanding of this is best developed at junior level by playing small-sided games, particularly if they are accompanied by knowledgeable coaching. As the boy grows and progresses to the 13-a-side game the coach should teach methods of creating this situation, which include:

1 **Centre-field.** By far the simplest method is to obtain a central position early in the tackle period, and then, as the ball is played, to move players from one side of the play-the-ball to the other.

The 1986 Kangaroos often used this tactic, an example being their second try in the first Test match. From a centre-field play-the-ball, as in diagram 106, Peter Sterling (7) counted heads and decided that Great Britain were light on his left. He

waited until the British defence was formed then moved from the right-hand side of the play-the-ball to the left, and launched an attack with a cut-out pass to Lewis (6) which resulted in O'Connor (2) scoring. Bob Linder (13) and Brian Niebling (11) followed Sterling, thus creating a six-on-four overload.

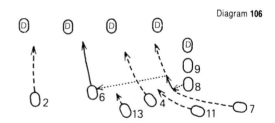

Diagram **106**

2 **Wide blind side.** A similar method is to move the ball infield from the touchline and then, from the resulting play-the-ball, move it back to an overloaded blind side. Parramatta, the most successful team in Sydney during the early 1980s, often used this tactic with Sterling bringing the ball to the back division of Kenny, Cronin, Ella, Grothe and Hunt.

Diagram **107**

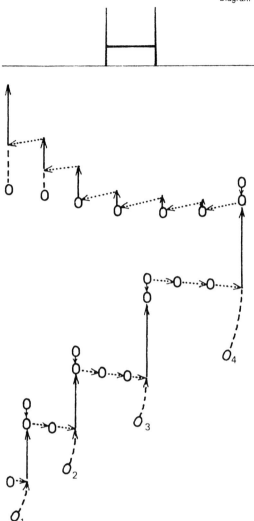

3 Wrap-around.   A more complex method is to attempt to manoeuvre the opposition out of position by combining several plays. The wrap-around play is an example which is used by several British clubs and was instrumental in Hull's success in the 1970s. Three or four plays are used to take the ball across field, with the attack being launched through the forwards from acting half-back, first or second receiver. In diagram 107 the forwards wrap-around to attack on the right and attempt to outnumber the opposition. If a clear break has not resulted the ball is passed back across field enabling the three-quarters, reinforced by a mobile back row, to attack on the wide side. Hull used the ball-playing skills of Steve Norton to launch the attacks.

The tactician needs two other assets:

1   The success of the plays depends entirely on a combination of several players, and it is essential that the tactician has the respect of his team-mates so that they will respond immediately to his prompting.

2   The tactician needs to have a complete knowledge of the game plan and the strategies to be used; indeed he must be an extension of the coach so as to implement the coach's tactics on the field of play. It is important, therefore, for the player and coach to have a close understanding, which will be achieved by a combination of discussion and practice to be explored later in the book.

Small-sided games

1 Passing and handling
2 Defending
3 Kicking
4 Gaining possession

1 PASSING AND HANDLING

A Passing allowed in any direction

1 Four against one (game 1)

Any number of passes is allowed
There is one grid
All players may move apart from the ball carrier
No body contact is allowed.

Objective: players make as many passes as possible. If the ball is intercepted or touches the ground, the defender exchanges positions with the attacker who made the error.
Aims: to develop skills in passing
   catching
   thinking: when to pass
      where to pass
      where to move
      communication

As with all games, manipulate the numbers to suit the ability of the group; for example, as they become proficient increase the pressure by reducing the numbers to three against one.

2 Four against four (game 2)

Any number of passes is allowed
There are two grids
The rules are the same as in game 1

Aims–as in game 1

3 Four against four: ball tig (game 3)

There are two grids.
Objective: the team in possession tries to touch the opposition with the ball. The ball carrier, ball and opposition must all be in contact to be effective. Players tigged either join the ball carriers, or are eliminated.
Aims: to develop skills in catching
   passing
   evasion
   thinking: where to pass
      when to run
      communication

4   Four against four: American touch (game 4)

There are two grids

All players are allowed to run including the ball carrier

The ball carrier stops when the opposition tigs him

The game is restarted with a pass

There is a turnover after two consecutive 'tigs'

Objective: to score by carrying the ball over the end line

Aims: as above, but with additional pressure to
develop creating space
methods of evasion
physical conditioning

This game can be played in a bigger area, using any number of players. Because it makes tremendous physical demands on the players all age groups benefit from it.

B   Passing by the rules of the game

1   With an overloaded offence (game 5)

Two grids

Forward passes not allowed

All players run with the ball

Players can tig, grip or tackle

Restart with a pass

Defence to be onside

Numbers to be determined by the ability of the group: for beginners five against one; as they become increasingly proficient reduce to four v. one, then three v. one. The next step is to increase the number defending to five against two, and so on.

Aims: to develop skills in passing
catching
thinking through: use and creation of
space
timing the pass
supporting the ball.

2   Three against three, equal numbers (game 6)

Two grids

As above

Aims: to develop skills in catching
passing
thinking through: attacking with equal
numbers, hence the in-
troduction and execu-
tion of run arounds,
drop-offs, and so on.

3   Channel rugby using shields: six against two, three, four or six (game 7)

Three grids, forming a channel

Identical rules to game 5, with the defenders holding shields

The ball carrier can either break the shield, or hit and off-load

Start with six against two, allowing two errors. Each time a try is scored increase the number of defenders.

Aims: to develop skills in passing in the tackle
breaking the tackle
catching a pressure situation
thinking through: creation of space
use of space
committing the de-
fence
timing the pass
supporting the ball.

C   Incorporating the play-the-ball

1   Incorporating overloaded offence: five, four, or three against one (game 8)

Two grids.

Rules as in game 4, but incorporating a play-the-ball.

The defender must act as marker

Aims: to develop skills in play-the-ball
pass from ground
passing
catching
thinking through: speed of ball
timing of run.

2 Four against two: defenders move back (game 9)

Two grids

As above, except that on a tig both defenders run back and touch the score-line before becoming 'alive' again

Aims: as above, but increased pressure requires
    increased speed.

3 Four against two: overloaded offence (game 10)

Two grids

As above, but no restrictions on defence apart from being onside

Aims: as above, but with increased pressure.

4 Three against one: acting half-back game (game 11)

Two grids

As above

Aims: ball carrier to stay 'alive'
    incorporating attacks off the acting half-
    back; for example, drop-offs, run arounds,
    switch plays, and decoy runs.

5 Four against three: defenders move back (game 12)

Two grids

As above

Defenders to touch score-line before coming 'alive' (see game 9).

Aims: as with all the above games, with emphasis
    on quick line readjustment and support
    play.

6 Four against three: overloaded offence (game 13)

Two grids

As above, but defence has no restrictions apart from keeping onside

Aims: as above.

7 No-error rugby: six against two, three, four, five or six (game 14)

Play on a half pitch

Normal rules

After each try an extra defender is introduced

Objective: to score a try within six tackles. Groups interchange when the offence is not successful

Each group can be allowed two handling errors.

2 DEFENDING

A Pass allowed in any direction

1 Four against four: number of passes (game 15)

Two grids

Rules as in game 2

Thinking: defence to understand principles of
    man-to-man marking.

2 Four against four: knock down (game 16)

Two grids

Rules as above except two cones are placed at each end of the court

Score by knocking a cone over with the ball

Thinking: defence to understand principles of
    defending a zone.

B Passing according to the rules of the game

1 Four against four: equal numbers (game 17)

Two grids

Rules as in game 6

Thinking: players to use both man-to-man mar-
    king and a zone defence, so as to
    demonstrate that a line zone defence
    is more effective. Offence should use
    run arounds, drop-offs, switches, and
    so on.

2   Three against four: overloaded defence (game 18)

Two grids
Rules as above but with more defenders
Thinking through: aspects of zone
                     keeping the line
Communication.

3   Three against three: equal numbers (game 19)

Two grids
As above.

C   Incorporating a play-the-ball

1   Three against four: overloaded defence (game 20)

Two grids
Rules as in game 13, but with one more defender
Ball carrier goes on one knee before playing the ball
Use one-marker defence.
Thinking through: marker duties
                     line
                     onside
Communication.

2   Three against three: equal numbers (game 21)

Two grids
As above.

3   Three against four: two-marker game (game 22)

Two grids
As above
Two-marker defence
Thinking through: marker duties
                     communication
                     line
                     blind-side drift.

4   Four against four, equating number game (game 23)

Two grids
As above: two markers
Thinking through: as in game 22, plus

equating numbers at either side of the play-the-ball
If the ball carrier counts to five before playing the ball, he will give the defenders time to think, readjust and realign.

3   KICKING

(a)   Kicking tennis (see page 99)

(b)   Punt forcing back (see page 102)

(c)   Five against five: kicks (game 24)

Four grids
Normal rules (tackle or touch) plus
(a)   A try counts 4 points; a try resulting directly from a kick 6 points
(b)   If the kick bounces into touch before the sixth play, the kicking team is allowed possession for a further two tackles
(c)   Grubber into in-goal with an onside tackle – drop out.

4   GAINING POSSESSION

(a)   Five against five: possession game (game 25)

Four grids
Rules as in game 24 plus
the team which gains possession is given six plays.
The team which infringes hands over possession.

1   Gymnasium

The majority of these games can be played indoors:

(a)   Move all equipment and apparatus to ensure that the playing area is safe
(b)   Score by touching the ball to the wall, eliminating the need for players to bend down close to the wall
(c)   When one game is being played, consider taking full advantage of the width; for example, play from side to side rather than from end to end
(d)   Large groups: sit the group down in line at the

bottom end of the gymnasium. If playing four against two, bring the four end players on the right to attack, then the next two to defend. If the attackers score, the defenders leave the area and join the end of the line on the left, being replaced by the next two in the queue on the right. If the ball carriers are unsuccessful, the two defenders become attackers and are joined by the first two from the right of the line, while the next two defend.

2   Shields

Shields may be used in most of the games, although they are not recommended for use indoors, or on hard surfaces, by inexperienced youngsters.
Variations:

(a)   A hit by the shields constitutes a tackle, but it must be a hit and not a glance
(b)   A hit by two shields consecutively constitutes a tackle
(c)   A hit by the shields does not constitute a tackle, so the attackers continue to hit and off-load.

TEAM SKILLS: ATTACKING WHEN IN POSSESSION

INTRODUCTION

One problem that the coach has to solve is the allocation of time between individual and team coaching. Many coaches devote too much time to the team, and too little to the individual. For that reason the previous two sections have deliberately concentrated on development of the individual.

It is time now to consider ways of blending the individuals into successful units. Although all players within a team must be encouraged to use their individual skill and flair, they must develop an understanding of the team's function and a responsibility to the overall tactical plan.

For a team to be successful it must first gain possession and then have the ability to attack from anywhere on the field. Once possession has been secured, the first step in team preparation is to develop its ability to move the ball quickly along the line. Only when the team is able to do this has it the foundation on which to launch attacks wherever the defence is at its weakest.

Garry Schofield (Leeds, formerly Hull, and Great Britain) is able to anticipate the movement of the ball with uncanny accuracy. During training sessions he makes himself aware of all the team's moves so that he can automatically adopt positions of support in match-play. His timing and angles of run are always superb.

Moving the ball wide

1   The defence
2   The team in possession
3   Attacking in more than one line

Senior teams need to perfect the ability to move the ball quickly across field. The team that persistently attacks close to the play-the-ball is far easier to contain than one that attacks anywhere along the line; while the team that can move the ball across field is able to move the opposition's defence about, create holes in its defensive pattern, and capitalize by moving the ball quickly to a player running straight through the gap.

Coaches introducing young children to the game may be tempted to reduce the number of errors by restricting passing, and concentrating on direct charges from acting half-back. This results in three-man rugby, relegating the rest of the team to the role of spectators. The coach has a responsibility to make the game enjoyable for all the players, and therefore the initial tactics should be to pass the ball along the line.

1   THE DEFENCE

Once a tackle has been made, the defenders – with the exception of the markers – must move back at least five metres. They are able to move forward as

soon as the ball has been brought into play. A well-organized defence will move back and quickly re-form. As soon as the ball is played, the defence will move rapidly forward and attack the ball carriers.

2   THE TEAM IN POSSESSION

A well-organized defence, with the ability to move quickly forward, considerably reduces the time the ball carriers have available. In order to move the ball wide successfully, the team in possession must fulfil the following requirements:

1   The ball carrier

The ball carrier must play the ball quickly and efficiently. Immediately he is grounded he should make every effort to regain his feet and play the ball. If this is done quickly, as in diagram 108, there is every chance that the ball will be brought into play before the marker defence has had time to reorganize and while the defensive line is still moving back the required five metres.

A slow play-the-ball movement will result in the ball being brought into play against a well-organized marker defence and a defensive line moving forward from almost a sprint position. The mechanics of the play-the-ball must result in the ball being rolled back smoothly. Once the ball has been played, the ball carrier should stay alive and support the attack.

the distance the second receiver stands being determined by the length of a good pass. Once the first receiver has passed he should follow the ball.

Diagram **108**

2   The acting half-back

When moving the ball wide the acting half-back needs to pass directly from the ground. Taking steps or even picking the ball up before passing wastes too much time. It is necessary, therefore, for the acting half-back to be aware of the position of the first receiver before the ball is played. Speed and efficiency are further helped if the acting half-back is early into position, encouraging the ball carrier to play the ball quickly. Once the acting half-back has passed he should follow the ball.

3   First receiver

On no account must the first receiver attempt to draw a man. He is a most important link in the chain and must do nothing more than catch and pass as quickly as possible. Some players pass well while stationary, but the majority are more efficient when on the move. Each individual should be encouraged to adopt the quickest alternative, and they should all realize that for every step they take the defence will be able to move two metres closer.

The first receiver is passing in a situation where he is not likely to be tackled, and so can be encouraged to catch and pass in one movement without bringing the ball into his bread-basket. He should be as far away from the acting half-back as possible – certainly a good passing length – and he should quickly tell the acting half-back where he wants the ball passed. His pass to the second receiver should also be a long one,

4   Second and third receivers

They should operate in the same way, ensuring that the ball is passed out quickly and efficiently, and should then support the attack.

5   Depth

The first three receivers should be aware of the dangers of standing too flat, thus enabling the defence to close them down. How deep these players stand will largely depend upon the speed of the opposition. A defence that is moving up quickly can be countered by the first few receivers standing further back than normal.

6   Width

Because the emphasis is on speed the first few receivers should stand as wide apart as possible, the distance obviously being controlled by the length of an efficient pass. Diagram 109 shows that team B, with fewer handlers in the line, will move the ball from 1 to 6 faster than team A.

7   Using the extra players

Once the team develops the ability to stand wide, players from the original line are released to adopt other roles. Many coaches encourage them to run in their original positions, but miss them out by either passing in front of them or behind. It is debatable whether decoy runners operating so close to the play-

Diagram **109**

the-ball, and in this case so far away from the opposition, achieve their objective. If not they are valuable players positioned out of the game. It would be far better for them to make a second line of support, particularly around the player who is to attack the opposition.

8   The runner

The deeper the attacking team stands, the more ground it has to make up. It is important, therefore, that the player straightening the line and attacking runs with speed and determination.

9   Support

The runner should be supported at all times.

Suggested practice

The practice described will enable those coaching children to introduce passing the ball wide for the first time. Coaches working with more experienced players may occasionally have to remind them of the complete practice, but more often than not will use the later stages only.

Numbers: groups of six, seven or eight
Equipment: one ball per group, and ten cones

Stage 1:   The groups move downfield passing the ball.

Coaching points

1   Good efficient passing

2   Catching and passing without bringing the ball into the bread-basket
3   Wide passing
4   Timing by the receiver to take the ball at speed.

Stage 2:   Introduce the play-the-ball. The group continues until the ball reaches the end man who, after sprinting with the ball for ten to fifteen metres, slows down. He then lies down, counts to five, regains his feet and plays the ball, which is then moved in the opposite direction. The practice continues.

Coaching points

1   Efficient play-the-ball
2   Acting half-back to pass from the ground.

Stage 3:   Introduce the groups to the duties of specific positions. Designate one player to be the acting half-back at all times; and have the same two players alternate between first and second receiver. The others in the group, the end man apart, always take up wide positions whichever way the ball is being passed.

Coaching points (diagrams 110 and 111)

1   The acting half-back, first and second receiver, pass, then follow the ball
2   Players other than the end man do the same, but as soon as the end man simulates a tackle they quickly adopt outside positions on the opposite side of the group.

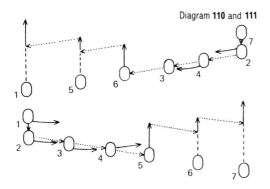

Diagram **110** and **111**

Stage 4:   Teach the first and second receivers to catch and pass in one movement, continuing as before with emphasis on moving the ball quickly to the third receiver without carrying it towards the opposition. When working with young children the first and second receivers may have to angle across field. The runner should straighten the line and take the ball at full speed.

Coaching points

1   Ball carrier – an efficient play-the-ball
2   Acting half-back – pass from the ground, and support
3   First and second receivers – catch and pass in one movement, then support
4   Runner – straighten the line and take the ball at speed.

Stage 5:   Cones are introduced to simulate the defence, as in diagrams 112a and b. One is placed

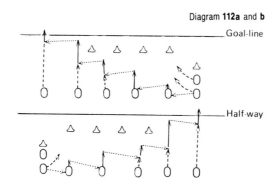

Diagram **112a** and **b**

where the ball is to be played, and four others are placed five metres back and four metres apart, in line. The ball carriers cannot carry the ball through the cones; their objective is to move the ball outside the cones to a player running hard and straight. The first three receivers are a link in the chain, and catch and pass as quickly as possible.

The groups are now able to interpass at speed down the field, starting at one goal-line, attacking two sets of cones, and scoring at the other.

Stage 6:   Increase the pressure by placing the cones in an arc so they represent a defence which is moving up quickly.

The ball carriers must again move the ball wide, round the outside cone to the runner.

Stage 7:   The cones can now be replaced by defenders using tackle shields. The defence should move up straight, in line and at match speed. The ball carriers have to move the ball round them to the runner.

When preparing to play against a team noted for the speed of its defence it is essential to practise against opposition.

3   ATTACKING IN MORE THAN ONE LINE

Players dropping out of the first line of attack should adopt positions of support at the back. A team which

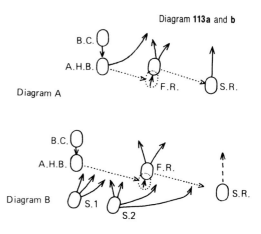

Diagram **113a** and **b**

adopts this formation with two or even three lines of attack creates more passing possibilities and attacking options, and is difficult to contain. This can be most clearly demonstrated in diagrams 113a and b. When a team uses one line of attack, its passing options and ability to support are severely restricted (see diagram 113a). In diagram 113b, the second line not only gives the handlers in the first line far more passing options, but is in a position to support attacks launched from several positions.

Because the support players at the back are not part of the first line of attack, they are free to move across field quickly. In diagram 83b, for example, S2 is able to support the acting half-back, first receiver and second receiver quite easily as play develops. An early call, perhaps made as the ball carrier regains his feet, would allow S2 enough time to move across field at the back of the first line of attack to support play almost anywhere.

The attacking significance of this can only really be appreciated when compared with the movement of the defence. It is essential to digest the information contained in Section 5, Chapter 2; here it is sufficient to point out that the majority of defenders drift sideways in line. The offence is therefore far more mobile than the defence, and should always be capable of overloading successfully anywhere on the pitch.

Kevin Ward (Castleford and Great Britain) hits the line strongly and prepares to off-load in the Great Britain v Papua New Guinea Test in 1987.

Attacking from a play-the-ball

All teams should be able to attack the opposition from anywhere on the field. The play-the-ball area is particularly vulnerable, and well-supported raids close to the play-the-ball often result in direct penetration or at least cause the defence to bunch. When this occurs, the gaps left out wide can be exploited from the next play-the-ball.

Attacks close to the play-the-ball should be controlled by either the acting half-back or first receiver. It is possible for either of these players simply to pass the ball to a strong running forward, but as most Rugby League players are sound tacklers such tactics are seldom successful, unless of course they are repeated to such an extent that the defence is battered into submission.

A more subtle and entertaining play is for the acting half-back and first receiver to develop the ability to open up defences by skilful football. Thus, this Chapter explores in detail:

1   Major principles of attack close to the play-the-ball:
   1   Play-the-ball
   2   Acting half-back
   3   First receiver
   4   Runner
   5   Support
   6   Decoy runners
   7   Sustained attacks.

2   The acting half-back: attacking possibilities
   1   Pass to the first receiver
   2   Pass directly to a runner
   3   Move attempting to create a hole
   4   Set moves
   5   Combination of outside and inside support
   6   Run around.

3   The first receiver: attacking possibilities
   1   Pass to the second receiver
   2   Move attempting to create a hole
   3   Set moves.

4   Wideout: attacking possibilities.

5   Blind side: attacking possibilities.

However, success can only be achieved by a thorough understanding of the various defensive patterns. In simple terms a Rugby League defence, from a play-the-ball situation, adopts a straight line across the pitch with either one or two players at the front operating as marker(s), then with a full-back, and sometimes a sweeper behind it. Unless the wingers are also back in anticipation of a kick, it is usual for the defensive line to contain between nine and eleven players. As soon as the ball is played the defensive line moves forward and tries to complete the tackle.

When using one marker the acting half-back cannot be pressurized until he moves. If the acting half-back carries the ball himself it is usual for the marker to tackle him. If he passes, however, the marker will make sure that he either pressurizes the first receiver or prevents him offloading to support on his inside.

A double-marker defence places immediate pressure on the acting half-back. A common method is for the markers to split once the ball has been played and to move at either side of the play-the-ball. This can be more easily exploited than a defensive pattern where both markers work together.

Defence will be fully discussed in Chapter 2 of Section 5.

1   MAJOR PRINCIPLES OF ATTACK CLOSE TO THE PLAY-THE-BALL

1   **Play-the-ball.** The chance of attacks being successful when launched directly through the play-the-ball area will be far greater if the ball carrier is able to play the ball while the tacklers are still regaining their feet. Attacks off the first receiver similarly will have greater chances of success if the ball is played before the defence has had time to reorganize.

The speed at which the ball carrier regains his feet and plays the ball is therefore a major coaching point, along with an efficient technique to provide the acting half-back with a smooth service. Once the ball has been played the ball carrier should maintain concentration and be ready to support any attack.

2   **The acting half-back.** The acting half-back has two major options: either to provide a fast and efficient service to the first receiver, or to be the springboard of the attack. If he is to adopt attacking

responsibilities himself he needs to communicate his intentions to his support players, move in a way that causes the defence to react and then give a perfectly weighted pass to a runner in the gap created. Once a ball has been passed the acting half-back should follow the ball and support.

3   **First receiver.** If the first receiver is to be the springboard of the attack, it is his responsibility to control the movements of the defence and to give a perfectly weighted pass to the runner in the hole that he has created.

4   **Runner.** The runner should concentrate on timing and the angle of run. It is usual for a collision to happen so he should carry the ball firmly in two hands, but be prepared to offload to support if the opportunity arises. Determination is essential.

5   **Support.** Good, intelligent close-support play is a most important principle, and sadly one which some coaches neglect. Many teams adopt intricate moves with decoy runners, then push a runner forward without support. Often the defence, though severely pressurized, is able to prevent the runner from making the break himself. A pass to a support player, however, often breaks down the defence, creating a try-scoring opportunity. If there is no support, the movement fails.

6   **Decoy runners.** Decoy runners attempt to draw the defence out of position, enabling the offence to attack the gaps created. Deception is important. The opposition will only be drawn to the decoy runners if it is apparent that they are to receive the ball. Decoy runs are therefore most effective near to where the attacks are to take place.

7   **Sustained attacks.** The attacking ploys to be discussed are not always initially successful. They do, however, often pressurize the defence and cause it to be moved out of position. The next play-the-ball is very important, for it is from this that many breaks are made. Attacks should be launched from successive play-the-ball movements with the team's tactician

assessing the position and directing the points of each subsequent attack.

Major problem

If the attacks are not carefully thought out the team will run short of players, and will be forced to resort to unsupported rushes from the first receiver. Not only are these boring for the spectator, but they take the pressure off the defence and allow it time to reorganize.

The team coach has to find a balance between

Creators
Runners
Support players
Decoy runners.

The problem is intensified by realizing that a well-supported attack from the next play-the-ball could well be the defence breaker.

2 THE ACTING HALF-BACK: ATTACKING POSSIBILITIES

1 **Pass to the first receiver.** When an attack is to be launched away from the play-the-ball, the duty of the acting half-back is to give quick efficient service to the first receiver. It is the first receiver who controls the direction, speed and weight of the pass, and it is important that he conveys his wishes to the acting half-back. Communication is important. Once the ball has been passed the acting half-back should follow the ball, and support play.

2 **Pass directly to a runner.** The acting half-back contributes little to the attack other than giving a perfectly weighted pass to a runner trying to break through the defensive line. The runner should be supported by at least one other player. After passing, the acting half-back should follow the ball, keeping in position to continue the attack or adopt acting-half-back duties at the subsequent play-the-ball. The runner should:

1 Run straight and attack the goal-line
2 Run with determination

3 Time his run, so that he receives the ball at speed almost level with the acting half-back
4 Hold the ball firmly in two hands if a collision is imminent, and then be prepared to offload if the situation arises.

The runner must always try to make as much ground as possible and should time his run to take a pass which is flat, almost forward.

If forward rushes are to be combined, the designated runner should be in position one play-the-ball early, and so be able to time his run at the earliest possible moment.

The opposition is placed under the greatest pressure when the time between each tackle and the play-the-ball is reduced.

(a) Normal. The acting half-back passes to the left to a runner coming from the left, or vice versa. In diagram 114 he passes to O1, supported by O3 and O4. Timing and determination of the run are important. The pass should be level to enable the runner quickly to reach the gain-line. The acting half-back should support play once the ball has been passed.

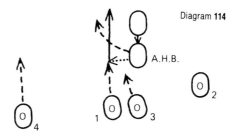

Diagram **114**

(b) Normal plus decoy. Aggressive double-marker defences have encouraged some teams to introduce a decoy on the inside of the runner. In diagram 115 O1 is the decoy, and the pass goes behind him to the runner O2. The acting half-back must be told that a miss pass is to be used.

(c) Switch. The acting half-back passes to a runner coming from one side of the play-the-ball to the other. In diagram 116 he turns to the right and passes to O2 going on a cross run to the left. O1, O3 and O4 are all able to support.

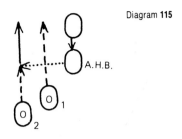

Diagram **115**

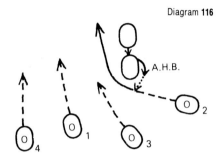

Diagram **116**

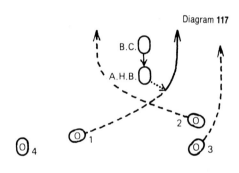

Diagram **117**

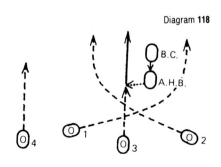

Diagram **118**

The angle of the run is important. The runner initially moves across field, but once in position it is important that the movement is straightened up before he hits the opposition. The runner arcs, therefore.

(d)   Decoy switch.   The acting half-back passes to a runner coming from one side of the play-the-ball to the other, after having first dummied a runner moving in the opposite direction.

In diagram 117, O_2 runs early, turning past the acting half-back who dummies and passes to O_1. The timing of both runners, and the angled arc, are major coaching points. O_3 and the acting half-back provide support.

(e)   Double decoy switch.   The acting half-back passes to a runner coming straight and close, after first of all sending a dummy pass to both decoy runners operating cross runs.

In diagram 118, O_2 runs early followed closely by O_1. The acting half-back dummies both players, and passes to O_3 supported by O_4.

The acting half-back should turn to face the support player, turning his back on the opposition. If the markers move up fast there is nothing to stop the acting half-back moving away from them towards O_3. Timing and the angle of run are the important factors. O_1 and O_2 will also provide support.

3   Move attempting to create a hole in the defensive wall.

(a)   Move forward and penetrate.   The acting half-back always has the option of moving quickly forward attempting to penetrate. This play has a chance of success if either the marker defence is slow to its feet, or if it has lost concentration. As with all attacks the movement should be supported. If possible the acting half-back should communicate with those players close to him, and the ball player should also be ready to support.

(b)   Move forward and pass.   The acting half-back moves forward as he did before, and as the marker is

drawn into the tackle a pass is made to a support player. An inside pass to a runner moving into the hole left by the marker is particularly effective. The player who played the ball is in an ideal position to support.

(c)   Move across and pass outside.   The acting half-back moves quickly across field away from the marker defence and tries to pull a player in the defensive line to him, thus creating a gap.

In diagram 119 the acting half-back has moved across field away from the marker defence. The marker has lost concentration. Defender D8 has been drawn to the acting half-back, and because D11 has been drawn to O13, O7 is in a gap between D8 and D11. The rest of the players must support.

(d)   Move across and pass inside.   The acting half-back moves quickly across field taking the marker defence with him. Before being tackled he passes inside to a support player.

In diagram 120, O8 is dropped off inside the acting half-back and inside the marker defence. Support is important. The ball player should also stay 'alive'.

A double-marker defence

A single-marker defence is susceptible to attacks directly from a play-the-ball, in particular to inside passes from the acting half-back. If these are well supported and the person playing the ball stays 'alive', the chances of a direct penetration are exceptionally high. For this reason more teams are now adopting a double-marker defence.

4   Set moves aimed at penetrating a double-marker defence.   An astute coach will have a series of set plays aimed at penetration around the play-the-ball. These could include:

(a)   Penetrating double markers moving left and right.   Double markers moving quickly left and right at a play-the-ball can be penetrated quite easily. The aim is for two of the offence to cause them to move as wide apart as possible and then to pass the ball to a runner going through the middle.

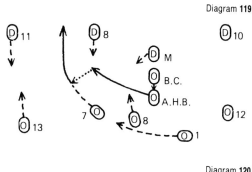
Diagram **119**

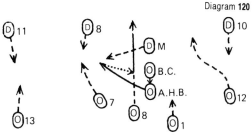
Diagram **120**

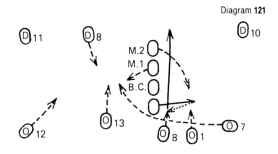
Diagram **121**

In diagram 121, the markers have decided to move left and right, while the rest of the defence move up very quickly.

O7 moves on a switch, acting as a decoy. The acting half-back shows him the ball then quickly moves in the opposite direction.

The markers move on to the acting half back and O7, leaving a massive gap in the middle. This is exploited by O8 who receives an inside pass from the acting half-back. Support is provided by the other players, with the ball carrier staying alive.

(b)   Penetrating double markers working together.   Double markers operating together and moving after the ball are far harder to penetrate.

In diagram 122, the acting half-back moves right and has two players advancing on his inside. O12 comes slightly later than O8, and angles directly through the area the ball was played. The double markers operating together are likely to take the acting half-back and O8, leaving O12 in a hole. Again support is essential.

A variation, as in diagram 123, is for another player quickly to follow the acting half-back, who moves quickly left with O7 moving directly behind him. As the acting half-back is about to be tackled by one of the markers he passes to O7, while O8, standing wide, runs towards the ball carrier, receives a pass from O7, and arcs inside the two markers. Timing and angle of run are essential to the move's success. Support must be supplied on both the inside by O12 and outside by O13.

5   A   combination   of   outside   and   inside support. Whether the acting half-back is involved with a set move or creating play, the success of his actions depends on how the defence reacts. It is always an advantage, therefore, for the acting half-back to have both an inside and outside passing option.

6   Run around. The acting half-back is in the ideal position to run around the first receiver. On doing so he can either straighten up, trying to break the line himself, or pass to a runner. The run around has been well covered on page 59. Support is again important.

Attacking options. It has become increasingly apparent that the ball carrier requires several passing options if he is to break down a well-organized defence. The more options that he has, the more problems the defence has to overcome, and this is even more difficult when the defence is outnumbered. It is not always obvious how the defence will react to any given problem, so the chances of success are increased if the ball carrier has the ability to make quick decisions.

The team in possession, therefore, should attempt to have:

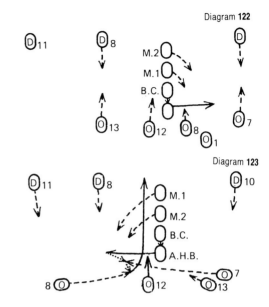

Diagram 122

Diagram 123

1   More players than defenders around the area to be attacked
2   A ball carrier able to pressurize the defence and then pass to unmarked players
3   The ability to support the unmarked player immediately he receives the pass.

3   THE FIRST RECEIVER: ATTACKING POSSIBILITIES

The first receiver has many passing options, several of them similar to those of the acting half-back. The major differences of the two positions is that the first receiver is further away from both the marker defence and the defensive line. It is necessary, therefore, for the first receiver to have a clear understanding of his role:

(a)   If an attack is to be launched away from the first receiver, then he should catch and pass the ball as quickly as possible. The manoeuvre should be completed well away from the opposition. The first receiver has to decide how wide and how deep to stand. This will depend on circumstances, particularly the speed at which the defence moves up. The tendency is, however, to stand too flat, and perhaps players in this position should be encouraged to stand further back than is usual.

(b)   If the first receiver is to launch the attack himself he must be far enough back to have time to pass, but close enough to the opposition to make them react. A complex manoeuvre too far away from the opposition means that they are not committed, and simply tackle whichever player emerges with the ball.

1   Pass to the second receiver.   The coaching points are similar to those already discussed regarding acting half-back. Communication, position of alignment, speed of movement and support are essential.

2   Pass directly to a runner.   It is common for the first receiver simply to hand the ball to a runner, either on the outside or inside. An outside pass allows the runner to attack the defence away from the attentions of the marker defence. The first receiver is doing nothing more than handing the ball on, so the pass should be made well away from the opposition. The runner should be determined and carry the ball firmly, preferably in two hands if a collision is imminent, but must be ready to make it available if the situation arises. Again the runner should (a) run straight, (b) be determined and (c) time his run to receive the pass almost level with the first receiver.

The runner needs support, so the first receiver and acting half-back should follow the ball once the pass has been made.

3   Moves attempting to create a hole in the defensive wall.

(a)   Move forward and penetrate.   Already described under attacking possibilities for the acting half-back. The first receiver needs to time his run so that he hits the defensive line straight and at full speed. He should always have support. Because he is running into the heart of the defence he should hold the ball firmly, preferably in two hands, and be ready to offload as soon as the defence has been penetrated.

If he is unable to break the defence, he should be ready to turn and make the ball available to a player behind him.

(b)   Move forward and pass inside.   When the first receiver moves forward with either determination or guile, two or more defenders can be drawn to him. This often creates a gap in the defensive line, and the ball should be offloaded for a team-mate running through. This ploy should not be confused with 2 above. If the first receiver is merely to hand the ball on it should be done early, as previously described in 2, otherwise the runner will be receiving both man and ball, which should be avoided at all costs.

In diagram 124, the first receiver, FR, angles in between defenders D1 and D3, with D1 moving to tackle FR leaving D3 to prevent an outside pass. However, S1 is free on the inside. It is important that S1 is supported, and FB, S2 and AHB are in position to do this.

Diagram **124**

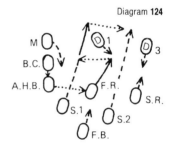

If on the other hand D1 moves towards S1 and D3 prepares to tackle FR, as in diagram 125, the unmarked player will be on the outside and a pass can be made to either S2 or SR. Support is again important.

Diagram **125**

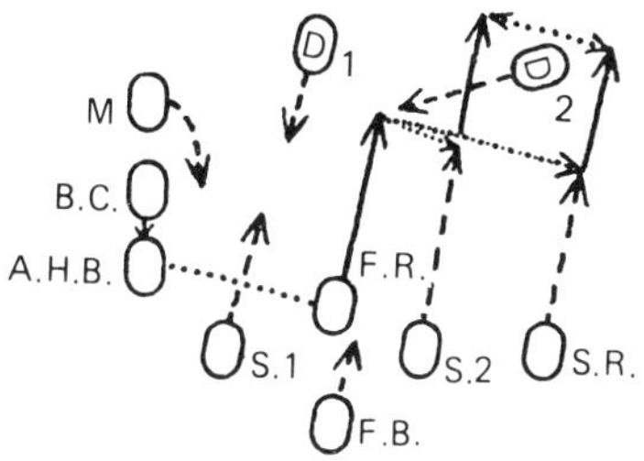

It may be that the markers will prevent FR passing inside to S1. In that case D1 is able to take FR, but the defence is still under pressure because D3 is overloaded. In diagram 126, D3 moves to tackle SR, leaving S2 free to come through the gap between D1 and D3. Support is provided by FB.

Even a double-marker defence can be exploited by FR passing inside, as in diagram 127. If AHB moves sideways before passing, one of the markers will probably try to tackle him. As S1 comes for the inside pass the second marker will move in. A quick and accurate pass from FR inside, across the front of S1 to S3 running into the play-the-ball area, can be most effective.

An astute double-marker defence undoubtedly makes raids on the inside of FR more difficult. They cannot, however, affect attacks on FR's outside. Well supported raids here certainly pressurize the defence and test its ability to drift into position.

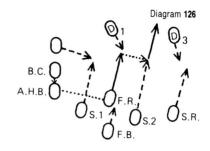

Diagram **126**

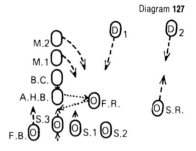

Diagram **127**

(c)   Moving forward and attacking with the outside pass.   (i) FR moves at the gap between D1 and D2, as in diagram 128. If D2 moves to make the tackle and D3 moves up on SR, then S2 will be in a gap. The gap will be widened if SR runs outwards and FR side-steps inwards before the pass is made. FB, S4, TR, S1, AHB are all in a position to support. (ii) If the double markers account for S1, allowing D1 to move up and attempt to tackle FR, then the situation changes. In diagram 129, if D2 moves up on SR then S2 will be in a gap. Support will be provided by FB, S1, S4 and AHB. (iii) However, if D2 moves towards S2 and D3 drifts in to take SR, then either TR or S4 could be free, as in diagram 130. (iv) Even when the defence all drift in there is an opportunity to break the line by introducing a runner coming late on an outside arc. In diagram 131, D1 moves to tackle FR and D2, D3 and D4 drift in to close down S2, SR and S4. However, if FR times his pass correctly, moves inwards and takes D1 with him, a gap for S1 could still be opened up with FB supporting.

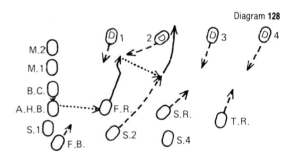

Diagram **128**

(4)   Run around.   An astute coach will devise set moves likely to break down even the best organized defensive patterns. These should suit his players'

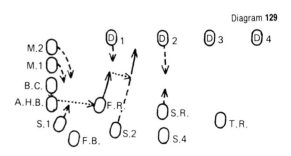

Diagram **129**

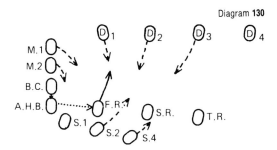

Diagram **130**

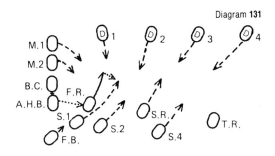

Diagram **131**

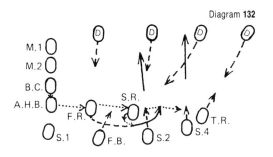

Diagram **132**

strengths. FR moves around SR and either attacks the defence directly, or feeds runners coming off him. Many variations are possible. In diagram 132, FR moves round SR and has runners on the inside (S2) and the outside (S4). FB supports.

4   WIDE OUT: ATTACKING POSSIBILITIES

Similar ploys can be executed off the second, third or even fourth receivers. It often happens that the defence will attempt to stifle any moves around the AHB and first receiver by moving in extra players. Obviously when this occurs gaps in the defensive line are created wide out. The ball carriers can exploit them by moving the secondary line in arcs across the pitch. It is far quicker and easier for them to move than it is for the defence to drift across, particularly if the area to be attacked is called early enough. In diagram 133, the defence has closed down the gaps around the AHB and first receiver. An early call by the offence will enable both second-row forwards to launch an attack between the stand-off (6) and inside centre (4). This area is then overloaded.

Set moves

Moves off the second and third receiver are often more successful than those off the first receiver, particularly when playing against a team with a well-organized double-marker defence.

The players must again be aware that the defence has to be committed and therefore the pivot must move into the defensive line. To do otherwise would

Diagram **133**

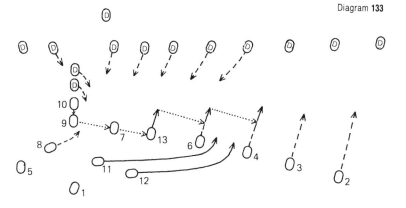

enable the defence to stand back and pick off the runners. Most coaches will develop their own set pieces. Two examples are:

1   Drop-off from second receiver (diagram 134). SR receives an early pass and angles across field, committing D3 and pulling D2 across with him. A gap can therefore be created inside D2.

SR has two runners in R1 and R2, both on his outside. R1 follows him staying on the outside, but R2 angles in late and receives a drop-off pass on the inside of SR while S1 supports. It is important that SR has the ability to perform the drop-off while committing the defence, and R2 must have the strength to offload in the tackle. Malcolm Reilly introduced a similar move to the Great Britain team when he took over as international coach in January 1987. Significantly, Lee Crooks was used as SR and Ellery Hanley as R2.

2   Run-around decoy (diagram 135). FR receives an early pass from AHB, gives it to SR, and executes a run around. TR almost immediately angles on an inside cross. SR has turned and has first FR then TR crossing. R1 from a position behind the play-the-ball runs across field and receives a short pass from SR on his outside. R1 should explode on to the ball – timing is important – while S1 supports.

3   Switch by second receiver (diagram 136). FR receives an early pass from the AHB. He passes outwards to the SR who runs back towards the play-the-ball, feeding runners angling through the play-the-ball area. The double markers will have been drawn across field towards SR, and the move exploits a lazy blind-side defence which does not drift inwards. R1 or R2 receives the ball, with FB supporting.

5   BLIND SIDE: ATTACKING POSSIBILITIES

Even at the highest level, blind-side attacks are most successful. Reasons for this include:

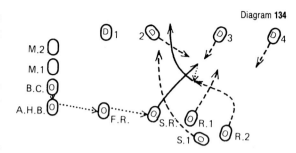

Diagram **134**

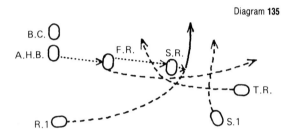

Diagram **135**

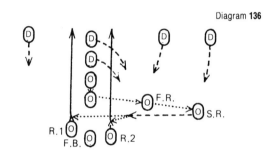

Diagram **136**

1   A short blind side is close to the play-the-ball, and can be overloaded easily by moving players across from the open side

2   Defenders on the blind side occasionally cover across the field anticipating an attack on the open side

3   Defenders on the blind side often lose concentration, have a rest or lose their discipline; as a result they fail to move up in the defensive line

4   The blind-side winger often moves back in anticipation of a line kick, leaving a gap in the defensive line next to the touchline.

Attacks can be launched directly down the blind side, but are often more successful when the initial movement has been infield. The ball can be brought back by a runner or by the first receiver quickly changing the direction of play. As with all attacks, the ball should be transferred to the unmarked player quickly, through as few hands as possible. In diagram 137, the blind-side winger D5 has moved back in anticipation of a line kick. Because of this the gap that he has left is quickly attacked. The first receiver O7 changes the direction of play and carries the ball blind, passing in front of O3 directly to O2, who sprints into the gap, carrying the ball through the defensive line. As D5 moves into the tackle, O2 passes infield to the supporting full-back O1. O9, O10, and O3 provide initial support while the rest of the team also move forward.

A similar move involving Andy Goodway, Tony Myler and Des Drummond created a spectacular seventy-five-metre try for Garry Schofield in the second Test at Brisbane's Lang Park in 1984.

In diagram 138 the blind-side defence has not moved up. D10, anticipating an attack on the open side, has begun to cover across field. The right centre O3 has been tackled by D4. From the resulting play-the-ball, the AHB passes infield to the first receiver O13. The double markers move infield, and the defence move up quickly apart from D10. He is on the blind side and begins to cover across. On realizing this, O13 switches play and passes to O8 who quickly runs through the gap left by D10 and carries the ball through the first line of defence. O1, O10 quickly support and the rest of the team follow.

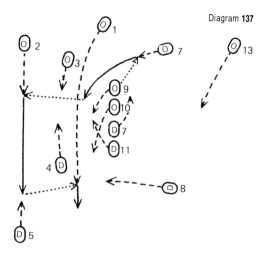

Diagram **137**

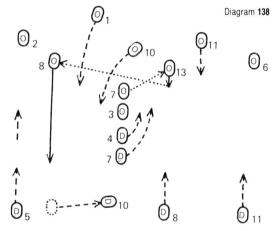

Diagram **138**

6   CONCEPTS OF GOOD COACHING

The various attacking plays discussed in this chapter are either:

1   Unplanned player combinations, or
2   Set moves.

1   Unplanned player combinations

These form the bulk of a team's offensive attacks, and depend on:

(a)   The ability of the team to
    (i)   Move the defence around
    (ii)   Move the ball quickly along the line to players in a position to launch the attack, and
    (iii)   Support to maintain the attack.
(b)   The ability of the ball carriers to read the movements of the defence, and pass to unmarked players.

Success therefore depends on:

(a)   Team coaching, and
(b)   Individual coaching.

(a)   **Team coaching.** The coach should continuously improve his team's ability to support the ball and move the ball quickly across the field. Work to this end should be included in the weekly training programme.

(b)   Individual coaching.   Players at the highest level must be able to carry the ball into a well-organized defence – causing it to move about – and then under extreme pressure must have the vision, awareness and skill to pass to an unmarked player. This depends on the player's rugby education and the quality of his previous coaching.

Individual coaching is always important, even at international level, and the senior coach should constantly devise conditioned practices for his players. This encourages them to attack in match-like conditions, pressurize the defence, read the opposition, select the correct option, and attack quickly in numbers.

2   Set moves

Set moves provide a team with most valuable attacking options, but their overall value must be put in perspective. In an average game a team will play the ball more than 170 times. If these include seventeen set moves, that is still only 10% of all attacks.

The junior coach must be aware that overemphasis on set moves will probably stifle the development of individual skill and awareness of the game. The senior coach should realize that although set moves are essential weapons in his team's attacking armoury, unplanned player combinations will provide most of the attacks.

Attacking from a tap penalty

1   To penetrate
2   To control the position of the defence
3   To obtain forward domination

Apart from kicking for goal, a penalty-kick can be taken in two ways:

1   A kick from the mark into touch, and
2   A tap ten metres in from where the ball crossed the touchline.

The attackers' aims are to penetrate, to control the position of the defence, and to obtain forward domination.

1   TO PENETRATE

Teams often try to penetrate on the first play of the tap. This is most unlikely to succeed because the defence will have had ample time to regroup and recover, so concentration will be high.

There are several plays used from a tap when direct penetration is the aim. The wall and fan are two examples:

The wall.   Three or four players stand shoulder to shoulder with their backs to the opposition. The ball is passed directly to them and the ball is shielded. The wall then has several options to catch the opposition unaware:

(i)   Runner going through the wall.   In diagram 139, O7 takes the tap and immediately passes to O8. He then runs round the back of the wall. The ball is handed from O8 to O9. O7 then appears at the other side of the wall, O10 steps infield, allowing O5 to take a short pass from O9 and burst through the gap. Players O8, O10, O11, O13, O6 and O4 are in position to support.

Diagram **139**

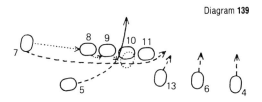

(ii)   Player in the wall taking the ball himself.   In diagram 140, O7 again passes to the wall and runs round while the ball is handed via O9 to O10. All four players in the wall move forward trying to create a hole in the defence. O8 and O9 move towards the touchline. O10 takes the ball infield and drops off O11 into any gap. Support is once again provided by O13, O6 and O4.

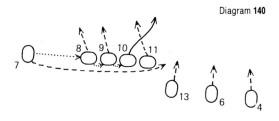

Diagram **140**

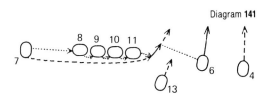

Diagram **141**

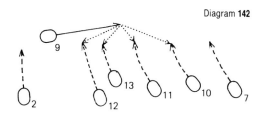

Diagram **142**

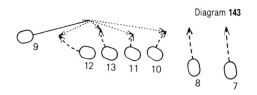

Diagram **143**

(iii)   The ball is passed infield.   In diagram 141, player passes into the wall, moves round, receives the return pass and feeds O6 going infield. Players O13 and the wall itself provide inside support while O4 and the rest of the team support on the outside.

2   The fan.   A group of players stand facing the acting half-back. As soon as the tap is taken they fan out and run towards the opposition. Any one of them may receive the ball.

In diagram 142, the forwards O13, O10, O12 and O11 run at different angles as O9 takes the tap. If O13 receives the ball he is supported by O12 and O11. If O11 receives the ball, support is provided by O13 and O10. If O10 receives the ball, O7 and the rest of the team provide support on the outside, while O11 provides support on the inside.

In diagram 143, the forwards O12, O13, O11 and O10 stand behind each other facing O9. Once the ball is tapped O9 runs infield while the four forwards fan out and any one of them may receive the ball.

Any defence unable to contain the opposition direct from a tap has a lot to answer for, and although immediate penetration may be the first priority of the team in possession it is most unlikely to happen. The fan does provide an important and additional advantage. The defence cannot be certain which of the forwards is to receive the ball, and must prepare to tackle all of them. This uncertainty prevents the gang-tackling which is prevalent when one forward carries the ball up. Gang-tackling is not only physically intimidating but also leads, inevitably, to a slow play-the-ball.

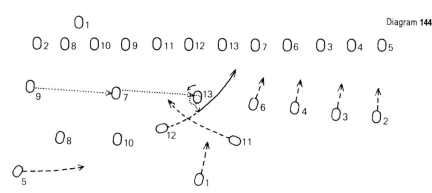

Diagram **144**

2   TO CONTROL THE POSITION OF THE DEFENCE

Because direct penetration is unlikely, an alternative tactic is to manoeuvre carefully and deliberately the opposition's defence to certain areas on the pitch.

Wide passing

In diagram 144, the ball is passed from the top via O7 to O13, standing as far infield as possible. A decoy runner, O11, moves in an arc towards the opposition's forwards in an attempt to reduce their crossfield cover, while O12 crosses behind the pivot, receives the pass, and runs determinedly at the opposition's half-back. Support is provided on the outside by O6 and the rest of the three-quarters, while the full-back moves to support inside, and the blind-side winger O5 covers. The strong running forward O12 attacks D7, but even so direct penetration is unlikely. However, from the next play-the-ball, problems can be created for the defence by:

1   Moving O7, O9, O8 and O10 across field to attack on the right, thereby considerably overloading that side of the pitch
2   Moving the three-quarters to the left, and overloading the left-hand side
3   Moving both sets of players at the same time, thus giving the ball carriers the option of attacking the defence's three-quarters via its forwards on the right, or attacking its forwards with the backs on the left.

The defence is presented with a problem which-ever variation the ball carriers adopt, and there is a possibility that players will try to interchange po-sition. It is as the defenders interchange position that they are most vunerable to an immediate attack.

Open up the blind side

Another play is for the ball carriers to try to move the opposition's forwards infield ten to fifteen metres, thereby creating a gap on the blind side which can be exploited on the next play. More often than not it will take the offence two plays to do this, with the attack being launched blind on the third.

In the left-hand section of diagram 145, the tap is taken by O9 who runs slightly infield before passing to O8, who attacks the opposition.

D9 and D10 make the tackle ten metres infield, and in the central section the offence again attack to the right with the AHB 9 passing to first receiver O7. He drops off D12 who is likely to be tackled by both markers while the AHB supports in case of a break.

In the right-hand section, the blind-side defence is likely to be short on numbers. The first receiver on the open side quickly transfers the ball blind and passes to O1 in the gap. The movement is well supported by O2, O10, O13 and O7.

3   TO OBTAIN FORWARD DOMINATION

Perhaps the most common tactic, particularly early on in the game, is to have the forwards running

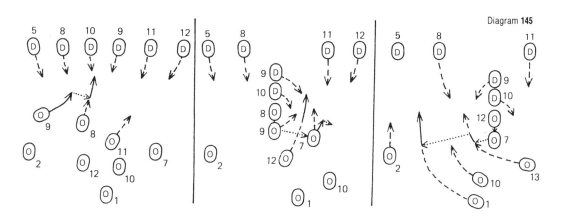

Diagram **145**

strongly into the opposition in an attempt to gain physical and psychological domination while gaining ground. It is important that the forward with the ball is closely supported. Close support play not only makes the continuation of play possible, but also gives the ball carrier immediate passing options, thus reducing the likelihood of gang-tackling.

Equally important is for the drives to be combined in as short a time as possible. As one forward takes the ball up strongly, another should already be in position to take it up on the next play. A quick play-the-ball will often result in him running at a disorganized defence.

Attacking from a scrummage

1 Tactical implications
2 Using an extra player
3 Using a player twice
4 Changing the direction of the attack
5 A kick

1 TACTICAL IMPLICATIONS

1 The scrummage ties up the forwards of both teams, so the three-quarters have vital space in which to attack. They should take advantage of this, particularly from those scrums when they have both head and put-in, when possession can be almost guaranteed.

2 Teams should try to score directly from the scrum, realizing that as soon as the ball has been won the opposition forwards will break quickly to arrive in position at the first play-the-ball.

3 The first option to be considered should be the giving of a quick early ball to the team's most dangerous attacker. This may be successful particularly if the opportunity is created for him to run at any of the opposition noted for weak defence.

Most players in the higher levels of the game are more than competent tacklers, so moves will be required which try to create gaps in the defensive alignment.

Broadly speaking the moves can all be categorized as follows:

1 Using an extra player
2 Using a player twice
3 Changing the direction of attack
4 A kick

2 USING AN EXTRA PLAYER

The players introduced into the line most frequently are:

(a) The full-back
(b) A blind-side attacker
(c) The loose forward

(a) The full-back

He is in the perfect position to assess the situation and arrive into the line as an extra man. He is able to time his run and select any option, and can join the line on the open side or blind, and in between any of the players. It is most common for him to be marked by the opposition full-back. The art of a good attacking full-back is, therefore, to arrive in a space before his opposite number. This can be achieved by a combination of timing and cunning.

The full-back is at his most effective when he spearheads the attack and tries to break through the opposition's defensive line himself. He should be encouraged to hit the line hard and straight, and his team-mates should be encouraged to support.

The full-back in diagram 146 enters the line between the stand-off and inside centre. Alternatives are to (i) enter the line in a catch-pass situation and

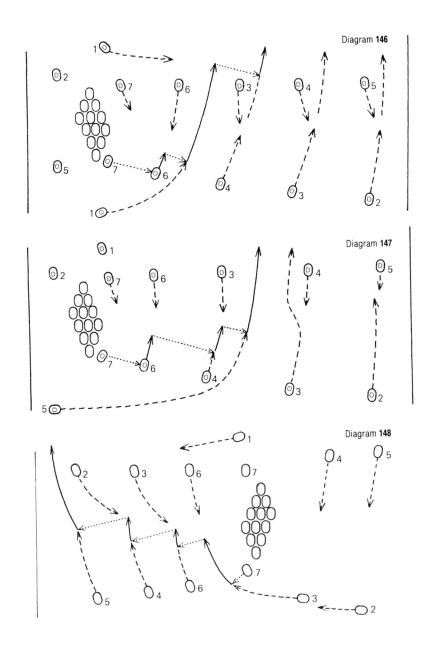

Diagram **146**

Diagram **147**

Diagram **148**

create extra men out wide, or (ii) be used as a decoy.

It is important for the blind-side winger to cover behind the line whenever the full-back joins the attacking line from a scrummage.

(b) Blind-side attacker

An extra man can be introduced into the line by using a winger or centre from the blind side. Again the ingredient of success is for the attacker to arrive on the ball before his opposite number, so timing is important. The extra man can either loop round and try to break the line himself, or join the line early and try to create the gap for someone else.

The blind-side winger O5 (diagram 147) times his run, and arcs off the inside centre breaking the line himself.

The blind-side centre O3 (diagram 148) receives the ball on the open side from the scrum-half. By slick handling the open-side winger O5 is given an overlap.

(c) Loose forward

The loose forward is perhaps the only other player who can enter the line from a scrummage and create the extra man. The laws of the game restrict when he can break, so it is usual for him either to pick the ball up himself or to combine with the scrum-half. In diagram 149, the scrum-half carries the ball forward,

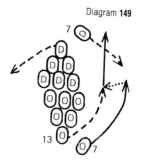

Diagram **149**

and off-loads to the loose forward on his inside, after first committing the defence.

3   USING A PLAYER TWICE

All the principles involved in this play are discussed in Section 2, Chapter 3, *Advanced Handling Skills*. From a scrum any of the three-quarters can carry out a run around, but usually it is the stand-off moving round one or both of the centres. The reason for this is that the scrum-half's run can be badly affected by a slow ball from the scrummage, while the defence has usually moved up by the time the centres receive the ball.

In diagram 150, the stand-off (O6) runs around both centres, while the full-back runs as decoy between them. The aim is to move the ball wide to the stand-off in space, after having brought the defensive full-back into the line. The blind-side winger covers for the full-back.

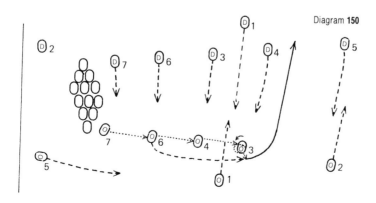

Diagram **150**

4   CHANGING THE DIRECTION OF ATTACK

Diagram 151 shows the first try scored by Great Britain in their 25–8 victory against New Zealand in the second Test at Wigan in 1985. Britain won the ball against the head; it was quickly passed to the inside centre Ellery Hanley (O4) via Deryck Fox (O7) and Tony Myler (O6). Hanley ran at speed across field towards New Zealand's outside centre, Gary Prohm (D4), taking James Leuluai (D3) with him. Both New Zealand centres were drawn towards Hanley who made a drop-off pass to Garry Schofield (O3), giving him the opportunity to finish strongly by scoring the first of his four tries.

5   A KICK

It is policy with some teams when defending from a scrum to position their full-back in the defensive line.

This is particularly the case when the opposition has a quick, elusive full-back, positioned to receive the ball in the line. When this occurs the defenders have no last line of defence and are susceptible to a kick either through or over them.

In diagram 152, O1 stands in the line from the scrum, between O6 and O4. D1, wary of the speed of O1, moves up into his defensive line to mark him. On winning the scrum, O7 passes to O6, who carries the ball towards the opposition, thereby committing them, but before being tackled chips over their heads.

The rest of the team are onside, and chase the ball. As long as the kick does not go dead they will have a good chance of scoring.

SUMMARY

1   The aim is to score directly from the scrum. Some teams use all their moves without first analysing

Diagram **151**

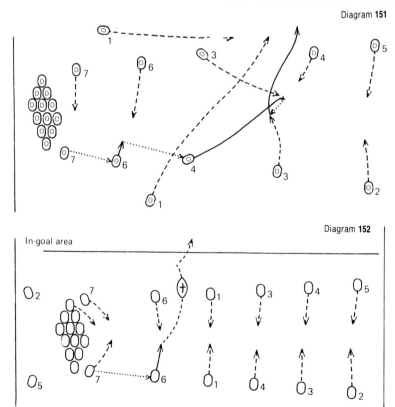

Diagram **152**

the weaknesses of the opposition. Whenever possible keep the game simple.

2   Teams should have a series of moves which enable them to attack anywhere along the line: these must be practised. Co-ordination, angle of run and timing are important.

3   If the full-back is to be introduced into the line, it is important that the blind-side wing provides cover.

4   Many moves have more chance of success if the pivot player has more than one passing option.

5   Support the player who is trying to penetrate the first line of defence. He may be successful but fall either to the cover defence or to the full-back, when support would ensure a try.

6   The ball carriers should understand where the next attack is to be launched. This is important when the move is foiled by a successful tackle, because a continuation of the attack will increase pressure on the defence.

7   A back row which breaks quickly from a scrum can often attack from the first play-the-ball, before the opposition arrives as in diagram 153a. This is helped if it is a set play and the back row knows exactly to which part of the field it is going. From the scrum, the stand-off (O6) takes the ball hard into his opposite number. Once tackled he plays the ball as quickly as possible, as in diagram 153b. The scrum-half moves into acting half-back, while the back three forwards (11, 12 and 13) loop round and attack on the first play.

8   Possession is vital. If there is any doubt at all in the ball carrier's mind whether his pass will go to hand, the move should be cancelled and possession maintained.

9   There are far fewer scrums in modern Rugby League. Teams should practise the moves, but beware of spending too much time on plays which will be used in frequently.

Diagram **153a**

Diagram **153b**

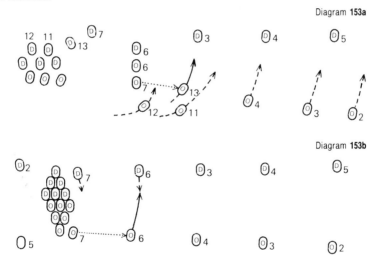

Attacking from the kick-off

1   LAWS OF THE GAME

(a)   Before the game begins, the two captains meet in the presence of the referee, one captain tossing a coin while the other calls. The captain winning the toss shall choose in which direction his team is going to play, and the other team starts the game with a place-kick from the centre of the half-way line.

(b)   After a goal or a try, the team against which the points have been scored kicks off to re-start the game.

(c)   The ball may be kicked forward in any direction, and is immediately in play when it has crossed the 10-metre line. The ball must bounce before it goes out of play. Opposing players must retire beyond the 10-metre line. Players in the team which kicks off must not advance in front of the ball before it is kicked. Any offence, by either side, incurs a penalty to be awarded at the centre of the half-way line.

(d)   A kick-off which goes out of play with a bounce:
 (i)   over the dead-ball line, results in the receivers restarting play with a drop-kick from between the posts

 (ii)   over the touchline, results in a scrummage being formed ten metres in from where the ball crossed the line with the kickers receiving the head and the receivers the put-in.

2   KICKING-OFF

1   The principles of kicking-off

(a)   To gain possession.   To gain possession from the kick-off is usually the priority, but is difficult to achieve. The kicking team can try to gain possession by:

(i)   Kick, follow and catch:
A short high kick will often enable a chaser to arrive underneath the ball and to catch it from an onside position.

(ii)   Kick causing the opposition to knock on:
In lower standards of rugby – particularly during inclement weather and on heavy, uneven pitches – it is sometimes possible to cause the opposition to fumble, thereby giving the kicking team the opportunity of gaining possession either directly or from

the resulting scrum, when they would have the head and the put-in.

(iii) Kick out of play, with a bounce over the dead-ball line. The game is restarted with the receiving team dropping out from under the posts, thereby returning possession to the team which has kicked-off.

(iv) Kick out of play, with a bounce over the touchline. The team kicking off will have the head at the resulting scrum, and although the receiving term will have the put-in, they will have, in theory, at least an equal opportunity of gaining possession.

(b) Place the receivers under pressure. When the chances of gaining possession from the kick-off are low, an alternative tactic is to kick the ball as far as possible and, with a fast, determined onside chase, try to tackle and contain the opposition close to their in-goal area. Many teams use the 22-metre line as a guide, and make sure that the receivers are tackled within their own 22.

2 Position of the team kicking-off

The team kicking-off should line up across the pitch four to five metres behind the ball. This will enable them to follow up at speed from an onside position.

Their alignment will depend on the tactics of the kicker. Certainly the player receiving the ball must be placed under immediate pressure, so a fast deter-mined chase is necessary.

The receiver has the option of

(a) attacking himself
(b) passing to support players
(c) immediately returning the kick.

If an immediate return kick is possible, a minimum of two players and possibly a third should remain back. The rest should spread across the pitch, move up quickly, and tackle the opposition as far upfield as possible.

The players kept back should all be safe catchers of a high ball, and either competent kickers or strong runners, depending on the team's plan.

3 The kicker

The kick-off is best performed by the team's specia-list kicker.

3 RECEIVING THE KICK-OFF

1 The principles of receiving the kick-off

It is essential that the team receiving the kick-off should gain possession. Good catchers should be placed in positions where the ball is likely to land, irrespective of their playing positions.

The receivers should be prepared to:

(a) Call clearly and early for the ball
(b) Move forward to catch the ball before it bounces
(c) Catch the ball cleanly, and
(d) Control difficult bouncing balls by either (i) dropping on the ball, or (ii) stopping it with the feet before picking it up.

The rest of the team should assist the receiver by either:

(i) Blocking the opposition within the laws of the game, or
(ii) Supporting the receiver.

Receiving the short kick

Players able to catch when under pressure must position themselves for the short high kick. Because the ball is best caught by moving forward, these players should wait around thirteen metres from the centre-line. They should be prepared to jump high and catch the ball, or act as blockers when leaving the ball for the second line of catchers. It is imperative not to give penalties away – particularly when receiving possession – so all blocking must be done within the laws.

Receiving the long kick

Players receiving the long kick must know the tactics to be used. But, whatever they are, it is essential that, first, the kick is taken cleanly.

Once the ball has been made safe it is usual to try to move as far upfield as possible. The catcher should either accept responsibility himself, or quickly transfer the ball to a strong direct runner. Criss–cross moves can be particularly effective. The rest of the team should support. If the ball is to be kicked immediately, the kicker must be close to the receiver. His kick should be strong, well placed and not rushed.

It is important that the rest of the team are aware of the tactics to be used so that they can act accordingly.

2   Positions when receiving the kick-off

Positions from the kick-off are affected by:

1   The skill of both teams
2   The tactics to be adopted
3   The size and conditions of the playing area, and
4   Weather conditions.

Because it is common sense for the receivers to be in position before the kickers, both sides of the pitch are defended by a mixture of forwards and backs. However the positions in diagram 154 are only guidelines and should be modified accordingly.

Drop-kick restarts

Similar principles apply to all drop-kick restarts from both the 22-metre and goal-lines.

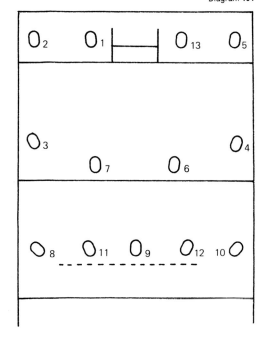

Diagram 154

PRINCIPLES OF PLAY

INTRODUCTION

It is now time to consider the overall principles of the game. What are we trying to achieve? How is it to be done? Perhaps the answer to the first question is straightforward. As with most team games the aim is to win, by scoring more points than the opposition. How to achieve this is a far more difficult problem, and one which can only be solved by coaches with a thorough understanding of the many complexities of the game.

Possession is the first principle of play, because it is impossible in Rugby League to score points when the opposition has the ball. The first step to winning the game must therefore be to gain possession of the ball, and to keep it for as long as possible.

However, the laws of the game, particularly the limited-tackle rule and the resulting handover of possession, ensure that no one team can completely monopolize possession. The opposition will have the ball for long periods during which they must be prevented from scoring. *Defence*, because of this, is the second most important principle of play.

Once a team's defence has been well established, the area in which most of the game is played will have a strong influence on the result. A team confined to its own 22-metre area is placed under tremendous pressure. Not only has its defence to hold firm, but any penalty conceded is likely to be converted into points. Territorial advantage can often be secured by inventive, strong running, attacking rugby, but this is not always the case when opposed by a committed and well-organized defence. An alternative method is to kick, and *an intelligent, well-executed kicking game* is the third principle of play.

It now becomes obvious that during periods of possession the opposition's defence must be placed under as much pressure as possible. This is achieved by strong running raids directed at every part of the defensive line. These raids have little chance of success if isolated, so combinations are necessary, with attacks in numbers, and because of this *supporting the ball* is the fourth and final principle of play.

Tony Myler, held up in a tackle by Bob Linder, in the Great Britain v Australia Test at Elland Road, Leeds in 1986, controls the ball firmly as he looks for support.

Control of the ball

1   Responsibility to the game
2   Winning rugby
3   The facts
4   Factors influencing possession
5   Methods of improving control of the ball
6   Specific practices

1   RESPONSIBILITY TO THE GAME

Attacking, free-flowing Rugby League football is the most exciting and entertaining game in the world, and a team moving forward in possession of the ball, passing it freely from one side of the pitch to the other, provides one of the greatest spectacles in sport.

35   Harry Pinner carries the ball into the New Zealand defence in the first Test in 1985, controls the ball firmly, and looks for support.

2   WINNING RUGBY

Rugby League is also fiercely competitive, and the players must enter the playing arena with one intention – to win.

Fortunately, winning rugby and entertaining rugby can be the same thing. A team which carries the ball to the opposition when in possession, controls the ball, and supports it well, combines the ingredients of success and entertainment. A team which squanders possession has little chance of achieving either.

3   THE FACTS

(a)   **Possession.**   Statistics from home and abroad suggest that when two teams of similar ability meet it is usually the one that has had possession the longest that wins the game. Statistics compiled by the National Coaching Scheme during the 1985–86 season at twenty-five games found that in all but three the team that had possession the longest won. These included the following internationals:

9 October 1985
Great Britain Under-21 12   (27 min. 11 sec.)
New Zealand 16   (29 min. 42 sec.)

19 October 1985, first Test
Great Britain 22   (25 min. 11 sec.)
New Zealand 24   (25 min. 20 sec.)

2 November 1985, second Test
Great Britain 25   (25 min. 39 sec.)
New Zealand 8   (23 min. 39 sec.)

9 November 1985, third Test
Great Britain 6   (27 min. 26 sec.)
New Zealand 6   (22 min. 5 sec.)

2 February 1986
Great Britain Under-21 6   (28 min. 50 sec.)
France Under-24 2   (22 min. 1 sec.)

1 March 1986
Great Britain 24   (25 min. 30 sec.)
France 10   (18 min. 28 sec.)

(b)   **Scoring opportunities.**   A team can only score when in possession of the ball. Using the international with France as an example, Great Britain had possession for 25 minutes 30 seconds out of a total of 43 minutes 58 seconds. They were therefore in possession for 58% of the time, compared with France's 42%, and had 16% more time in which to score.

(c)   **Physical conditioning.**   It is far more physically demanding to make a series of tackles than to run the ball. Any coach or player who doubts this can quickly test the theory at training. Have one group of players running and passing the ball, while another group adopts defensive duties. The group which has been moving up in line, tackling, quickly regaining their feet, moving back and then repeating the exercise experiences fatigue far sooner than the ball carriers. The team that is tackling for the greater length of time is likely to be using up more energy, and therefore is more likely to become fatigued during the game.

(d)   **Mental pressures.**   An individual lapse in concentration, an incorrect decision or a breakdown in skill, is likely to have a greater effect on the result of a game when made by the defence. The mental pressures are therefore far greater on the team not in possession.

4   FACTORS INFLUENCING POSSESSION

(a)   **Scrummaging.**   It is important to win as many scrummages as possible. A team should ensure it wins all those with the head and put-in, and make a concerted effort to win as many others as possible.

Although the average number of scrums in the game is declining, there are still enough for scrum wins to influence the result. It is therefore advisable for teams to improve their win/loss ratio by regular scrummaging practices.

(b)   **Penalties.**   Often there are more penalties awarded in a game than there are scrums, so playing within the rules has important strategic implications. An undisciplined team will have great difficulty in controlling the ball.

Discipline, a complete knowledge of the laws, and a desire to play within them should be part of a team's strategy. This places a considerable onus on match officials to referee honestly, competently and not to make any pre-match judgements.

(c)   Defence.   Exerting pressure on the opposition when they have the ball will often result in them making errors of judgement and cause a breakdown in skill, as a result of which they lose the ball. A strong defence, which will be fully discussed in the next Chapter, is an important strategic factor influencing possession.

(d)   Winning loose balls.   Possession is so important that any loose ball should be quickly regathered. Controlling, picking up and falling on loose balls are most valuable skills which have a positive effect on a team's efficiency.

It has been emphasized that skills practices considerably improve reaction time. Players of all ages and abilities should practice regularly the skills of regaining possession. All training games and unopposed practices should encourage players to fall on the ball, and to regain possession quickly.

(e)   Reduction in handling errors.   The reduction of errors when in possession is affected by many factors, not least a correct mental attitude. Players need to be aware of the importance of possession when making decisions, particularly when carrying the ball. The golden rule at all times is that responsibility for possession belongs solely with the ball carrier. Irrespective of how strong the calls are from supporting players, a visual check should first be made and the pass given only when the ball carrier is certain that it will go to hand.

Efficiency in the skills of the game will also improve a player's ability to control the ball. Skills practices should dominate the coaching programme for youngsters, and should also be included in the weekly plan for more senior players. The coach should observe all his players, analyse faults, and then organize individual skills practices whenever required. The importance of practising skills under pressure needs consideration. Many players perform well in training but find that errors occur in the game. They can be helped by simulating controlled pressure situations during training sessions.

5   METHODS OF IMPROVING CONTROL OF THE BALL

(a)   Scrummage:
   Knowledge of the rules
   Sound hooking technique
   Correct scrummage formation
   Strong co-ordinated push
   Correct mental attitude of the pack
   Regular practice
   Match statistics to identify scrum wins, both with and against the head.

(b)   Penalties:
   Knowledge of the rules
   Discipline
   Control
   Match recognition, plus the possibility of punishment by the club for players guilty of persistent infringements.

(c)   Defence:
   Sound tackling technique
   Well organized defence
   Speed of the defensive line
   Good kicking game with chase
   Attitude: to attack the opposition and obtain possession
   Match statistics to identify work-rates on defence.

(d)   Winning the loose ball
   Proficient level of skill
   Regular practice
   Habit building by having to fall on the ball in training games
   Match statistics to identify the players who win possession.

(e)   Reduction in handling errors
   Recognition of the importance of possession
   Proficient levels of skill
   Skills practised in pressure situations
   Match statistics to identify the players guilty of losing possession
   Individual coaching.

6   SPECIFIC PRACTICES

Although control of the ball can be improved with constant encouragement by the coach and under-standing by the players, during every coaching session and game, there are specific practices designed to assist its development.

(a)   Control of the ball.   Coaches may insist that players control the ball at all times, even during training sessions. Balls should be carefully passed from hand to hand, placed in the corner out of the way when not in use, and never handled carelessly.

(b)   Piggy in the middle.   This game is ideal for developing support play. It is played in a grid where three players have possession, and attempt to keep the ball from the fourth. All players can move, apart from the player with the ball, so the two free attackers have to move into open space and communicate with the ball carrier. 'Pass' and 'support' are the key words at first, and the aim of the game is to make the highest number of successive passes. The game can be physically demanding as the players combine, especi-ally when the man in the middle is highly motivated. The three controlling the ball try to make twenty consecutive passes, while the man in the middle tries to gain possession. If the ball is intercepted or touches the ground, the player guilty of the error changes places with the one in the middle. The emphasis must be on error-free football. Body con-tact is not allowed, so the player in possession must hold the ball safe until he is certain of making a successful pass.

(c)   Four against four possession.   Piggy in the middle can be extended to increase pressure on those controlling the ball, with three against two, for example. The final stage is to have two four-a-side teams competing in a twenty-metre grid. The rules are identical, and the objective is still to make twenty consecutive passes. This drill develops support play, makes physical demands on the players and makes control of the ball the overriding principle.

(d)   Conditioned games.   These training games, as close to the game of Rugby League as possible, should play a part in all weekly training programmes. The games can be tackle, grip, two-handed touch or tig. Various rules can be devised which encourage control of the ball.

(i)   Six against three, four, five, or six.   Twelve players in two teams use half the pitch. Control of the ball is being developed so the offence is overloaded at first, then made equal as the attackers experience success. Team A attacks with the ball and lines out to receive a goal-line drop-out. At first only three of team B take part. They drop-out then move up while team A tries to score within six tackles (or touches), playing normal Rugby League rules. Once a try is scored the three defenders change places with their team-mates. After the second try has been scored four defend, after the fourth try five defend, and after the sixth try all six defend. If after any drop-out team A loses possession or commits an infringement the teams interchange, and the same occurs if team B completes six consecutive tackles.

(ii)   Unlimited-tackle football.   A game of tackle, grip, two-handed or one-handed touch can be played under the old unlimited-tackle rules. The offence keep the ball until they lose possession or contravene the laws. Pressure may be increased by having fewer players in the team with the ball than the opposition.

(iii)   Conditioned   unlimited-tackle   football.   A similar game can be developed in which the team with possession takes a tap on their own 22. Their objective is to reach the half-way line. They are allowed unlimited tackles, but if they infringe or lose possession the other team receives the ball. Once the half-way line is reached, they are allowed a further six tackles to score. Grubber-kicking is encouraged. If the opposition are tackled within their in-goal area following a grubber-kick, they re-start play with a goal-line drop-out.

Defence

1   Definition
2   Defensive organization
3   Communication and understanding
4   Physical conditioning and commitment
5   Attitude
6   Improving the team defence

36   Wigan's success in the 1986–87 season was based on a well organised defence. In the 1987 John Player Cup final Warrington's Gary Sanderson is dealt with most efficiently by Ian Roberts and Brian Case while Ian Potter is ready to lend a hand.

1   DEFINITION

Defence is the function of the team when not in possession of the ball. The major objective of the defensive line is to prevent the opposition from scoring, but it will be far more effective if it tries to

1   Exert pressure
2   Gain ground
3   Win possession, and
4   Physically dominate the opposition.

   Some coaches, particularly those in the highest grades of rugby, will argue that in big matches defence has a greater influence on the result than any other factor. Jack Gibson, the famous Sydney coach, says players do not relish playing against teams with well-organized and vigorous defences. 'Who would you rather play against, a team noted for its attacking play and capable of scoring many tries, or a team with a strong, aggressive defence?' Gibson is occasionally criticized, both in Australia and Great Britain, for concentrating too much on defence, but he explains:

(a)   the opposition will have the ball for approximately 50% of the game
(b)   what can you do in that time but defend as well as possible?

It is hard to argue with such logic.

   Most agree that the biggest difference between Australian and British team play in the 1980s has been the Australians' superior defence. While the British concentrated on improving individual smother-tackling technique, the Australians improved their defensive organization. They developed ways of defending against the run-around and drop-off, ensured that their defensive line was not pulled out of position, and produced methods of equating numbers quickly. They concentrated on speeding up the defensive line, thereby reducing the opposition's thinking time, and pressurizing them into error. Their thoroughness proved conclusively that thought and preparation produce results.

2   DEFENSIVE ORGANIZATION

Communication, understanding, physical conditioning and commitment are essential ingredients of successful defensive play. The first step is to understand fully the following aspects of defensive organization:

1   Individual tackling skill
2   The defensive line
3   Positional play in the defensive line
4   The marker defence
5   The sweeper
6   Drifting to reduce gaps
7   The two-man tackle
8   The gang-tackle
9   Controlling the speed at which the opposition play the ball
10   Equating numbers
11   The speed of the line
12   Gaining possession
13   Cover defence
14   Line defence

1   Individual tackling skill

Rugby League, perhaps more than any other sport, requires all players to have a solid defence. Individual tackling technique is most important, therefore. The coach of youngsters should ensure that every player under his guidance is proficient in all forms of tackling. He must spend time observing, analysing and improving each player individually. Those coaching the more senior players must also devote time each week to improving the tackling ability of the squad. The individual performance of each player should be analysed and individual coaching offered whenever necessary.

   More often than not, players needing improvement should tackle opponents, but for competent tacklers frequent drills on tubes and tackle bags will be more beneficial.

   When improving individual defence the coach should concentrate on:

(a) *Technique* (see Chapter 4, Section 2).

(b) *Balance and footwork*: the defender must be agile, and capable of moving quickly into the tackle. He should adopt a boxer's footwork on the balls of his feet, with weight equally balanced first on one foot and then on the other.

(c) *Head down*: the player's chin should be close to his chest, eyes observing the opposition, as he gets ready to pounce. Players who lift their heads may flinch away from a hand-off, resulting in a missed tackle.

(d) *Shoulder contact*: the shoulder should always make contact, being driven with determination into the target area. When hitting with the left shoulder the player should drive with his left foot forward, and vice versa.

(e) *Tackle low*: the first man into the tackle should always tackle low, thrusting his shoulder into the target area, to ensure that the ball carrier is stopped and quickly grounded.

(f) *Timing*: of the tackle is an important consideration. Players must concentrate on this aspect of defending.

2   The defensive line

It is vital for the defence to maintain a straight line across the pitch. The end men should be slightly outside the opposition's end men at each side of the line, but gaps between players should be as small as possible, particularly around the area of attack. The defence should have the same number of players as the offence at each side of the play-the-ball. The line should extend at each side of the play-the-ball and move forward together.

Players should guard against the following errors:

(a)   The line being too short

In diagram 155, the defenders are bunched, and by quick passing the ball carriers are able to move the ball to an unmarked player (O4) who penetrates.

(b)   An individual moving up faster than the line

Any player moving up in front of the rest of the team

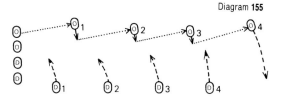

Diagram 155

leaves a gap, which can be exploited either by individual evasive skills or passing combinations.

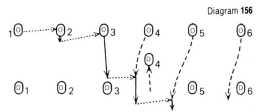

Diagram 156

In diagram 156, D4 has moved up in front of the defensive line leaving a gap which is exploited by O3 carrying the ball forward and offloading to O4 in the gap created. O4 has the option of coming on a short pass (as in the diagram) or moving into the hole around the back of D4.

(c)   An individual moving up slower than the line

Similar evasive skills or passing combinations can exploit an individual who is left behind the defensive line.

In diagram 157, O4 simply runs at D4, carries the ball through the first line of defence, and off-loads to support.

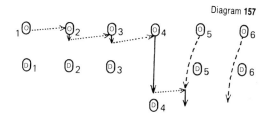

Diagram 157

(d)   An individual being drawn across field

A defensive player in the line who moves quickly across field leaves a hole which the rest of the team find difficulty in covering.

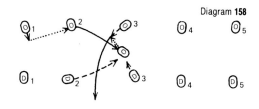

Diagram **158**

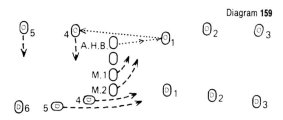

Diagram **159**

Diagram **160**

across at the back of the open-side line is susceptible to a quick reverse of play, as in diagram 159.

O1 upon receiving the ball on the open side quickly changes the direction of attack, by passing blind to O4.

Because the blind-side defence, D4 and D5, have anticipated an open-side attack and covered across, O4 and O5 are able to penetrate the defensive line.

(f)   The defence should mark players not space

The defence has four players on the blind side marking D2. As a result the attackers have more men on the open side, and are likely to penetrate with additional runners off O13, as in diagram 160.

In diagram 158, the attacker (O2), on receiving the ball, sprints across field taking D2 with him. A gap is created on the inside which is exploited by O2 dropping off O3.

The defenders should not get involved in crossfield running, and must not adopt a man-to-man marker system.

Communication and understanding between players are vital, and in the above example D2 should leave O2 and be prepared to cover any inside pass. As O2 moves across field he will be tackled by D3 or D4.

(e)   The blind side covering across

A blind-side defence which is too quick to cover

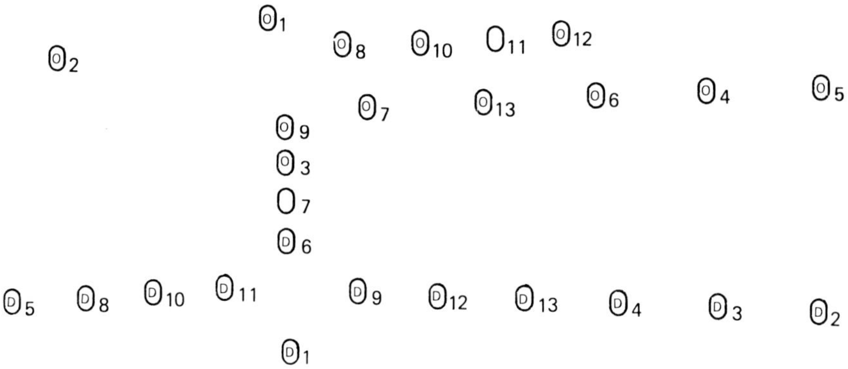

3   Positional play in the defensive line

Scrum

A team that has both the head and put-in should win possession and immediately attack the opposition, who need a well organized defence.

(i)   The backs

The back division should form a defensive line across the pitch, lying flat as close to the opposition as the rules allow. They should line out, marking their opposite numbers. If the opposition places its centres on either side of the scrum, the defenders should follow suit; if the stand-off takes position on the open side, then the defending stand-off should stand on the corresponding side in direct opposition to him. If all the back division, apart from the blind-side wing, line out on the same side of the scrum, the defence should do likewise.

It is usual for the defenders to stand slightly on the outside of the opposition, so that both their opposite number and the movement of the ball from the scrum can be seen clearly. Such positioning tends to prevent an outside break, and catches the opposition in a pincer movement of backs and covering back-row forwards. Some teams regularly, and others on specific occasions, will position themselves on the inside of their opposite number, thereby shepherding the offence to the touchline. In this way each player is travelling in a covering direction, and the attacking moves of the opposition can be combated more easily. However, the dangers of showing the outside gap to fast runners should never be underestimated. Each coach should be aware of the advantages and disadvantages of both systems, and only adopt a formation after weighing these against the strengths and weaknesses of his players.

(ii) The forwards

It is imperative that all the forwards carry out their scrummaging duties in an effort to win the ball, or at the worst try to push the opposition backwards so they have poor ball. However, once the opposition has won possession, the forwards should be ready to break as quickly as possible in an attempt to stifle any attack.

(iii) Defence around the scrum

The backs mark the opposition as previously mentioned, lying as flat as possible. Once the opposition is in possession, the defending scrum-half should try to tackle his opposite number. The loose forward assists, with responsibility for blocking the blind side and assisting the scrum-half in preventing any attack around the base of the scrum. (If the scrum-half has had to put the ball in from the blind, then the loose forward is responsible for the open side.)

(iv) Scrum-half

The scrum-half should pressurize the opposing scrum-half. But if the attacking scrum-half gives a quick service to his stand-off, the defending scrum-half should follow the ball, and therefore becomes the first cover defender.

(v) Loose forward

Once the ball is out of the scrum the defending loose forward should break as quickly as possible. The blind side is his first priority, but if the ball has moved to the open side he should assist the defensive line and cover any possible breaks. (Again, if the ball has been put in from the blind side, the loose forward breaks to the open side.)

(vi) Open-side second row

The open-side second-row forward should break as quickly as possible, following the scrum-half across the back of the three-quarters in a covering position.

(vii) Blind-side second row

The blind-side second row should break as quickly as possible, and ensure that the blind side is well covered. If the ball has moved to the open side he should then cover across following the loose forward.

(viii) Front row

The front row, once the ball has been lost, should make every attempt to rejoin play, but the coach should understand that it is unrealistic to rely on any member of the front row to make a tackle direct from the scrum. Because of this, at the first tackle from the scrum, the second-row forwards should be prepared to adopt the defensive duties normally carried out by the props, covering each side of the ruck. As the tackle periods develop, the front row should drift inwards to adopt their normal positions.

(ix) Full-back

The full-back should be aware of the defensive capabilities of his own team, as well as the likelihood of his opposite number joining in the attack. It is most important that he not only communicates, but has a clear understanding, with his back division. If the scrum is in a central position, with split centres, the full-back should position himself behind the scrum.

If the scrum is close to the touchline and both attacking centres adopt positions on the same side of the scrum, it may be possible – if the previously mentioned points are adopted by the defensive team – for the full-back to move infield and adopt a position in line with the posts. This will enable him to pick up his opposite number wherever he may come into the line. Even so, some coaches will prefer to have their full-back in a more orthodox position behind the scrum. In this intance, it may not always be possible for the defensive full-back to get across field and take his opposite number. The full-back and backs must therefore combine and fully understand who is to take whom.

(x)   Blind-side winger

The blind-side winger must take a positive role in the defensive formation of his team. His first priority is to cover any blind-side attack, but if the opposition move the ball away from his wing he should be ready to cover. Many coaches expect the blind-side winger to be the second line of cover after the scrum-half, but this is a little ambitious and can leave the blind side open to a kick, especially if the full-back has adopted a position in line with the posts. The blind-side winger should block his side but should be prepared to cover when it is obvious that the opposition are mounting a concerted attack away from his wing. He should also cover for the full-back when he comes into the line. He will, therefore, possibly cover across slightly behind the open-side second row.

Summary

Whatever defensive formation a team uses, it is important that every member clearly understands his responsibility to tackle quickly and efficiently, or adopt the necessary covering role. The importance

of understanding and communication cannot be overemphasized. Defensive formations should be practised in training, and any resulting problems put right.

Tap-penalty

The basic defensive formation from a tap-penalty is identical to that from a play-the-ball, with the exception of a marker system. The defensive line, with a full-back and sometimes a sweeper at the back, stretches across the width of the pitch, outside the opposition. Usually the ball carriers group their forwards around the tap and have their three-quarters outside them, stretching to the far touch-line. In such instances the defence will line out in a similar formation, with forwards and backs in direct opposition.

Some teams, in an attempt to reduce crossfield running, encourage the blind-side centre to stay next to his winger. This is safe as long as:

(a) The centre has a strong front-on defence, capable of stopping determined running forwards.

(b) The opposing centres are closely marked.

Play-the-ball

There are three basic areas which should be covered at every play-the-ball:

(i)   At the side of the play-the-ball (ruck)

Two players, ideally front rowers, should stand six metres apart, three metres either side of an imaginary line running back from the centre of the play-the-ball.

(ii) Right centre and right wing

Assuming that the centre has the ability to tackle strong running forwards, the two players should stay together on taps and on all occasions except where a narrow blind side exists, or from a kick-off. The winger positions himself outside his opposite number, while the centre follows his opposite number to the left side of the pitch only when he is confident that the defence on his side is formed. The centre, upon moving, should tell his winger that he is going, and also, as he moves across, encourage the other players to move outwards so that no gaps are left. Once on the other side of the pitch, the centre should be aware that he has a responsibility to move back when his flank is under attack. The team should understand that a reduction in defensive crossfield running is good policy, and that at no time should any gaps be left in the defensive formation.

(iii)   Left centre and left wing

Their responsibilities are identical to those listed in the paragraph above.

All the other areas between the centres and the ruck must be filled on each side of the field. In an ideal situation the second rows should be second men to the props, on either side of the ruck. The two half-backs and the loose forward have a roving commission, and fill all the gaps between the second rows and the centres.

It is important for these players to read the game and to be where play is developing. If time permits they may run round the back of the ruck to fill gaps, but the normal way is for players to drift across.

It is important that players do not follow the ball in a swarm, otherwise criss-cross moves will exploit the defence and open up gaps. It is also important that players space out evenly and move up in the line together.

(iv)   Full-back

The full-back should be behind the defensive line following the ball, continually communicating with his players, encouraging them into positions and ensuring that no holes are allowed to form. He should also meet attacking players on equal terms: if he allows the ball carrier time to set up support, a try will result. He must either tackle, rush or shepherd, and should also be alert for the kick.

(v)   Wingers

Wingers have a special job. The open-side winger should position himself on the outside of his opposite number. A winger who can move quickly in and crash-tackle the opposing centre may be useful in defence, but it is imperative that the ball is stopped, otherwise the flank will be wide open. The message is clear: do not go in unless certain that the ball will be stopped. A problem does occur when the winger is left with two attackers. Some wingers, relying on speed and experience, move in to encourage the pass then tackle the winger from the side. An alternative ploy is to tackle the inside man and rely on the cover and full-back to prevent the wing from scoring. On no account should the winger move in and be caught in no-man's-land.

The blind-side winger should be prepared to cover across to the other side of the pitch, and assist the full-back in receiving any kicks.

4   Marker-defence

More often than not, the player(s) who made the previous tackle take(s) the position of marker(s). A team can adopt either a one-marker or two-marker defence.

(i)   One marker

The marker should be alert and ready to take part in play. He should try to finish the tackle on top of the ball carrier; control the speed of the play-the-ball movement by regaining his feet before the tackled player; take one step back; and concentrate on preventing the acting half-back making ground.

He should not be baited by the opposition, nor should he move around the ball carrier as the ball is played, otherwise he would leave the gate open for the acting half-back to break around the other side. He should stand his ground and wait for the acting half-back to move. If the acting half-back moves forward, the marker should immediately tackle him. He should also be prepared to follow the ball if passed and either tackle the first receiver, or ensure that the first receiver does not pass the ball back inside.

(ii)   Two markers

There is an increasing use of two-marker defence, particularly at the top level of the game. Many teams adopt a two-marker defence in both 22-metre areas, others adopt a two-marker defence early in the tackle counts, while others adopt a two-marker defence at every play-the-ball.

Some argue that the defensive line cannot afford two markers as they result in gaps being left out wide. This may occur in teams that have a poor commitment to defence, but the advantages of a two-marker defence are too important to ignore. Attacking ploys were discussed in the last chapter and it became obvious that a one-marker system is open to well-supported raids by either the acting half-back or first receiver.

Not only does a well-organized two-marker defensive system prevent most plays, but it also allows the defence to exert immediate pressure on the ball carrier, and so control the game.

It is essential that:

1   The marker defence is set up before the ball carrier regains his feet

2   Both markers concentrate, and

3   Both markers expect to make the next tackle.

37   The two markers work together: Lee Crooks and John Fieldhouse (no. 10) are alert as the Australian hooker, Royce Simmons, passes to the first receiver in the third Great Britain v Australia Test in 1986.

It is also necessary for both of them to work closely together. The acting half-back is their first priority. If he moves, one of them should tackle him, while the other prevents an inside pass. Similarly, if the acting half-back passes to the first receiver one of the markers should move quickly across to tackle him, while the other prevents an inside pass. In this way they always operate as a unit. On no account should they split, otherwise they would be vulnerable to a runner going between them.

In diagram 161, the acting half-back has passed to the first receiver. M1 moves quickly to FR, with M2 tracking across behind, preventing FR from passing on the inside. The open-side defence (D1 and D2)

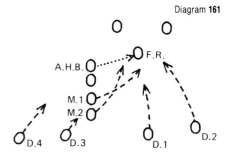

Diagram 161

also move up in line, quickly eliminating all passing options. The blind side have a very important duty. Not only do they move forward maintaining the line, but in unison they drift inwards allowing D3 to move into the play-the-ball area vacated by the markers.

The team should adopt a set pattern at every play-the-ball. There are many variations which include:

(a)   M1 having responsibility right and M2 left. If the opposition move the ball right, M1 would quickly move in to make the tackle with M2 following to prevent an inside pass. Alternatively, if the ball carriers move the ball left, M2 would move quickly into the tackle, with M1 following to prevent an inside pass.

(b)   Think left, think right. The markers operate an identical pattern to the above, but M2 controls in which direction they move. It is imperative for him to give the necessary instructions to the first marker (M1) before the ball carrier regains his feet.

(c)   The first marker (M1) always chases the ball with the second marker (M2) following to prevent an inside pass. M1 would first of all be responsible for the acting half-back, but would then quickly chase the ball when passed, followed closely by M2.

(d)   The second marker (M2) chases the first receiver. The system is identical to (c) but with the second marker chasing, and the first following to prevent an inside pass.

(e)   The first marker (M1) charges the first receiver. This system is usually adopted if the opposition's first receiver is a very talented tactician and is the springboard of most of the team's attacks. The second marker (M2) is responsible for stopping the acting half-back. If a pass is made, M2 follows M1 across, and prevents the first receiver from giving an inside pass.

5   Sweeper

Many teams use a sweeper, who lies approximately five metres behind the defensive line and moves across fractionally behind the ball. This is a most demanding role with three major objectives:

(i)   to collect any short kicks
(ii)   to tackle the ball carrier front on immediately the line has been penetrated
(iii) to read the game, communicate, and organize the defensive line.

Some teams use a sweeper all the time, while others bring a player out of the line to sweep late on in the tackle count when the opposition is more likely to kick.

Since using a sweeper takes one person out of the defensive line, it may be a luxury that a team using double-marker defence can ill afford. An alternative is to give two players the responsibility. If two players are used, they should position themselves at either side of the play-the-ball, and be prepared to carry out normal defensive duties in the line. When the opposition mounts an attack the sweeper directly opposite stays in the line and becomes heavily involved with normal tackling duties, while the

sweeper on the other side of the play-the-ball is free to move across and adopt the sweeper's duties. As the opposition attacks the other side of the ruck, the sweepers switch roles. The player who has been sweeping joins the defensive line, while the player on the other side of the play-the-ball now adopts the role as the sweeper.

This is a more efficient method, but depends on the players having a deep personal understanding coupled with the ability to read the game. It may also be necessary to have a third player on standby, ready to adopt a similar role in case one of the sweepers is involved with marker duties.

6   Drifting to reduce gaps

Whatever defensive formation a team adopts it will be unable to defend against skilled opposition unless it masters the drift.

(i)   Individual drift

As a player goes up to tackle his opposite number, he should be prepared, once the ball has been passed, to at least follow the ball to the next man. If this is done he can assist in tackling the next receiver and also prevent him off-loading an inside pass. In this way gaps between players are filled by the next player in the line drifting across.

In diagram 162, O3 on receiving the ball from O2 draws D3, then offloads inside to O5 who has arrived after making a crossfield run behind the line. D1 and D2 have moved up on their men, and O5 penetrates.

Diagram **162**

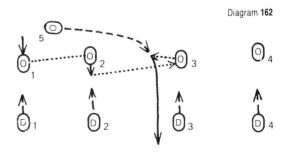

In diagram 163, D1 and D2 move up on O1 and O2 to make a tackle. However, as they pass, the defenders drift after the ball by at least one man and fill the gaps. O5 would then be tackled by D2.

Once the tackle has been completed, it is important for the defence to realign correctly, and for players who have moved forward and drifted in to move back and drift out to their positions. Unless this happens, some of the opposition will be left unmarked.

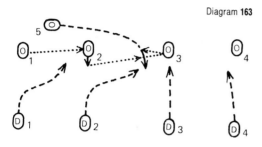

Diagram **163**

(ii)   Blind-side drift

The blind-side defence should move up in line, otherwise the team will be susceptible to a change in the direction of play. As the ball moves open, the blind side should move up and drift across slightly, allowing the first defender on the blind side to move into the gap left at the play-the-ball. When this occurs the markers are free to move across to pressurize the first receiver.

Diagram 164 illustrates the dangers that occur when the blind-side drift does not take place. The ball carriers have moved the ball open. Both markers have quickly chased the ball to the first receiver and the blind-side defence have moved up leaving a gap in the area of the previous play-the-ball. This gap can be exploited by the first receiver changing the direction of attack.

In diagram 165, the danger has been eliminated by the blind-side defenders moving up and drifting

Diagram **164**

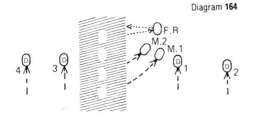

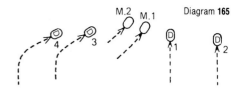

Diagram **165**

infield as D3 blocks the previous play-the-ball area. The other blind-side defender must then drift in with him.

Once the tackle has been made, the blind side should regain position by moving back and drifting out.

(iii)   Open-side drift

As soon as it becomes clear where the defensive line is to be attacked, defenders on the outside should drift in to eliminate all passing options. It is important that the defenders on the open side drift in together. The open-side drift requires more experience than the blind-side drift. If the open side drift too early, their over-eagerness can be exploited easily by the ball carriers.

When the tackle is completed, the open side should move quickly back, and drift out to regain their original position.

7   The two-man tackle

The first defender should move in with determination, and more often than not execute a low tackle to stop the ball carrier.

A second defender, as long as he does not leave an unmarked player for the ball carrier to pass to, should move quickly in to prevent a pass. This necessitates a high tackle, with the target being the ball.

It is imperative that the second tackler ties up the ball, otherwise the ball carrier will have taken two defenders out of play. He should also finish on top in the tackle, and be back on his feet before the first tackler and the ball carrier; and immediately adopt the required defensive position.

8   The gang-tackle

This involves more than two defenders, and has two major objectives:

(i)   To gain physical domination.   Once the player has been stopped by defender 1, and the ball tied up by defender 2, additional tacklers are free to pile into the ball carrier, intent on knocking him to the ground. As long as the tackle is within the laws it is an accepted tactic, which places the opposition under intense physical and mental pressure.

(ii)   To control the play-the-ball.   An important consideration is to slow down the game when the opposition have possession. This stops them from combining plays at speed. It is often possible for the ball carrier to regain his feet quickly in a one-man or even a two-man tackle, then play the ball before the defence is reformed. If the defence use delaying tactics they will be penalised. A gang-tackle prevents this. Sheer weight of numbers controls the ball carrier, and as long as those involved attempt to regain their feet the referee is powerless to penalize them. Quite naturally, three or four players take longer to regain their feet than one.

Danger

Teams employing gang-tackles have to ensure that the players involved:

1   Move quickly into the tackle
2   Force the ball carrier to the ground
3   Regain their feet quickly
4   Join the defensive line
5   When joining the defensive line, are aware of opposition movements and are ready to move to equate numbers.

These tactics require high levels of fitness, discipline and understanding.

9   Controlling the speed at which the opposition play the ball

The defence should always be organized before each play-the-ball. Naturally, the slower the ball carrier is in regaining his feet and playing the ball, the greater the advantage the defence has.

The tacklers must make every attempt to finish on top of the ball carriers, and should always regain their feet first. A useful play is for the first tackler to slide down the legs of the ball carrier and to keep hold of his ankles until the last possible moment. It is, however, equally important to play within the rules and not give away penalties. With this in mind players should try to finish on top of those they tackle, and to regain their feet first.

If three men are involved in a tackle the ball carrier must be grounded, otherwise the defenders will have three men out of play. In such instances it is imperative that the last man in is the first man on his feet, and goes quickly back in line communicating with his team-mates.

10   Equating numbers

The advantages that ball carriers can gain by overloading one side of the play-the-ball have been discussed in previous chapters.

The defence must try to cancel this by:

1   Controlling the speed of each play-the-ball, and
2   Counting heads to ensure that there is the same number of defenders as attackers on each side of the play-the-ball.

Players at each side of the ruck have the greatest responsibility and must be prepared to move from one side to the other if the need arises. Any realignment must be made before the ball is played, and this places added responsibility on those involved in the tackle to move back into line noting the position of the opposition. The importance of intelligent communication cannot be overemphasized.

11   The speed of the line

The most important consideration in advanced team play is to increase the speed at which the defensive line moves up. As long as the line is maintained, a team which moves up quickly will cause the opposition all kinds of problems:

(a)   *Time.*   It will reduce the amount of time the opposition have to think, causing them to be harassed into error. Quite often the defence will be able to gain possession.

(b) *Contain play close to the play-the-ball.* The ball carriers will more often than not be tackled before they have had time to move the ball wide. Play will therefore be contained around the play-the-ball, frustrating the ball carriers. A team which is prevented from putting together a series of passes is easily contained, particularly as the defence will not be required to interchange positions.

(c) *Depth of attack.* The ball carriers, in an attempt to move the ball wide, will stand deep giving the defence an opportunity to gain ground and a psychological advantage.

(d) *Possession.* A common play to reduce the speed of the defensive line is for the ball carrier to kick, particularly grubbers or chips, into the area behind the line. In this case the defence has a favourable opportunity to gain possession.

12   Gaining possession

Gaining possession should be the ultimate objective of the defence. It should try to move up quickly, reduce the time the opposition has to think, physically intimidate them by strong determined tackling, and harass them into error. Once they have dropped the ball the defenders should quickly react by falling on it and securing possession.

13   Cover defence

The team should beware of defenders covering too quickly and leaving gaps in the defensive line. In an ideal situation, the defence should move up simultaneously at either side of the ruck. If the line is penetrated all players should be trained to chase back at maximum speed.

There are, however, certain exceptions to the rule:

(a) *Scrum* (see page 176).

(b) *Play-the-ball,* involving

(i) *The sweeper* (see page 181).

(ii) *A blind-side winger.* The blind-side winger should drop back and begin moving infield behind the full-back when the open side is under attack. In this way the winger – often the fastest player in the team – is in a perfect position to cover. The proviso is that he must move up in line alongside his centre as soon as the opposition changes the direction of play and launches an attack towards his flank.

(iii) *A back-row forward.* Some coaches have at least one back-row forward covering behind the line. They should be aware, however, of the dangers that can occur when the opposition changes the direction of play and attacks the area which the covering player has left, leaving unguarded areas through which the opposition can strike hard for the try-line. The back-row forward must be always alert for this possibility and take alternative action immediately.

14   Goal-line defence

When defending the goal-line there is an immediate danger that the acting half-back or some other player close to the play-the-ball will dive underneath the defence and score. This will be prevented by:

(a) *Reducing the gaps around the play-the-ball* by having the defenders closer together.

(b) *Adopting crouch positions* similar to the defence in American football, thereby preventing the ball carrier from diving underneath the defence.

(c) *The full-back* positioning himself directly behind the marker. Although the full-back will be over the goal-line, he will be in position to
   (i)   make safe any kicks through or over the defence
   (ii) move forward and prevent any attacker held up by the defenders from grounding the ball.

If the ball carriers are forced to move the ball wide, they must stand very deep. Nevertheless, the defensive line will be required to realign immediately to stop any wide receivers.

Advanced variations

There are several variations to this defensive organi-zation which include:

1   The umbrella defence (diagram 166)

The outside defenders move up quicker than those in the centre of the pitch, in an attempt to contain the opposition close to the play-the-ball. The system requires discipline, fitness and understanding, but can be extremely effective.

It is vulnerable

(a)   On the edge of the ruck where the defensive line is irregular (A)

(b)   To a short kick behind the centre and wing (B).

Teams employing an umbrella defence therefore generally use a sweeper.

2   Wedge defence (diagram 167)

The wedge may be used against a team intent on

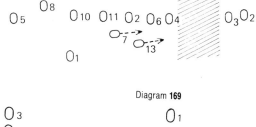

Diagram **166**

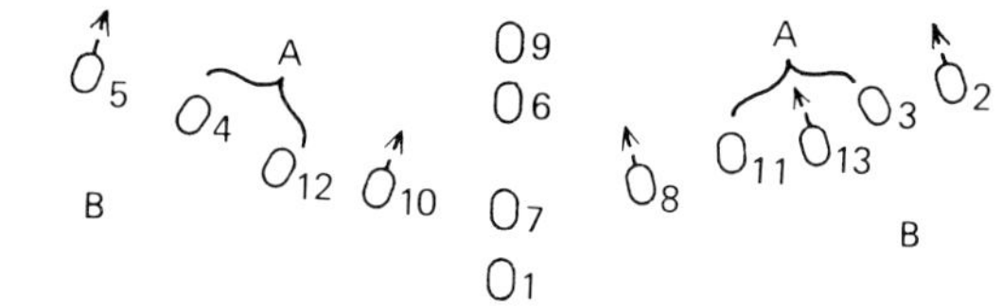

Diagram **167**

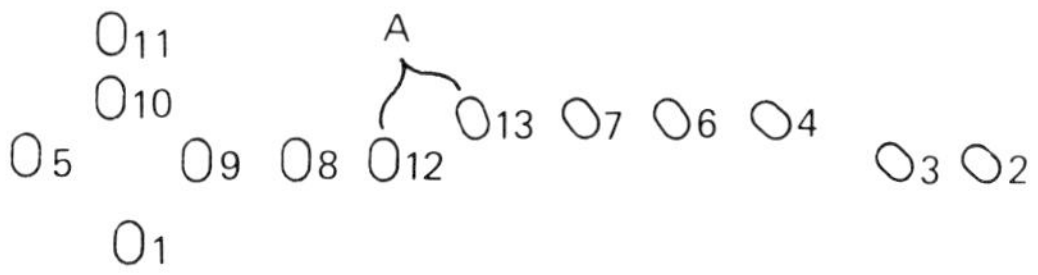

Diagram **168**

Diagram **169**

moving the ball quickly across field. As with the umbrella, the objective is to contain the attack. Defenders on the edge of the ruck move up very quickly to stop the progress of the ball by driving a wedge into the attacking line.

As with the umbrella, the wedge is vulnerable on the edge of the ruck where the irregularity occurs (A), but is effective if the opposition have not the skills necessary to exploit it.

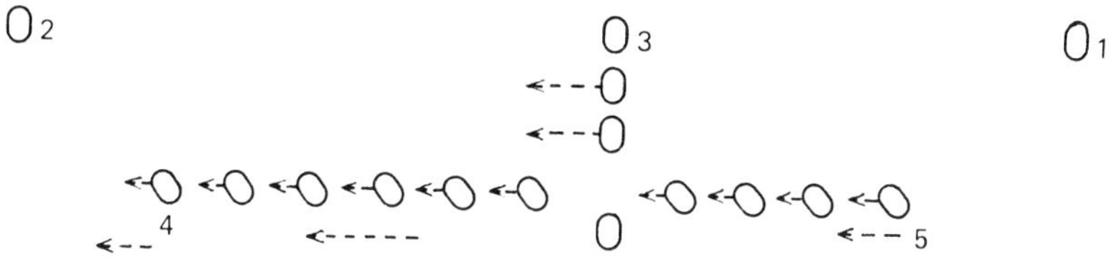

3   Channel (diagram 168)

This is a dangerous technique more applicable to Rugby Union. It is used against teams that attack well, with the defence leaving a deliberate hole for the

ball carriers to run into. Because the defenders know where the ball carrier is to be directed, the cover defence is able to move into position early and make the tackle.

4   Drift (diagram 169)

The defensive line shortens, thus reducing the gaps between players. This is efficient against teams which are incapable of quickly moving the ball wide. However, the system can be modified and advanced to provide an efficient defence against any team, as long as the wall of players is capable of drifting across the pitch as a unit. Communication, discipline and organization must be precise.

It has already been established that the ball can be passed quicker across field than players can move. Thus the defence would be vulnerable to attacks down the flanks. However, it should be realized that while the ball has to move from point 3 to 2, the defence has only to move from 4 to 2. As long as the defensive line drifts across as a unit it will be faster than the ball.

3   COMMUNICATION AND UNDERSTANDING

A successful team defence depends on each player understanding the defensive plan and being able to make correct decisions as the game unfolds. Communication is also essential.

Players should talk to one another:

1   When equating numbers at either side of the play-the-ball
2   At the opposition's play-the-ball, whether marking or in the line
3   As the opposition moves the ball, identifying the player to tackle, particularly if the opposition use run arounds or any other criss-cross moves; and
4   Giving encouragement when tired.

Players who understand the pattern, think, make correct decisions, and communicate are vital assets to the team.

4   PHYSICAL CONDITIONING AND COMMITMENT

The defence of any team can be improved by increasing the individual's work rate. This necessitates an increase in both

1   Physical fitness
2   Commitment

Physical fitness

Conditioning for Rugby League football is explained in Section 6. However, the advantages of including defensive conditioning drills in each week's training programme cannot be overemphasized. They include:

1   Improved physical conditioning
2   Increased work rate
3   Improved understanding of the requirements of the game
4   Faster player reaction. The drills speed up the conditioned reflexes
5   Increased enjoyment: although the drills are physically demanding, most players realize their importance and find them more enjoyable than unrelated physical conditioning.

Most of the drills discussed in this chapter develop all five aspects, but particular emphasis should be placed upon:

1   Reducing the time players are on the ground, and therefore out of the game. Once a tackle has been completed the tackler should regain his feet before the ball carrier and be fully prepared to tackle immediately.
2   Making powerful tackles ('big hits').

Commitment

Players respond to encouragement and challenges, and the importance of making tackle counts available to the players cannot be emphasized enough. It gives them a guideline and something to beat, acting as a spur to those who are not doing enough work and complimenting those who are. It is common coaching sense that the more progress a player can be seen to be making, the more the player will be encouraged to practise.

It must be remembered by the coach that players in mid-field will make more tackles than those on the flanks, and it is equally important to be able to motivate every player whatever his position. One way is to work out an average tackle count for every position, and encourage team members to make more tackles than the average for that position.

Statistics were compiled by the Rugby League National Coaching Scheme during the 1983–84 season at over thirty games. The average tackle count and maximum tackle count for each position were:

Tackle Counts (player's team in italic)

Position	Average	Maximum
1	5	10 (Patrick Wosniak) 4/12/83 Great Britain Under–24 v. *France* Under–24
2	5	12 (Paul Prendeville) 20/11/83 *Leeds* v. Hull K.R.
3	12	24 (Paul Fletcher) 12/2/84 *Bramley* v. Wigan
4	11	26 (Gary Prohm) 18/9/83 Warrington v. *Hull K.R.*
5	5	11 (Gary Prohm) 16/11/83 *Hull K.R.* v. Queensland
6	15	36 (Steve Peters) 28/9/83 Warrington v. *St Helens*
7	18	44 (Peter Sterling) 8/1/84 *Hull* v. Bradford Northern
8	22	40 (Steve O'Neil) 21/9/83 Swinton v. *Widnes*
9	20	43 (Howie Tamati) 12/2/84 Bramley v. *Wigan*
10	20	36 (Lee Crooks) 4/12/83 Great Britain Under–24 v. France Under–24
11	24	32 (Mick Worrall) 4/12/83 Great Britain Under–24 v. France Under–24
12	24	33 (Mick Scott) 12/2/84 Bramley v. *Wigan*
13	24	32 (Terry Webb) 14/1/84 *Leeds* v. Widnes

5   ATTITUDE

Attitude of mind is the most important factor in the improvement of defensive qualities. Consider these two philosophies of play:

1   *Philosophy adopted by most team sports in Europe*

In any game there is attack and defence. Attack is when a team has possession, defence is when the opposition have possession. The object of the attack is to go forward and score; the object of the defence is to stop the opposition from scoring.

Conclusion: the game is similar to snakes and ladders. The team in possession attacks and moves upfield, while the defending team is content to move backwards as long as it prevents a score.

2   *Philosophy of American grid-iron football*

There is offence and defence. Offence is work in possession, defence is work when the opposition have possession. The object of the game is to attack at all times. Attack with the offence to move forward and score. Attack with the defence to move forward, pressurize the opposition into error, and gain yardage.

Conclusion: the game is similar to draughts. The players attempt to move forward at all times.

Rugby League must be prepared to learn from other sports, and the grid-iron philosophy of defence has numerous advantages.

Perhaps the attitude of defences in British Rugby League should be far more positive, and have the objectives not only of preventing a score but of:

1   Attacking the opposition when they have the ball
2   Gaining ground
3   Exerting pressure
4   Forcing error
5   Winning possession
6   Controlling the game, and
7   Demoralizing the opposition.

Be positive. There is offence and defence. Attack in both.

6   IMPROVING THE TEAM DEFENCE

The defensive pattern should be within the capabilities of the team and fully understood by the players, so it is worth formulating the pattern during player-coach discussions. Once the players know the roles they have to play the pattern can be gradually modified and updated.

The coach needs to observe the games closely, and analyse any weakness. Improvement begins with players accepting the need for improvement and understanding the steps to be taken. This is best achieved during discussions with individual players and at team meetings.

Training drills and practices are the next stage to improvement, but it cannot be overemphasized that players need to understand the aims and objectives of what they are doing.

Finally, it should be accepted that the team will defend for approximately 50% of each game and that a subsequent concentration of training time is necessary to improve defence.

Practices

Listed below are several practices recommended to improve defence. Coaches should be aware of them, but should also develop drills and practices of their own.

1   Individual tackling skills

Many practices are contained in Section 2, Chapter 4. It is relevant to emphasize the need for players of all ages and abilities to practise regularly the skills of tackling, so tackle bags and shields are invaluable training aids.

It is recommended that players involve themselves in individual tackling drills every week, and at times concentrate upon making powerful tackles – big hits – emphasizing the drive of the legs and the determined thrust of the shoulder into the target area.

A progression is to encourage players to drive into tackle bags and then fall on to a ball placed nearby, thereby emphasizing the aim of gaining possession through defence.

A similar emphasis can be placed on controlling the tackle, by insisting that each player drives his shoulder powerfully into the tackle bag and then crawls on top of it before attempting to regain his feet.

The chief aim of the practice is to develop technique. The other aims are:

1   To gain possession

2   To control the play-the-ball
3   To build determination.

2   Small-sided grid games

Touch football in a fifteen-metre × thirty-metre corridor (two grids). There is no play-the-ball, so the game is re-started after a touch with the ball carrier passing. Encourage the team in possession to use every possible attacking combination. The defence should be encouraged to maintain the line and adopt a zone defence in the line, rather than man-to-man marking. In this way they will not be pulled out of position. Communication is very important. The defence should move up and drift across together to control the game.

Begin with four defenders v. three ball carriers. As the defence improves, reduce to three v. three and finally to four ball carriers v. three defenders.

The chief aims are: maintaining the defensive line
zone defence
communication, and
thinking.
Other aims are: enjoyment
improvement of handling skills.

3   The defensive line

The players form up across the pitch, as in diagram 170. The unit moves forward and backward as one, always facing upfield, but visually checking to each side. All players should be encouraged to call out 'forward', 'backward', 'together' and so on.

Cones are then placed upfield at ten-metre intervals. The defensive line starts on the goal-line, jogs to the first cone, back to the goal-line, up to the second cone, then back to the first. In this way they progress up field and the unit develops the habit of moving forward when defending.

It may help if young children initially hold hands and later position themselves as in a match for a mid-field play-the-ball, with the props in the middle at either side of the ruck, the second rows at either side of them and the wingers and centres outside near the touchline.

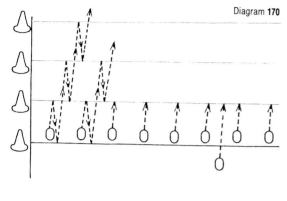

Diagram **170**

players retreat they quickly adopt their original positions, covering the entire width of the pitch.

The chief aims are: quick realignment
                           maintaining the defensive line
                           communication.

The other aim: warm-up.

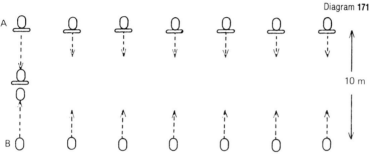

Diagram **171**

10 m

Although this is a very basic practice, senior coaches will find that it has value as a warm-up drill.

The chief aims are: maintaining the defensive line
                               communication
The other aim: warm-up.

4 Defensive line and drift

An extension of the above, incorporating the drift and emphasizing the importance of correct realignment at the play-the-ball.

The group moves downfield obeying the following commands:

Forward : they all advance in line
Right   : while advancing the players drift to the right. The right winger stays on the field while gradually the other players drift up to him. The line must be maintained, but is being pulled across field.
Left   : As above, but to the left.
Back   : the line moves back ten metres. As the

5 Defensive line using tackle shields

There are two groups, both in line, ten metres apart, as in diagram 171. Group A hold shields firmly in front of them covering the target area for a block-buster tackle, while group B crouch, alert and ready to move. Group B aims to move forward in line as quickly as possible to make strong defensive hits on the shields. A player or players, preferably in central positions, are defensive captains.

On a command, the shield-holders jog forward. Group B, in line, moves quickly to them and collides as hard as possible. Care should be taken, however, to ensure that there is no clash of heads or lower limbs. When hitting with the left shoulder, players should lead with the left foot, group B forcing group A backwards over its original starting line. This simulates a tackle, and group B quickly returns to its starting position. The practice continues with group

B working together, moving forward at the same time and maintaining the line.

Although the coach will control the first few practices, the players should quickly take over so that communication and organization are developed.

When working on technique a good practice is for the players to make four consecutive hits, with the coach checking the line, the speed of the line and the quality and intensity of the collisions. The drill can be extended to incorporate conditioning by having the players work for a minute with the target of making a dozen hits. The groups then interchange following a thirty-second rest, each completing three repetitions.

The chief aims are: maintaining the defensive line
                  speeding up the defensive line
                  communication
                  big hits
The other aim: physical conditioning.

6 Defensive line using tackle aids and incorporating realignment

The squad is divided into groups of around six players. One group, holding the equipment, line out approximately four metres apart. The second group, in single file, line out at a point ten metres in front of the end man. Shields, tackle bags or inner tubes may be used.

In diagram 172, the first player in group B moves forward and makes a heavy tackle on the tackle bag. Quickly on his feet, he drifts across and backwards, then on reaching the starting line he moves forward towards the first inner tube, being joined by the second defender who is now opposite the bag. The players move forward together. After each hit they drift across and back and are joined by another team mate until they are all working together. By the time the first defender is approaching the last bag he will be tired, and it is up to the rest of his team to talk and encourage him to maintain the line.

The chief aims are: communication
                  physical conditioning
                  maintaining the defensive line
The other aim: building team spirit.

An extension is to use a ball placed close to the equipment. As soon as the collision has been completed, the player should gain possession by quickly falling on the ball. Immediately the ball has been secured, it should be released in readiness for the next player.

Diagram **173**

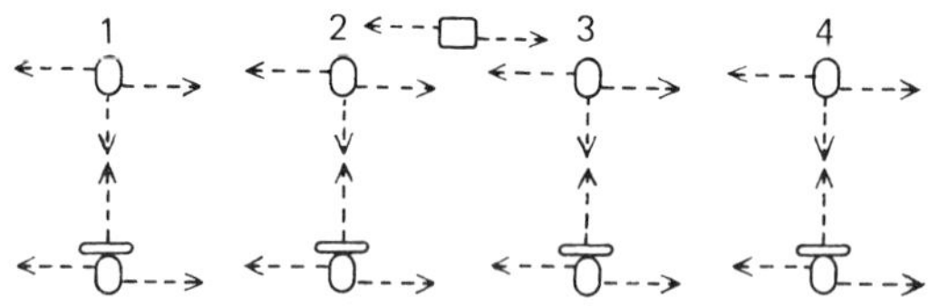

7 Reaction drill

Divide the squad into two groups with the offence holding shields, as in diagram 173. The coach stands behind the defenders and controls the movement of the offence while the defence reacts to their movements:

(a)   The coach moves right, the offence follows him, the defenders react accordingly

Diagram **172**

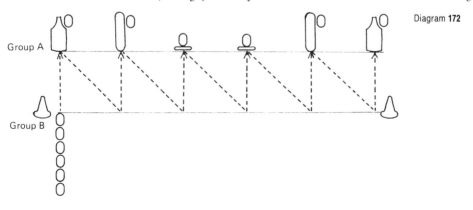

(b) The coach moves left, the offence follows him, the defenders react accordingly

(c) When the coach moves his hands upwards the offence jogs forward; the defenders move up in line to hit the shields.

8   Unequal numbers drill

The squad is divided into groups of odd numbers (eleven, for example), as in diagram 174. They are then subdivided so that six oppose five, and are

Diagram **174**

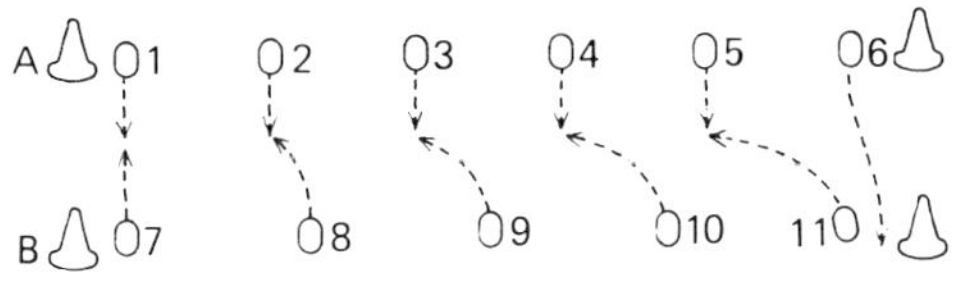

A⬠ ◯1   ◯2   ◯3   ◯4   ◯5   ◯6⬠

B⬠ ◯7   ◯8   ◯9   ◯10   11◯⬠

placed in line ten metres apart. The group with the extra players (A) are the ball carriers and on a command they jog forward to line B. Line B also jog forward, and each player grips one of group A around the waist to halt his progress. The additional player should always be allowed through.

The command the coach gives to start each drill is important. On the command 'Left!' the defenders move forward in line and stop players 1 to 5 while ball carrier 6 jogs through. On the command 'Right!' the defenders move forward in line and stop 2 to 6. Ball carrier 1 is this time free to jog through.

As the players become proficient, the drill is extended to include:

(a) The defenders immediately upon hearing the command name the player they are to halt

(b) The speed of the line is increased

(c) On moving back to the starting line the ball carriers interchange positions, so that on the next drill the defenders will be stopping someone different.

It is likely at first that:

(a) Two defenders will stop the same ball carrier, and

(b) A player in the middle will be allowed to penetrate.

As the players begin to think, become aware, and communicate, the success of the drill will improve.

The chief aims are: games awareness
thinking
communication
speed of the line
The other aim: physical conditioning.

9   Sweeper drill (diagram 175)

This is a similar drill to the above, but a ball is used. The six ball carriers line out at an angle with the ball at the end, while four defenders face the last four ball carriers with the additional defender in line with the play-the-ball. On a given command, one passes from the ground and the other players jog forward as they pass the ball to the end player 6. As soon as the ball is passed the four defenders angle in, with 8 moving on 2; 9 on 3; and so on. They try to stop the flight of the ball. The sweeper 7 sprints along the back of the line with the objective of stopping the end ball carrier 6 immediately he receives the pass.

The chief aims are: sweeper duties
speed of the line
communication
The other aim: quick, accurate passing.

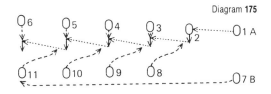

Diagram **175**

10   Marker-defence

The following practices test a two-marker system, operating think left, think right. They can, however, be modified to suit any other marker system which the coach might put into operation:

1   Tubes (diagram 176)

Divide the squad into groups of six: player 1 has a
ball and 2, 3 and 4 have tubes to test double markers
5 and 6. 5 in the diagram thinks left, and 6 right. 1
plays the ball, and either 2 or 3 rolls an inner tube
forcefully forward. (They decide beforehand which
one is to roll the tube; on no account must both be
rolled.) 4 rolls his tube every time, after and towards
the first tube, at the same side of the play-the-ball. If
2 and 4 roll their tubes, 5 will tackle 2's and 6 will
tackle 4's. On the other hand, if 3 and 4 roll their
tubes, 6 thinking right will tackle the far one with 5
tackling the one rolled by 4.

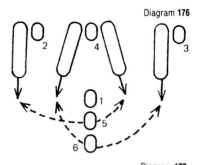

Diagram **176**

2   Shields (diagram 177)

Player 1 is the acting half-back while 2 and 3, holding
shields, are ready to drive the ball in. 4 and 5 are the
double markers, 4 thinking right and 5 left. 1 starts
the practice with the ball in front of him on the
ground: he can either run with the ball himself, or
pass to 2 or 3. If the ball is passed to 2, he ignores it
but runs forward strongly holding the shield.

   5 should be prepared to tackle:

(a)   1 breaking to the left of the diagram
(b)   2 running forward on the left, or
(c)   3 off-loading inside, having followed 4 to the
      right.

4 should be prepared to tackle:

(a)   1 breaking to the right of the diagram
(b)   3 running forward on the right, or
(c)   2 off-loading inside, having followed 5 to the
      left.

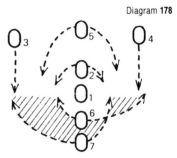

Diagram **177**

3   Real opposition (diagram 178)

Working in a confined space, the double markers 6
and 7 should be able to prevent:

(a)   The acting half-back 2 attacking in any direc-
      tion, or
(b)   The acting half-back 2 moving across and
      dropping off any player
(c)   The first receivers 3 or 4 running straight, or

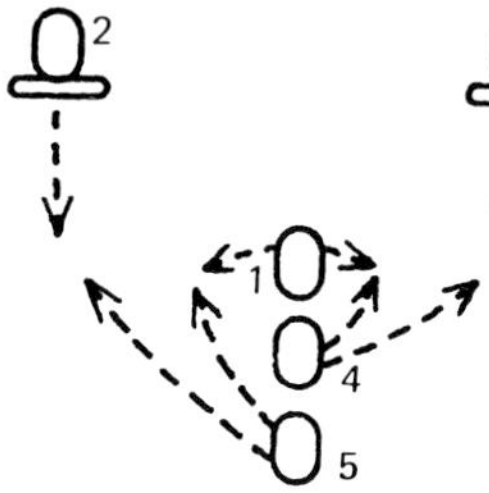

Diagram **178**

(d)   5 when running on the inside of either 3 or 4.

   The two markers, operating think left, think right,
will be vulnerable only when:

(a)   3 or 4 run across field
(b)   3 or 4 pass the ball back inside, across 5, to each
      other (that is, 3 to 4, or 4 to 3).

In a game each of these plays would be prevented by
the next player in the defensive line.
   Players should practise marker-defence regularly.
The chief aims are: marker defence
                    alertness
                    communication
                    thinking
The other aim: work rate (match involvement).

11   Ruck defence

The defence around the ruck can be severely pressurized by seven players attacking seven defenders within the confines of a grid about fifteen metres wide, as in diagram 179. The marker defence is certainly tested, but so too are the speed, drift and combinations of the first two defenders in the line on each side of the play-the-ball. M1 thinks left and M2 right. The ball is moved to O1 while D2, D4 and D6 move up; both markers move towards O1, and D1 and D3 move up in the line but drift inwards, thus blocking the area around the play-the-ball.

Diagram **179**

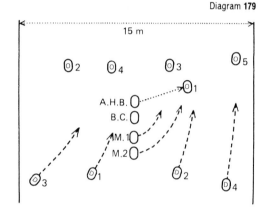

The chief aims are: marker-defence
                   drift
                   speed of line
                   alertness
                   communication
                   thinking
The other aim is: work rate.

12   Scrum defence

(a)   Backs

The backs are required to perfect their defensive duties against opposition. Another team from the club, whether the reserves or simply another age group, will provide a stern test. The opposition should use a full repertoire of moves so that the defence can develop understanding.

(b)   Cover defence of backs and forwards: two practices

(i)   Tubes. It is possible to test the awareness, understanding and covering ability of the back row by adopting the following practice, as shown in diagram 180.

Diagram **180**

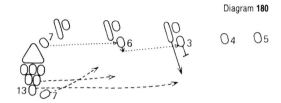

The forwards form a scrum, packing down if at all possible against another pack or a scrummaging machine. It is important that they exert themselves in the scrummage.

The backs line out against them with additional players holding tubes behind the scrum-half, stand-off and centres.

The ball is fed into the scrum, and as soon as possession is won the backs simulate a match attack. When the coach blows a whistle, the player with the ball stops while the man who has been following him rolls the tube vigorously in a forward direction. The forwards break within the laws of the game, and adopt the defensive duties described previously in this chapter, with one of them tackling the tube. The coach can pressurize individual pack members by telling the others to break slowly.

(ii)   Opposition. Quite simply the pack of forwards can be put to the test when competing against their own back division. But the practice must be realistic: the forwards must pack firmly, and not break too early. The attacking qualities of the backs and the cover defence of the forwards can both be developed.

The three-quarters should be able to move the ball to the flanks before any cover arrives. Once they are able to do this successfully, moves should be developed that turn the ball inside. These will provide a realistic test for the forwards.

The chief aims are: understanding
                    alertness
                    communication
The other aim: physical conditioning.

13   Team defence

(a)   Unopposed

The entire team line out in defensive formation for a play-the-ball in the middle of their 22, and the ball is placed on the ground in front of the markers. Both markers are ready and communicating. The line is alert, with the full-back (and sweeper if necessary) at the back. The coach side-foots the ball across the ground, simulating a play-the-ball. As soon as the ball is touched by the coach's foot the defence quickly move up in line and the player in front of the ball drops on it. The player who has fallen on the ball regains his feet quickly, counts to five and places the ball in front of him, then the practice continues.

The team should count the number of tackles and react accordingly. The coach may pick the ball up and kick to the full-back and wings, or put grubbers through the defence, who react as they would in a match. The coach should test in particular:

(a)   Marker-defence
(b)   The line
(c)   Speed of line
(d)   Drifting across so no gaps appear immediately around the tackle
(e)   That at each play-the-ball the line stretches the required width
(f)   Catching abilities of the full-back, winger, and others, plus blocking of the rest of the team
(g)   Ability to gain possession from grubber kicks
(h)   Reorganization after a tackle.

The coach should also test the defence from all restarts, for example, by

(a)   Drop balls
(b)   Chasing kicks from the field of play
(c)   Chasing kick-offs, from the centre, the 22, and the goal-line
(d)   Scrums
(e)   Tap-plays.

These must be practised in each quarter of the field.

(b)   Opposed

There are two teams, one defending for a period of time while the other has possession. The game begins with a tap on the half-way line.

Objective: although under pressure, the defence should force the ball carriers back by making them commit errors.

The coach stands behind the defence, observes, analyses and corrects.

The number of defenders in relation to the offence should guarantee success.

Development: as the defence becomes more efficient, (a) the number of defenders in relation to ball carriers is evened up, and (b) the distance the ball carriers are taken back after dropping the ball and losing possession is reduced.

The rules should be modified as the defence becomes more competent. At first there are:

(a)   More defenders than ball carriers
(b)   The width of the pitch is in proportion to the number of defenders involved
(c)   The coach must decide whether players should tackle or grip
(d)   If the ball carriers drop the ball but regain possession, play is restarted with a tap ten metres back
(e)   If the ball carriers lose possession the ball is given back to them and play is restarted with a tap twenty metres back.

Support play

1   Developing support play
2   Various types of support play
3   Contract system
4   Analysis

38   Kevin Ward offloads after a tackle by Gene Miles, with Ian Potter in close support: a good example of support play in the second Great Britain v Australia Test in 1986.

The importance of support play in Rugby League football cannot be overemphasized. Indeed, there is little doubt that purposeful, intelligent and sustained support play makes the difference between successful and unsuccessful teams. The team that keeps the ball moving causes problems for the opposition, and always has a chance of beating the defence. Combination passing, a direct result of persistent support play, is not only difficult to stop but provides one of the most exciting sporting spectacles.

1   DEVELOPING SUPPORT PLAY

Specific practices to develop support play are referred to later, but it is essential for the coach to understand that he must always instil in his players the importance of having more men than the opposition around the ball, on both offence and defence. To make the most use of this numerical advantage and convert it into points needs:

1   Skill
2   Correct decision-making
3   Physical fitness, and
4   Mental ability.

1   Skill

To play a vital part in support play the individual player must develop his ability to pass the ball and to support it. Support play depends on the ball carrier having the ability to make the ball available to the right person at the right time. He must be able to make a correctly weighted pass, in addition to making the ball available in the tackle. Players must also support the ball, and develop good timing and the correct angle of run.

2   Correct decision-making

Players must be able to decide correctly:

1   Whether to pass
2   Who to pass to
3   The split second the ball should be released
4   The angle to run at, and
5   The timing of the run.

3   Physical fitness

It is necessary for players to try to increase their work-rate, to become more involved, and to improve their ability to support the ball carrier. Improved work-rate often depends on increased physical fitness, particularly endurance. This is an important factor which will be discussed in Section 6.

4   Mental ability

Even a fit player will not support the ball without first making the correct mental decisions:

1   To get off the ground and become quickly involved.
2   To play the ball quickly, then immediately be involved again in play.
3   To pass off the ground and follow the ball.
4   To pass and follow the ball.
5   To move across field in an arc and support the ball carrier.

All these factors have been referred to previously. However, it should be understood that intelligent support play is first and foremost a mental skill. The player has to make the decision to support, and he can be encouraged to do this during each and every coaching session, 'Follow the ball!', 'Stay alive!', and 'Get involved!' are key instructions that the coach should be using all the time. It is far easier for players to adopt good supporting positions in a well-coached team. If they are aware of the various team moves, the tactics to be adopted and the game plan, they can anticipate and move into position early.

Communication is also important. If, for example, a team decides to move the ball wide from a play-the-ball to the centres, an early call to all the players will enable them to adopt supporting roles around the area the penetration is to be attempted. The runners in the forwards, for instance, will have time to move out wide ready to support whichever centre is to hit the line.

Conversely, if the attack is to be launched close to the play-the-ball, not only will the forwards adopt their required positions, but the three-quarters will know that the ball is not coming out so they can close ranks, move flatter, and be ready to support any break.

2   VARIOUS TYPES OF SUPPORT PLAY

There are several types of support play, but for simplicity they are categorized as follows:

1   Supporting the break
2   Using the overload
3   Hitting the defensive line and offloading
4   Hitting the defensive line and keeping the ball alive.

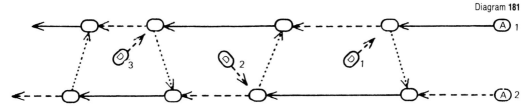

Diagram **181**

1   Supporting the break

Defences in modern Rugby League are becoming increasingly efficient, so direct penetrations are less frequent. It is therefore important that the most is made of every break, and support is necessary to maintain the impetus of the movement. The individual who breaks the line will very quickly be tackled by the full-back or cover defence so it is essential that colleagues arrive alongside him quickly. Anticipation, communication, prior knowledge and timing are the necessary ingredients of success.

Positive encouragement to follow the ball will help players at every level of their development. However, specific practices can be structured.

Practices

1   Unopposed drills

(a)   Single-file passing (see page 54), in order to develop

anticipation
communication
timing, and
weighting of the pass.

(b)   Long and short passing (see page 55), in order to develop

anticipation
communication
timing, and
weighting of the pass.

2   Small-sided games with the emphasis placed on continuation: two against one, three against two, and so on.

In diagram 181, O1 draws D1 and passes to O2. Because the drill is continuous, O1, after passing, has to follow and support as O2 approaches D2, then off-loads to O1. The practice continues through the channel.

This should develop

continuous 'pass and follow', and
communication.

3   Group games

(a)   *Three against one* (see page 50)
(b)   *Four against four* (see page 50)

This should develop

continuous 'pass and follow'
decision-making on when to pass
communication.

(c)   *American touch* (see page 131)

This should develop

close support
numerical supremacy
communication
anticipation
concentration, and
decision-making.

4 Unopposed drills to develop speed, support and communication (see page 65).

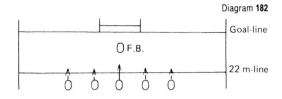

Diagram **182**

5 Conditioned games

(a) Ball carriers against full-back (diagram 182). A specific number of players (five, for example) carry the ball forward and attack a full-back.

The coaching points emphasized in the earlier two against one and three against two practices should be adhered to.

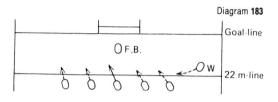

Diagram **183**

(b) Ball carriers against full-back and wing (diagram 183). This is a slight extension of the previous game with the ball carriers attacking away from the extra defender.

(c) Ball carriers against full-back, wing and cover defence (diagram 184). The ball carriers are confronted with a more difficult problem. It is recommended that they attack a flank rather than the middle, thus moving away from one of the defenders and creating a five v. two situation rather than five v. three. The support players should position themselves to give the ball carrier as many passing options as possible, and he should then pass to an unmarked player.

Depth is especially important.

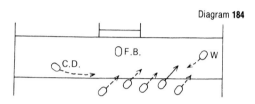

Diagram **184**

(d) Ball carriers against first line of defence, full-back, wing and cover defence. The ball carriers now attack three shield holders defending a twelve-metre channel (diagram 185).

The full-back, wing and cover defence line up in the positions in the diagram, but cannot move until the ball carriers penetrate the shields. The ball carriers, therefore, have to penetrate the shield using close support play. The moment they break into the clear they are confronted by the match-like situation of the full-back and cover defence.

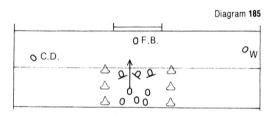

Diagram **185**

(a) The points awarded for the try are made dependent on the number of passes made:

no passes, 1 point,
two passes, 2 points,
three passes, 3 points, and so on.

(b) The score is allowed only if the player who breaks the defence makes a pass before the touchdown.

This is a positive attempt to eliminate the 'stand and observe' syndrome, replacing it by an automatic reaction in all players to 'support the break'.

6 Small-sided games

In all the many and varied small-sided games used in the training programme, the coach can insist that the player who makes the break passes to a colleague before a try is scored. There are several ways of doing this.

2   Using the overload

Teams should attempt to have more players around the ball than the opposition, but they need the ability to take advantage of the overload situation. As important in developing support play is for the coach to ensure his players make the correct decisions once the overload has been created. Practices previously discussed in Section 3: two v. one, three v. two, and four v. two drills, allied to playing small-sided games with an overloaded attack, will be of considerable assistance as long as the players are fully aware of the key factors:

(a) *Fast action*: the opposition will be trying to equate the overload by moving additional defenders into the area, so the overload will not last long. Move quickly.

(b) *Straight running*: the overload has been created so there is no necessity for run arounds, drop-offs and so on. Keep it simple, act quickly, and run straight.

(c) *Passing options*: create as many passing options as possible by supporting on the inside and outside in addition to having players at different depths.

(d) *Least number of passes*: an over-elaboration of passes can cause problems. Once an overload has been created the ball should be transferred as quickly as possible to the player in the gap. If this can be done with only one pass, so much the better. The more passes that are made, the greater is the opportunity for the defence to readjust.

(e) *Decision-making*: players must make the correct decision dependent on the actions of the opposition. Once an overload has been created, planned moves should be replaced by intuitive action.

3   Hitting the defensive line and off-loading

A ball carrier running strongly and hitting the defensive line with determination will be hard to handle, and will often cause two or even three defenders to be drawn into the tackle. Unless the defence is extremely well organized and has the ability to drift in, gaps will be created alongside the runners. These gaps should be exploited by support players arriving after the gap has been created but before the ball carrier is grounded. Timing is important.

Practices

1   Passive opposition (see page 65)
2   Shield opposition (see page 65)
3   Continuous runs (diagram 186)

The acting half-back passes to the first receiver, who immediately off-loads to R1. He attacks the shields

39   Keith England (Castleford and Great Britain) runs with determination in an attempt to break through the French defence in the Great Britain v France World Cup match at Headingley, Leeds, in 1987.

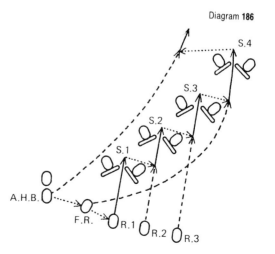

Diagram **186**

and off-loads on impact. R2 does the same. R3 also runs determinedly and off-loads to FR who has followed the ball. FR hits the last bank of shields and off-loads inside to AHB. All players should support.

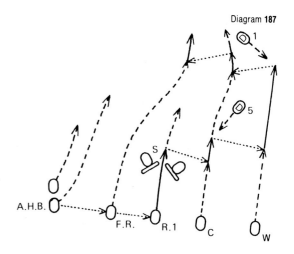

Diagram **187**

Combinations (diagram 187)

Combinations can be developed which will enhance team play. Runner 1 takes the ball from the first receiver, hits the shield determinedly, and off-loads to the centre. He draws D5 and passes to his wing, then supports and takes an inside pass as the wing commits D1. The acting half-back, first receiver and the ball player are encouraged to support.

4   Hitting the defensive line and keeping the ball alive

Players carrying the ball up strongly and trying to break the defensive line are often aware that they are going to be tackled a split second before they are grounded. A good player will use this split second to try to turn so he can off-load to a team-mate directly behind.

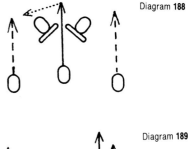

Diagram **188**

Practices

1   Individual skill (see page 65)
2   Three against two shields

In diagram 188, three players, the ball carrier in the middle, attack two shields. The players holding the shields are instructed to be firm, but to allow penetration as long as the ball carrier runs strongly with determination.
Major coaching points are:

Ball carrier: determination
                 hold the ball firmly
                 break shields with shoulders and chest.
Support: timing.

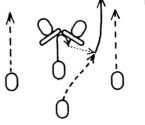

Diagram **189**

3   Four against two shields

In diagram 189, the practice is extended to include an additional support player at the back. The players holding the shields try to prevent the ball carrier

breaking. If he does break, he off-loads as in diagram 188. If the defence is too strong he turns and off-loads to the support player at the back, who must follow the ball, always reading the situation, and when the ball is made available, time his run to arrive at the correct side at the correct time.

The practice can then be developed to encourage team play. The support player at the back will always follow the ball and should have the option of penetrating himself or immediately off-loading as soon as he receives possession of the ball.

4   Continuous and combination practices

These are practices similar to those described in diagrams 186 and 187, but with the ball carrier hitting, turning and off-loading.

5   Corridor football

This is a practice in a confined area against shields.

(a)   *Six against six.*   A narrow corridor is marked out about ten metres wide. Six ball carriers have to move down the corridor and score a try. To begin with, three defenders, holding shields, try to prevent them, and each time the ball carriers are successful an additional defender is introduced until all twelve players are involved.

The coach should ensure that all the players have an opportunity to run the ball.

(b)   *Forwards against backs.*   The forwards attack the backs in a narrow corridor, combining as they would in a game. If necessary the scrum-half joins them. The backs, holding shields, defend. When it is the backs' turn to attack the corridor is widened.

6   Team play

A coach should devise team moves aimed at overloading the various areas of the pitch. These should include:

(a)   *First play following a scrum.*   For the team's forwards to break faster than the opposition, and overload at the first play-the-ball following a scrum.

(b)   *Blind side.*   For the team to open up a wide blind side and then saturate it with players.

(c)   *Wide.*   To move the ball across the field to the three-quarters, and move the forwards over ahead of the opposition's.

(d)   *Midfield.*   To move the ball into midfield, and from the resulting play-the-ball overload the more weakly defended side.

3   CONTRACT SYSTEM

One method of improving support play is to pair off the forwards. For example, the open-side prop with the open-side second row and the blind-side prop with the blind-side second row. The hooker is used as acting half-back, and the loose forward as a floater. The open-side prop and second row therefore sign a contract. Every time the prop takes the ball in, the second row supports, and when the second row takes the ball in, the prop supports. Support is ensured and the work rate is shared.

Combination attacks need to be well thought out but any difficulty can be overcome by careful planning.

Examples (diagrams 190a,b,c,d)

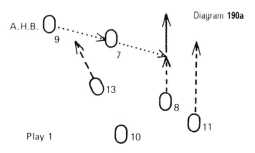

Diagram **190a**

A.H.B.

Play 1

Play 1 : Tap
9 passes to 7
13 has decoy duties
8 takes the ball in
11 supports
(10 is not involved in this play. Instead he adopts a position to be able to quickly drive the ball in on the next play. 12 similarly is not involved.)

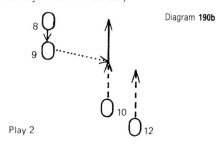

Diagram **190b**

Play 2

Play 2 : 9 is AHB
10 drives infield
12 supports

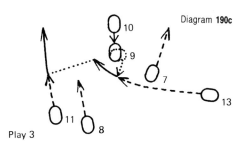

Play 3

Play 3 : 9 is AHB
       7 runs infield as a decoy
       13 brings ball from open to blind
       11 comes on the ball
       8 supports

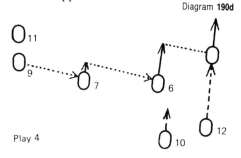

Play 4

Play 4 : 9 is AHB
       7 passes infield to 6
       12 comes on the ball
       10 supports
Play 5 : Repeat the play 3 with 8 running, 11 supporting
Play 6 : Grubber-kick into the in-goal area

Backs support.
  On play 1, if 8 off-loads to 11, then on play 3, 8 comes on the ball with 11 supporting.

4   ANALYSIS

The various drills will help to encourage better support play, but feedback from the games is also necessary. An astute coach will carefully analyse each player's performance in the game and then positively encourage improvement (see Section 7, Chapter 2).

Tactical kicking

1   Important aspects
2   The kicking game

1   IMPORTANT ASPECTS

Although control of the ball, support play and a well-organized aggressive defence are the cornerstones of any team's success, recent rule changes – particularly the limited tackle rule and the subsequent turnover of possession – have elevated kicking to a place alongside them.

This is important for those coaching all age groups:

The junior coach should spend time developing the correct techniques of the various kicks in all players.

The youth and open-age coaches should continue the process, but give specialist attention to:

40   Tactical kicking: Peter Sterling (Australia) causes Great Britain problems in the third Great Britain v Australia Test in 1986.

(a) The player who adopts first-receiver duties: it is an advantage if he has the skills to punt, grubber-kick and kick over, as well as the ability to make correct tactical decisions.

(b) The full-back: it is an advantage if the full-back possesses a long accurate punt.

2 THE KICKING GAME

A team with a well-thought-out kicking game has the ability to:

(a) Control the area of the pitch in which the game is played

(b) Regain possession, and

(c) Overcome a well-organized defence.

(a) Controlling the area of the pitch in which the game is played

The mental pressures of defending close to the goal-line are severe, because:

(i) The first line of defence must hold. Any break by the opposition will almost certainly result in them scoring a try.

(ii) If penalized, the opposition are in goal-kicking range.

(iii) The opposition are in drop-goal range.

(iv) The opposition are in position to regain possession by kicking into the in-goal area.

It is often a good strategy, therefore, to play position rugby and attempt by astute tactical kicking to play the game in the opponents' half of the pitch. This strategy is only effective if the team has a solid well-organized defence. Certainly there is far more sense in a team kicking the ball downfield than in handing over possession close to its own goal-line.

It is within the rules for defenders in an onside position to move downfield as soon as the ball has been played and be in position before the kick arrives, as long as they give the receiver the required five metres.

Teams adopting these tactics should consider the following:

1 Length

The kick must be long; there is little point in a team turning possession over on the half-way line. Kicking practice is needed.

2 Kick from a central position

Kicks from a central position cause the opposition far more problems as they have to defend both sides of the pitch. If only one defender is back the kicker can easily kick away from him into space. Previous plays should establish this central kicking position.

3 Previous plays

Plays prior to the kick should also attempt to gain ground. Strong rushes close to the play-the-ball should be considered rather than stringing a series of passes together, which may lose ground.

4 Good pass to kicker

The kicker will be concentrating on the execution and direction of the kick, and will almost certainly be under pressure from the opposition. A good pass directly to his hands is essential.

5 Position of the kicker

It is usual for the kick to be executed behind the play-the-ball. The kicker is therefore further away from the opposition and has a little more time to execute the kick.

6 Blockers

One or two players, usually the front row, can be placed in front of the kicker thereby giving him some protection as the opposition will have to move round the blockers to reach the kicker.

On no account should the blockers move, or they will be penalized for obstruction. In addition, they should beware of hindering the kicker.

7   Dual kickers

Certain opponents, particularly with astute markers, will be able to pressurize the kicker severely. When this occurs a useful play is to have a second kicker within passing distance of the first. If the first kicker is pressurized he has the option of passing the ball to the second kicker.

8   The chase

There is little use in kicking downfield if the opposition is allowed to carry the ball back again. The objective is to contain the opposition as far downfield as possible. It is usual, therefore, for a number of players to move downfield before the kick and position themselves to tackle the receiver as soon as the rules allow. The chase must not set off before the ball is played, and must give the receiver the required five metres. It is usual for three fast men to lead the chase, usually the stand-off and centres, while the rest of the chasers follow in line. The aim must be to tackle the receiver within five metres of catching the ball.

The chasers should be wary of an immediate counter-attack, and ensure that the chasing line stretches across the field.

9   One chaser onside

Occasionally the receiver will stand still to assess the position. The players who have moved downfield in front of the ball may not approach within five metres if the catch was clean, so it can be an advantage for the kicker to follow his kick. He is onside, and every player he passes becomes onside. If the kicker himself does not move downfield, it is an advantage to have one player from an onside position moving to put the receiver under pressure.

10   Returning the kick

The receiver may immediately return the kick, particularly as most of his team are likely to be in front of him. It is therefore worth considering having the kicker stay back in anticipation of the return, and for

him perhaps to have one additional team-mate back with him.

11   A call

It can often be an advantage to plan this as a move. The first step is to give the downfield kick a name, 'downtown' perhaps is a favourite. Once downtown has been called – it is vital that all the players hear the call – they are all aware of the strategy to be used. It is usual for the call to be made as a colleague is being tackled and for a steadying drive to take place immediately afterwards, prior to the kick. This enables the kick to be set up correctly and gives time for the players to adopt their chasing role.

The success of the move depends entirely on where the opposition is tackled in possession. If the kick is short, if the receivers are allowed to carry the ball back upfield, or if a penalty is conceded for obstruction or offside, the play is a failure.

Additional tactical considerations

1   Downtown will be anticipated by the opposition, particularly on the fifth and sixth plays. They may drop additional players back, particularly wingers. The result will be that their first line of defence will be weak and susceptible to a direct passing movement.
2   Downtown made before the fifth and sixth tackle periods could take the opposition by surprise.
3   The tactical kickers in the team, particularly the first receiver, may be given the responsibility of making snap decisions. If a long downfield kick is one of them, the rest of the team must be ready to chase quickly. Anticipation and organization are important.
4   External conditions, a strong wind blowing directly down the pitch, for example, or an excessively sloping ground, may affect the way the downtown is used.
5   The downtown may be called as a decoy move and the ruck area attacked by a runner with support. This is more likely to work against an alert and committed defence which has anticipated by moving up quickly on the kicker.

Defending the downtown

In most instances the receiver is under no immediate pressure when he receives the ball, particularly if the chase is from an offside position, and therefore he should be able to catch the ball cleanly. However, it is necessary for him to understand that both teams are involved in a struggle for territorial advantage and that each metre of the pitch is important. The receiver should, immediately upon catching the ball, try to gain as much ground as possible. He then has three options:

1   To run strongly and try to gain as much ground as possible himself
2   To return the kick
3   To launch an immediate counter-attack using support players.
    It is usually one of the wingers who assists the full-back, and these three players should accept the following responsibilities:

1   If the full-back receives the ball and is quickly tackled, the nearest winger should move to acting half-back and be prepared to carry the ball in strongly.
2   If a winger receives the ball and is quickly tackled, then it should be the full-back who attacks from acting half-back.
3   If the full-back receives the ball and has room to run, he should angle towards the touchline with the winger coming inside him. The ball can be passed inside to the winger, or alternatively the full-back can attack, using the winger as a decoy. On no account should the full-back run close to the touchline and run the risk of being tackled out of bounds.
4   If the winger receives the ball and has room to run, he should angle infield with the full-back crossing.

Diagram **191a**

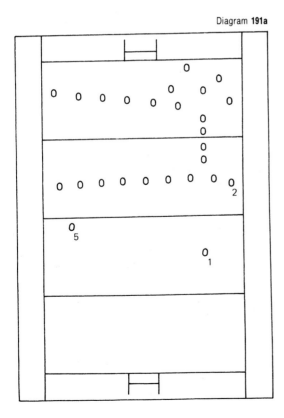

Diagram **191b**

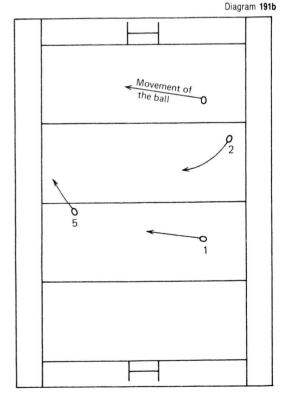

5 If the chase is poor and the receiver has a lot of room in which to work he should, after receiving the ball, attack the weakest part of the chase with support.

Wingers therefore have the added responsibility of assisting the full-back. Although their first priority must be to stay level with their centre and in the defensive line when under attack, they are free to move back when able to do so.

In diagram 191a play is on the right-hand touch-line of the defensive line. The right winger liable to be under direct attack is level with his centre. The left winger, however, has moved back and infield, so the area at the back is being patrolled by the full-back O1 and the left wing O5. As the ball is moved infield the left winger must begin to move forward into position. The speed of his movement forward is controlled directly by the speed with which the opposition move the ball, and he must be level when his wing is under direct attack.

As the ball moves toward the left-hand side of the defensive line the full-back moves across tracking the ball (diagram 191b) and the right winger is released to move back to assist. However, he must be prepared to move forward if the direction of attack is changed and his wing is approached.

Intelligent understanding is a requirement of good wing play. It is also important that the defence tries to pressurize the kicker.

(b) Regain possession

1 The bomb

The bomb is a kick which places the receiver under intense pressure. The key to success is the chase, so the height the ball is kicked is determined by the distance the chase has to cover. A long chase necessitates a high kick. On no account will the bomb be successful if the chase is not underneath it when it lands. The bomb that lands in the in-goal area causes the most pressure, because the receiver has to out-jump the chasers and catch the ball safely to prevent a try. The posts also increase the difficulty. However, if the ball is safely caught the receivers keep possession and play is restarted with a 22-metre tap.

The bomb requires:

1 Length. A bomb without a chase is of little value, so the kick must not be too long otherwise the chasers will not be able to get underneath.

2 Height. The higher the kick goes the more time the chase has to get underneath the ball.

3 The chase. Those chasing the ball must come from an onside position, and it must be clear to the referee that all the chasers were behind the kicker when the bomb was launched. The chase should be determined and those involved should jump in an attempt to catch the ball. The more players involved, the better.

4 Position of the kicker. It is usual for the bomb to be kicked by the first receiver so that the majority of the team will be onside and in a position to chase. If the opposition exerts tremendous pressure on the kicker, he may of course stand deeper, but when this occurs those in front of him must not follow the ball unless they do so behind the kicker himself. Only the kicker can put these players onside.

5 Kick on the last play. More often than not the bomb is used close to the opposition's in-goal area so the team should not waste plays setting the kick up. Usually the kick is made on the last play. The rest of the team should be aware of this, and be ready to act quickly and decisively.

Defending the bomb

1 The first priority is most certainly for the full-back at least to have the ability to leap high into the air and catch the ball. But in general more advanced coaching methods must be learned than those described on pages 97 and 98 of Section 2.

The receiver should attack the ball, and catch it as high as possible above the heads of the chasers. There are three instructions to remember when attacking the ball: move late, move quickly, and take the ball at the highest possible point of its trajectory.

There are three advantages in delaying the movement to attack the ball:

(a) More time is given to asses its trajectory
(b) A later movement means that the receiver must move more quickly, so greater height is achieved when jumping for the ball
(c) Because greater height is achieved, the ball can in fact be taken earlier in flight than would be the case if the receiver moved early but slowly.

What at first may appear a contradiction is in fact completely logical and sensible. The important factor is that this technique allows the receiver to take the ball at the highest possible point in its trajectory.

The greatest possible height will be achieved by a one-footed take-off. By adopting this technique, it will be easier to maintain balance and transfer the body momentum in an upwards direction. In a two-footed take-off, the body momentum must be stopped from moving forward before it is transferred upwards. Not only is less height achieved, but timing and balance become much more difficult.

The arms should be outstretched in order to take the ball at the greatest possible height. The head, of course, should be steady throughout. Once the catch is made, it is important that the ball is brought into the body and secured as quickly as possible. Some protection can be provided by the front knee being lifted high and bent.

An early call will allow the rest of the team to clear the receivers' path and to adopt protective positions.

2   The rest of the team, assessing the trajectory of the kick and responding to the receiver's early call, will move towards the point of landing. Their first priority is to give the receiver room; on no account should they restrict his movements. The second priority is to offer protection and to form, within the rules, a block between the receiver and the chase. The blockers must not be penalized for obstruction. Every movement they make should be within the rules, but if they simply keep their eyes on the ball, move towards the landing point, and stop in front of the receiver, they will automatically be in the path of any direct chase. A couple should perhaps move

behind the receiver to cover any possibility of the ball being dropped.

3   Before the kick is made, the defence should read the situation and be prepared to pressurize the player who is about to kick the ball.

1   Additional tactical consideration

Since the full-back has the ability to jump high for the ball, he is the ideal player to lead the chase, but teams using the full-back in this attacking role must cover at the back, probably with a winger or half-back.

2   The grubber and chip-kick

The grubber-kick in particular is a skill which can be used to regain possession, especially when play is close to the opposition's in-goal area. A team tackled in its own in-goal area, after receiving a grubber-kick, restarts play with a goal-line drop-out, thereby returning possession to the kicking team. A cleverly weighted kick, pushed through a defence and coming to rest in the in-goal area, therefore, will place the opposition under considerable pressure as long as the chase is good. The chase, as with the bomb, should be from an onside position. This play can be used only when close to the in-goal area, otherwise the chase will have difficulty in arriving on time. The kick over the first line of defence is harder to control, but if accurate will have the same effect as long as it is not caught on the full.

Once a team has obtained the territorial position to launch such a kick it may be worth considering always using this tactic. Then the team would realize that the grubber would always be kicked on the sixth play. A team doing this and controlling the ball would be able to place the opposition under the severest pressure.

When the action is away from the in-goal area, an alternative play is to strike a grubber-kick hard at the feet of the approaching defenders, hoping to regain possession from the ricochet or force them to knock on. This should be attempted by a skilful kicker close to the defence. An over-ambitious kick could sit up, allowing the opposition easy possession.

3   The line kick

Perhaps the most common kick is the one that goes into touch with a bounce, which because of the scrummaging law should ideally be made before the sixth play. It is usual for this kick to be intuitive, and to be made by the tactical kicker operating usually at first receiver. The rest of the team should react to the kick and quickly move up together, making sure that the opposition is unable to counter-attack if by any chance the ball does not go out of play. The ball should be directed into space which can often be found behind the winger and in front of the full-back. The kicker should be wary of being too ambitious, for this will often allow the full-back easy possession.

A team possessing a skilful tactical kicker, and which wins more than a fair share of scrum possession, will adopt these tactics far more frequently than the downtown.

(c)   Overcome a well-organized defence

A defence may be penetrated, particularly one that moves up quickly, by kicking the ball into the area immediately behind it for the kicker or a team-mate to regather.

1   Weighting.   The kick, either a grubber between players or a chip-kick over the top of the first line of defence, has to be so weighted that it is regathered before the full-back has time to arrive, and be directed away from any sweeper.

2   Timing.   The kick should be executed close to the defence so that it is fully committed, and will be slow to turn and chase.

3   Intuitive.   It is usual for the kick to be intuitive. Because the chase determines its success, the kicker and players surrounding him must react quickly and chase.

Tactical considerations

A team which plays a skilful short-kicking game will always cause problems for the opposition. The opposition in their pre-match planning may be forced to modify their defensive plan either by using a sweeper to collect the kicks or by slowing down the speed of their defensive line.

Malcolm Reilly, appointed Great Britain's coach in 1987, has always been convinced that physical conditioning standards must be improved throughout the game in Britain. Here he watches Ian Potter working out in the gymnasium.

SECTION 6

PHYSICAL CONDITIONING

Excellence in performance is achieved only after hours of dedicated training. Des Drummond (Warrington and Great Britain), British 'superstar' champion in 1983, always sets an outstanding example in training.

Rugby League: Comparison with other sports

1   Association football
2   American football
3   Rugby Union
4   Rugby League

When planning a conditioning programme for a player it is necessary to understand fully the requirements of the sport he plays. A careful comparison of the demands made by Rugby League with other major sports is also a help.

1   Association football.   In an average game of soccer the ball is in play for approximately sixty minutes. Speed is an essential requirement, but physical contact is restricted mainly to clashes of the lower limbs, and collisions seldom knock anyone to the ground. Endurance and speed are the main requirements. Most professional soccer players train or play six days of the week.

2   American football (grid-iron).   A stop-go sport, with games lasting approximately three hours, but with continuous action seldom lasting for more than ten seconds. The roles of the players are specific: tremendous agility and speed are the requirements for some positions, while sheer physical strength is a requirement for others. The physical confrontations are intense and the collisions severe. The training programmes are the most advanced of any team sport in the world, with speed and strength the major prior-

ities. The commitment demanded of the players in their pre-season build-up and during the season will be a surprise to most people, as the players begin preparation at 9.30 am and work continuously until 4.00 pm. They have one rest day a week.

3   Rugby Union.   This is another collision sport in which the tackled player is usually knocked to the ground. The roles of the players vary considerably. The forwards, for example, are often involved in more than thirty scrummages, thirty line-outs and forty rucks or mauls per game, but seldom handle the ball. The wing forwards are the specialist tacklers and may make as many as twenty tackles in any one game. The backs are the handlers who require speed and agility, but are seldom asked to make more than ten tackles a game. Statistics from the All Blacks' camp suggest that in international Rugby Union the ball is not often in play for more than twenty-five minutes. Speed, strength and endurance are the major requirements. Most of England's top players are involved in two games a week, and train on two further occasions. Official coaching sources consider that the playing commitment is too demanding, and prevents adequate physical preparation being made.

4 Rugby League. This is a collision sport in which the ball is in play for approximately fifty minutes. Scrummages, reduced to an average of 19.4 a game, take place outside the fifty-minute period. There is a definite movement within Rugby League to reduce specialization, so the work performed by the players varies less from position to position than in the past. Wingers and centres are expected to share the work load far more, while forwards have become much faster.

During the fifty minutes the ball is in play, each player covers between 5,000 and 7,500 metres at differing speeds – sometimes walking, sometimes jogging, occasionally moving backwards, and at all times ready to explode into maximum effort.

While covering such distances, it is the intensity of the physical confrontations that makes Rugby League unique. Those connected with the game will testify to the ferocity of the tackling and the commitment of the defence. The average number of tackles per position has been well illustrated in Chapter 2 of Section 5. It is safe to assume that most players will be involved in as many as twenty physical confront-

ations per game, and for some players this will rise into the forties. Most of these confrontations will cause the players to be forcefully knocked to the ground, after which they have to regain their feet as quickly as possible.

The statistics set out below, compiled during the third Test match played at Wigan between Great Britain and Australia in 1986, show the commitment needed to play top level Rugby League.

Although the ball in Rugby League is in play for ten minutes less than in soccer, the physical confrontations are far more intense. The ball is in play twice as long as in Rugby Union, and the action is far more continuous than in American grid-iron football. There is less specialization in League when compared with other collision sports. All the players are required to handle, be mobile and run with the ball. The physical collisions are intense and more numerous.

The conclusions are that physical conditioning standards necessary to play Rugby League are far higher and more demanding than in any other team sport.

PLAYING POSITION	NAME	TOTAL INVOLVEMENT			PHYSICAL INVOLVEMENT		
		HANDLED BALL	TACKLES MADE	TOTAL	TACKLED IN POSSESSION	TACKLES MADE	TOTAL
Full-back	Joe Lydon	21	14	35	1	14	15
Wing	Henderson Gill	18	10	28	6	10	16
Centre	Garry Schofield	26	17	43	3	17	20
Centre	David Stephenson	7	9	16	4	9	13
Wing	John Basnett	14	9	23	9	9	18
Stand-off	Tony Myler	26	20	46	3	20	23
Scrum-half	Andy Gregory	66	18	84	6	18	24
Prop	Kevin Ward	20	24	44	16	24	40
Hooker	David Watkinson	70	35	105	1	35	36
Prop	Lee Crooks	31	30	61	14	30	44
Second row	Chris Burton*	9	15	24	8	15	23
Second row	Andy Goodway	28	18	46	16	18	34
Loose for- ward	Harry Pinner	38	20	58	7	20	27
Back sub- stitute	Shaun Edwards						
Forward sub- stitute	Ian Potter	5	11	16	3	11	14

*Chris Burton was sin-binned for ten minutes, and then replaced by Ian Potter

Training facts

1   How much training?
2   What kind of training?
3   How intense should the training be?
4   Does the training have to be continuous?
5   How do we make training interesting?

1   HOW MUCH TRAINING?

Although the standards of fitness required to play
Rugby League are higher than in other team sports,
the commitment to physical preparation by many
players is totally insufficient, and compares unfavour-
ably with the commitment of other sportsmen.

Athletes, swimmers and gymnasts are among a
multitude of sportsmen throughout the world who
train hard every day of the week, every week of the
year. Peter Coe, describing to the 1985 Birmingham
conference on Competitive Sport and the Growing
Child, his son's training commitment said: 'Seb tends
to train for quality. He does not run as many miles as
most of his competitors, and perhaps, therefore, does
not devote as many hours to training. However, his
training is very intense and of an extremely high
quality. *Even so he trains an average sixteen hours a
week*.'

Cynics might say that giving the example of Seb
Coe, one of the world's most successful athletes,
provides a false picture. But those who have attended
Rugby League coaching courses at the Lilleshall
National Sports Centre and discussed training pro-
grammes with the national gymnastics squad; or who

41   Dedicated players must supplement club training by training
in their own time. Here Andy Platt (St Helens and Great Britain)
performs a heavy strength training programme.

have attended those at Carnegie College in Leeds and enjoyed similar discussions with athletes working with Wilf Paish, will be fully aware that a sixteen-hour commitment per week is not by any means abnormally high.

Others may argue that the majority play amateur Rugby League for the pure enjoyment of the sport, while the top performers play professional Rugby League, which is part-time anyway. Commitment to training, therefore, cannot possibly be expected to be in excess of two club-training evenings per week.

Amateurs motivated purely by enjoyment, and not striving for excellence, will certainly not wish to embark on a too strenuous or time-consuming training programme. They have to realize, however, that Rugby League is a physically demanding sport, and that injury could be the result of inadequate preparation.

Those striving for excellence, particularly in the professional game, have to accept that standards have changed markedly in the last ten years. British athletes, swimmers and gymnasts need to devote several hours a day to their sport to have any chance of competing on equal terms in the world arena. One of the reasons behind Australia's success in Rugby League in the 1970s and 1980s is that their top players have accepted this fact, and train most days of the week.

A survey of graded players in Sydney, published on 21 May 1986 in *Rugby League Week*, showed that 32% train from 10–12 hours each week, while 56% train more than 12 hours a week (the figures exclude time spent in competition). Because of the competitive nature of the Sydney League these figures will undoubtedly increase over the years. Britain is in direct competition with them, and will not succeed unless similar standards are adopted.

The problem is intensified in a team sport like League because there is so much to do and so little time to do it. Club sessions are usually restricted to two evenings per week, although some clubs now demand an extra session from their players. Excellence depends on the continuous development of the individual and the team. Skill, correct decision-making, tactical knowledge, physical conditioning and attitude have to be nurtured in the players, in

addition to blending them into a unit. This all takes time. Those coaching senior players have two solutions to the problem:

(a)   Draw up a list of priorities for the club training sessions. Physical conditioning and tactics must dominate the programme, leaving little time to improve individual skills, awareness of the game or decision-making.

(b)   Insist that players do most of their conditioning on non-training nights, so that club sessions can be devoted to individual coaching and team improvement.

Only when the second solution is adopted by all professional clubs, and those amateur teams with outstanding juniors, will British Rugby League be able to compete on an equal footing with Australia.

This chapter emphasizes, therefore, that:

1   It is normal for those striving for excellence in any sport, whether professional or amateur, to devote some hours each day to preparation.

2   Most physical conditioning must take place on non-club-training days, but as the players are mainly involved in full-time employment the training schedules will have to be realistic as far as time and equipment are concerned.

3   Club sessions will contain some conditioning, but most of the time will be devoted to individual and team improvement.

2   WHAT KIND OF TRAINING?

It is important that coaches offer the players realistic guidelines on conditioning. It is unrealistic to expect players to devote six full evenings a week to the sport, so training programmes have to be devised which allow the players to train in their home environment. It is equally important that players devoting so much time to preparing for the sport have sound advice and perform the right kind of training.

Gone are the days when enthusiastic but ignorant coaches merely ran their players to exhaustion. It is necessary for training to be specific to the event for it to give maximum benefit. The physical requirements of the game have to be analysed. It is normal for a player in a match to cover between 5,000 and 7,500 metres at varying speeds, moving forwards and backwards. Players have to be able to perform various skills at maximum speed, and withstand the rigours of harsh bodily contact. They must be prepared to make around thirty tackles a game, as well as being tackled with the ball. In most tackles the player is knocked to the ground; the speed with which he gets up and rejoins play contributes to the team's effectiveness. Such considerations determine training.

It is also important that training is specific to the player. Although in modern Rugby League the tendency is for all thirteen players to share a similar work load, wingers obviously have a role different from front-row forwards. The natural strengths and weaknesses of players must also be taken into consideration in planning individual fitness programmes. Although playing such sports as squash and tennis may be enjoyable, it does little to prepare the players for Rugby League football. The coach must test each of his players physically and plan an individual training programme specific to their needs and to the role that they are expected to play in the game.

All players must develop their:

Suppleness
Stamina
Strength, and
Speed.

In addition, the training must be specific to both

The game, and
The individual.

3   HOW INTENSE SHOULD TRAINING BE?

It is important to understand that training is an ongoing process, and that improvement does not occur without a great deal of hard work. Training depends on the principle of overload, adaptation and progression.

(a)   Overload

Unless the body is subjected to stress, its condition is unlikely to improve. Below this stress level the player will at best maintain his current level of fitness. If a training programme is to be effective, it must make demands on the body's systems. The principle of overload is based on three factors:

(i)   *Frequency*: the number of sessions per week, per month, per year,

(ii)   *Intensity*: the training loads per week, per month, per year, and

(iii)   *Time*: the duration of training in hours per week, per month, per year.

The principle of overload is used in a number of different ways, by lifting heavier and heavier weights to improve strength, for example, or by running longer and longer distances to increase endurance. There are a number of changes which occur: the nervous system encourages the formation of more muscle fibres; the circulatory system changes to distribute more blood to the muscles that need it; and the overload stimulates the muscular system to produce extra protein to help meet the extra demands which the body anticipates.

(b)   Adaptation

As a result of the body being overloaded it adapts, and in so doing overcompensates in preparation for more strenuous efforts. The result is an increase in endurance or strength, and a greater capacity to perform work.

(c)   Progression

As the body adapts it is able to tolerate activity of a greater intensity. Training must progress, therefore, and it helps if a careful record is kept in order to monitor this progression. The coach must remember that the player should do more work tomorrow than he did today.

The balance between work and rest is important both within and between training sessions. Improvement through training is simply the result of the body's response to carefully graduated stress. The body needs a recovery period between successive periods of exercise, so players and coaches should beware of simply piling on heavy exercise loads. A point is quickly reached where there will be diminishing returns from further training. Although players may train daily, they should never train hard more than three days a week, with a game counting as a hard session.

The balance between hard and easy weeks should be three hard to one easy week. It is in the easy week that the training stimulus has its full impact:

(a) Each training session must be intensive enough to reach the critical training threshold.
(b) Alternate hard and easy days; never train very hard on consecutive days.
(c) Enough time must be left for the body to rebuild. If you exercise before full recovery you defeat your purpose.
(d) Each workout must be progressively more strenuous than the last.

4 DOES THE TRAINING HAVE TO BE CONTINUOUS?

Once training ceases, levels of fitness deteriorate rapidly – far more rapidly than they have taken to increase. A perfect example can be seen by the muscle wastage that occurs when an athlete has his leg in plaster for any length of time. Similar deterioration occurs in all aspects of fitness.

This is relevant to the injured player. Every effort must be made to continue with some form of training when a player is side-lined. A player with an arm injury can more often than not continue with his running and sprinting, while a player with a leg injury must continue to work out his upper body. In both cases every effort must be made to continue exercising the heart, lungs and circulation.

Similarly it is not possible merely to train a player at the beginning of the season, and then expect him to maintain this level simply by playing. Evidence suggests that when this occurs an individual loses 30–35% of his fitness during the season. *This is a strong argument for the governing bodies to reduce the number of fixtures played, so that clubs play a maximum of one game per week.*

Reversibility should also affect the work performed during the close season. Examine diagram 192. The continuous line represents the fitness level of a player who:

(a) Trains for six weeks prior to the season.
(b) Trains hard during the season until February, when his club becomes involved in mid-week fixtures (36 weeks).
(c) Rests from May until pre-season training begins (10 weeks).
(d) Trains for six weeks prior to the season.

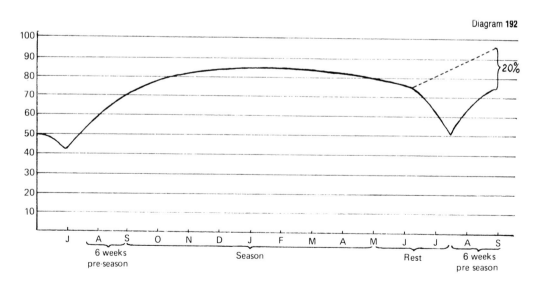

Diagram **192**

The broken line represents the fitness levels that the same player could expect if he trained throughout the year. The difference is considerable, but understandable when one considers that fitness levels fall during inactivity more rapidly than they can be increased by training.

There is little doubt that players do require a psychological or mental break at the end of an intense season. However, a total rest will cause the loss of most of the physical gains made previously by hard sweat and tears. Freedom from the pressures of competition, perhaps allied to a change in training programme and locality, will provide the athlete with the mental rest he requires. Physically the work can be intensified, for the close season is when most gains in fitness can be made. Surely to do any other is completely illogical.

5   HOW DO WE MAKE TRAINING INTERESTING?

Training needs to be interesting otherwise the players will become bored and disillusioned, so performance will suffer. The following considerations should be made:

1   *Variation*

It is important to vary the exercises and training routines, to maintain motivation and stimulate interest: hard sessions should be followed by easier ones, and work should be followed by rest. Follow a long workout with a short one, an intense session with a relaxed one, high speed with easy distance. When training becomes dull, change it.

2   *Measurement*

The more progress a player can make, the more he will be encouraged to continue. A training diary should be kept by players and coach alike. Times taken, distances measured, and repetitions counted should be logged so that progress can be seen to be made.

3   *Relation to the game*

Whether professional or amateur, players take part in the game primarily for enjoyment. The more closely training activities can be related to the game, the more enjoyable the training will become.

4   *Competition*

Games players are highly competitive. A clever coach will use competition to motivate his squad.

Suppleness and warm-up

1   INJURIES

Lack of flexibility is one of the most frequent causes of strain and tear injuries in sport. Records suggest that a regular flexibility programme will reduce the number of strains, tears and pulls by over 80%. There is evidence, however, that unaccustomed stretching directly before competition can overexcite the muscle and actually result in injury.

It is therefore essential for a Rugby League player to adopt a regular stretching programme, which should be incorporated in the warm-up before every training session and game.

2   SPEED AND ENDURANCE

Poor flexibility also hinders speed and endurance, since the muscles have to work harder to overcome the resistance to maximum length of stride. By increasing the possible range of movement in the shoulders, hips, trunk and ankles, it is possible to increase stride length, and therefore increase both speed and agility, as well as save energy. This in turn means that the performer can play harder and longer.

It is should be understood, however, that the amount of stretch achieved will not be beneficial unless it is accompanied by an increase in muscle strength.

3   STRENGTH

There is a danger that crash programmes of strength training could restrict range of movement, directly increasing the possibility of injury. An all-round increase of strength is necessary for the modern Rugby League player, but the strength programme should incorporate flexibility work, and the weight-training exercises should also involve a wide range of movement.

4   FLEXIBILITY DEVELOPMENT

How is it possible to increase the range of movement? Unless the muscle is stretched beyond its habitual length, then the exercise can be of little value. There are two main types of stretching exercise which are used to increase flexibility: static stretching and ballistic stretching.

(a) Static stretching involves slow, sustained exercise: a muscle is lengthened and then held in position for a few seconds. Static stretching may be further assisted by using a partner to extend the final range of travel, and this is usually referred to as passive stretching. Partner work is to be recommended, because it is easier to relax the parts of the body which are not being exercised if these are supported. The fact that the partners can communicate with each other means that each muscle can be stretched as far as possible without risk of injury.

(b) Ballistic stretching is *not* advisable. It involves a bouncing or jerking movement, which produces a certain momentum in the part of the body concerned, stretching the muscle even further. The quick, repetitive bouncing actions commonly used in warm-ups will produce a stretch reflex permitting only a momentary lengthening of the muscle. Researchers have also suggested that these exercises can make muscles sore or less resilient and elastic.

Static and passive stretching are preferable, mainly because the muscles are more relaxed and there is no induced stretch reflex involved. Static stretching is also beneficial before and after workouts as a way of reducing (and sometimes even eliminating) muscle inflammation, and of assisting recovery from soft-tissue injuries.

5 GUIDELINES FOR STRETCHING

1 Make sure you are fully relaxed before starting your stretching routine.

2 Do not begin stretching until the muscles are warmed up.

3 Ease into the stretch to the point where it is comfortable; it should never be painful. Never strain because this may damage the muscles.

4 Stretch so that the pull is felt in the bulky central portion of the muscle. It may be helpful to concentrate on relaxing the muscle or muscle group which is being stretched. Excess tension in the joints can often be relieved by slightly shifting your arms and legs.

5 As the feeling of stretching decreases, you should stretch a little further, making sure it still feels comfortable.

6 Do not bounce in the end position, because of the strain on the muscles being stretched.

7 Do not hold your breath: try to breathe calmly and rhythmically to help you relax.

8 Concentrate on stretching the weight-bearing muscles in the lower back, hip, knees and ankles.

9 Stretch both before and after each workout. This is the minimum requirement. Stretching after a workout should be particularly encouraged because not only does it help you to relax and recover, but also the muscles are warm and hence easier to stretch.

The following section gives various flexibility exercises, but you should be able to devise others.

6 STATIC STRETCHING

(Demonstrated by Brian Case, Wigan and Great Britain)

1 Neck (illustration 42)

Starting position: sit or stand in a position which is comfortable.

Movement: slowly roll the head around in a full circle while keeping the back straight.

Repetitions: ten times, each time reversing the direction.

2 Arms and top of shoulders (illustration 43)

Starting position: sit or stand with legs apart. With arms behind the head, hold the elbow of one arm with the hand of the other arm.

Movement: gently pull the elbow across behind the head.

Time: fifteen seconds with each arm.

42–53 Brian Case demonstrates a series of stretching exercises:

- 42   neck
- 43   arms and top of shoulder
- 44   arms, shoulder, back
- 45   front of legs (quadriceps)
- 46   back of legs (hamstrings)
- 47   groin
- 48   back of legs (hamstrings)
- 49   groin, hips, and inner thighs
- 50   hips and front of legs (quadriceps)
- 51   groin and inner thigh
- 52   back of legs (hamstrings)
- 53   calf

44

42

43

45

3 Arms, shoulders and back (illustration 44)

Starting position: stand with legs apart and inter-lace fingers above the head, with palms facing upwards.

Movement: gently push the arms slightly back and up.

Time: ten seconds.

4 Front of leg (quadriceps) (illustration 45)

Starting position: assume a bent knee position with heels flat and toes pointed straight ahead.

Movement: push the knees gently forward.

Time: thirty seconds.

5 Back of legs (hamstrings) (illustration 46)

Starting position: stand, feet shoulder-length apart.

Movement: slowly bend forward from the hips, keeping the knees slightly bent. Let arms and neck relax.

Time: thirty seconds.

Do not: bounce, lock knees, or overstretch.

6 Groin (illustration 47)

Starting position: sit with soles of feet held flat together, and grasp toes.

Movement: gently pull forward from the hips. Squeeze knees down, exerting pressure from the elbows.

Time: thirty seconds.

7 Back of leg (hamstrings) (illustration 48)

Starting position: sit down with left leg straight, and the side of the right foot touching the inside of the left thigh.

Movement: keeping head and back flat, reach down with both hands towards the toes. Extra stretch can be obtained by pointing the toes back towards the head, or by grasping the ankle and pulling the chest down to the knee.

Time: thirty seconds each leg.

8 Groin, hips and inner thighs (illustration 49)

Starting position: sit up with legs spread as wide as possible, and knees locked.

Movement: slowly bend forward from the hips keeping the quadriceps relaxed. Try to keep the hips from rolling backwards, and put the hands out in front for support.

Time: thirty seconds

9 Hips and front of leg (quadriceps) (illustration 50)

Starting position: place the right foot forward until the knee is directly above the ankle and the left knee is almost touching the floor at the back. Both feet should be in line, facing forwards.

Movement: bring the hips downwards, keeping them straight. Use the hands to maintain balance if necessary.

Time: thirty seconds each leg.

10 Groin and inner thigh (illustration 51)

Starting position: stretch the right leg out as far as possible to the side, with the left leg bent and bearing the weight.

46

48

49

47

50

51

52

53

Movement: gently push the body down, and stretch the left leg out.

Time: twenty seconds each leg.

11   *Front of leg (quadriceps)* (illustration 52)

Starting position: stand upright, grasp the right foot with the right hand, and pull the foot close to the buttocks. If need be, hold on to a partner for balance.

Movement: pull the foot towards the buttocks.

Time: twenty seconds each leg.

12   *Calf* (illustration 53)

Starting position: lean against a solid support with the body angled back, legs and feet together. Stand on tip toes.

Movement: gently place both feet flat against the ground.

Time: twenty seconds.

7   PASSIVE STRETCHING (diagram 193)

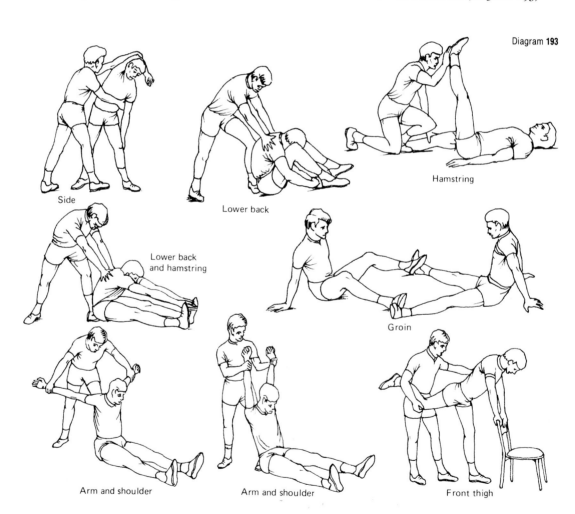

Diagram **193**

Side

Lower back

Hamstring

Lower back and hamstring

Groin

Arm and shoulder

Arm and shoulder

Front thigh

8   THE WARM-UP

1   Warm up before every game and training session
2   Raise the body temperature and increase circulation first by jogging or running on the spot
3   Do each of the flexibility exercises until the stretch is felt, and then hold
4   Do not bounce: achieve the stretch position gently
5   Do not over-stretch: the position should be tight but not painful
6   Stretch before and after weight-training
7   On match days finish the warm-up and flexibility programme ten minutes before kick-off.

Stamina

1   IMPORTANCE

The conclusion in Chapter 1 of this section was that a Rugby League player requires higher levels of stamina than those taking part in other collision sports. High levels of stamina are so essential that endurance training must be the foundation of the training programme of all players, irrespective of their position.

2   ENDURANCE TRAINING

Without becoming too scientific, it is necessary for coach and players to understand clearly the major principles of endurance training.

Perhaps a comparison can be made with an individual selling a car. He realizes that the would-be buyer will expect the engine to be efficient, and the bodywork in good condition. Likewise endurance can be split into two similar components:

(a)   The engine, that is, the energy systems, and
(b)   The bodywork

It is essential that Rugby League players achieve high levels of endurance in both. An overemphasis in training on either, with neglect of the other, will cause inefficient performance.

3   DEVELOPING THE ENERGY SYSTEMS

The body has two energy systems, and Rugby League needs both. They are:

(a)   Aerobic – working with oxygen
(b)   Anaerobic – working without oxygen

(a)   Aerobic endurance

Aerobic endurance is also known as cardiovascular endurance, and involves the efficiency of the heart, lungs and circulation. Every muscle in the body requires energy, supplied by the blood which receives oxygen in the lungs and is pumped through the body by the heart. The bigger and stronger the heart, the more efficient will be its pumping capacity, and the more fuel will be supplied to those muscles which are working. Greater efficiency is shown by a drop in the pulse rate.

Training details

A long continuous run is the recommended exercise to develop aerobic endurance. This form of long continuous exercise:

1   Makes the lungs work more effectively, allowing more air to reach the blood as it is pumped through them.
2   Increases the number of red cells in the blood, allowing even more oxygen to be extracted from the air which enters the lungs.
3   Increases the size, thickness and strength of the heart muscle. With the chambers of the heart increasing in volume, the whole heart becomes bigger, stronger and more efficient.

Pulse rate

Scientific studies suggest that the heart rate is the best indicator of the intensity of continuous exercise such as running. It should be held at 130/160 beats per minute for at least thirty minutes, and all coaches should learn to measure the heart rate accurately. An easy and effective way of doing this is to take the radial pulse: to do this, place your fingers on the underside of the wrist in line with the base of the thumb. Count the number of beats for fifteen seconds, and then multiply by four to give an estimate of the heart rate per minute.

Training

The continuous runs should vary over different routes and distances. Players who find such training difficult should begin steadily, and be encouraged by all the middle-aged people who have recently taken up jogging. 'If they can do it, so can you.'

Gradually, the duration of the run should be lengthened to around thirty and eventually to forty minutes. The players should be encouraged to run in a relaxed frame of mind, and there is no need to time the runs. As long as the pulse rate is maintained in excess of 130 beats per minute the training will have its desired effect.

54   Taking the pulse.

It is more enjoyable to run through countryside and on grass, but this is seldom possible. For running on hard surfaces, insist on a good pair of trainers with thick soles and be wary of the camber of the roads.

During early season training two or three long runs a week may be necessary, but gradually as the levels of aerobic endurance are improved other forms of training can be introduced into the programme. Even then, however, players should do at least one run every week.

To perform the long runs as part of the club training session would be a waste of valuable training time. The player can run in the early morning before breakfast, during the lunch hour, or in the evening. The total training time, including changing and showering, is less than one hour – no more commitment than a middle-aged jogger is giving.

(b)   Anaerobic endurance

'Anaerobic' literally means 'without air', or effectively without oxygen'. So anaerobic endurance implies muscular work done without oxygen.

Perhaps the best example is a 400-metre runner who comes round the last bend and experiences extreme fatigue. His legs feel heavy, they wobble, and all strength appears to have disappeared. The fatigue cannot be overcome merely by breathing in more air. The athlete is using two energy systems, with the anaerobic cycle supplementing the aerobic mechanism. This occurs during relatively short intense activity, after ten seconds to two minutes, and is therefore relevant to the Rugby League player.

The anaerobic cycle involves chemical changes which take place in the muscle. There are two major considerations:

(a)   The production of anaerobic power
(b)   The removal of the waste products in the muscle.

Without going into confusing detail, training should develop the body's ability to do both, and this is best achieved by interval training. A more detailed explanation can be obtained from most books on the physiology of exercise, but the National Coaching

55   Aerobic endurance: Ellery Hanley (Wigan and Great Britain), Ian Potter and Brian Case during a long thirty-minute run, part of Great Britain's squad training in the summer of 1987.

Foundation's Resource Pack 5, 'Developing Endurance' by Dr. Craig Sharp, is highly recommended.

Interval training

Rugby League football consists of short bursts of intense running. Interval training, therefore, should be specific to the game's requirements, and it is an advantage in early season training to supplement the long continuous runs (aerobic), with interval training which includes runs of no longer than thirty seconds. When the training plateau has been increased, and as the season approaches, the interval training should consist of shorter more intense bursts over 60–120 metres. Runs of this distance should be included in each week's programme throughout the season, because quality runs repeated after a rest period will considerably improve the player's ability to produce anaerobic power.

Many people unfortunately underestimate the importance of the rest period, which is not only to allow the heart rate to come down but also to allow time for the lactic acid which the working muscles have produced to be cleared out of the system. This is best achieved if the rest intervals are between five and six times as long as the work period, and include activity approaching 65% of the working intensity. If this is not adhered to the lactic acid will be locked up in the muscles causing fatigue and soreness.

The variables in interval training are, therefore:

1 Length of run
2 Speed of run
3 Number of runs, and
4 Rest periods between runs.

Examples:

1 Early season training – longer runs

Restrict these to 400- or 800-metre runs, all of which should be individually timed. Each player can be timed over 1600 metres, divided by four, giving an average 400-metre time which is related to the 1600-metre speed. Take two seconds off this to work out the 400-metre target, and double this to obtain the 800-metre target, for example:

the 1600-metre time is 5 min. 20 sec.

the average 400-metre time is $\dfrac{5 \text{ min. 20 sec.}}{4}$
= 1 min. 20 sec.

the 400-metre target time is 1 min. 20 sec. − 2 sec.
= 1 min. 18 sec.

and the 800-metre target time is 1 min. 18 sec. × 2
= 2 min. 36 sec.

Training example

2 × 800 metres in under 2 min. 36 sec.
Recovery, 10 minutes jogging.
4 × 400 metres in under 78 sec.
Recovery between runs, 5 minutes jogging.

2 Pre-season training — faster runs

Work out each individual's training target.

Training distance (sprinting)	Target time	Work–rest ratio
50 metres	Add 1.5 sec. to best 50-metre time from running start	1 : 5
100 metres	Add 3.0 sec. to best 100-metre time from running start	1 : 5
150 metres	Add 4.0 sec. to best 150-metre time from running start	1 : 5
200 metres	Add 5.0 sec. to best 200-metre time from running start	1 : 5

Examples of three pre-season and in-season interval training sessions

Session A	8 × 100 metres under 14 sec.
	Recovery: walking 70 sec.
	2 × 150 metres under 19 sec.
	Recovery: walking 95 sec.
	2 × 200 metres under 30 sec.
	Recovery: jogging 150 sec.
Session B	6 × 50 metres under 8 sec.
	Recovery: walking 40 sec.
	4 × 100 metres under 14 sec.
	Recovery: walking 70 sec.
	2 × 150 metres under 19 sec.
	Recovery: walking 95 sec.
Session C	4 × 200 metres under 30 sec.
	Recovery: walking 150 sec.
	8 × 100 metres under 14 sec.
	Recovery: walking 70 sec.
	8 × 50 metres under 8 sec.
	Recovery: walking 40 sec.

Interval training is very demanding and severely tests the commitment of the players. It may have to be carried out on a club training evening. The players should be placed in groups of similar speeds, and their individual times would act as no more than a guideline in determining both the target time and rest interval. Even so, the coach should consider timing and recording each run. This will show the commitment of the players and help to motivate them.

Important considerations

1   Interval training develops endurance and not speed. Even interval training consisting of extremely fast fifty-metre runs will not develop pure speed.

2   Both energy systems need developing. Each week's training should consist of one thirty-minute run (aerobic) and one interval training session (anaerobic).

3   Training should be specific to the individual. Certain players have high levels of anaerobic endurance, but find difficulty in running for any length of time. They need to perform more long continuous runs than the player who finds this type of training relatively easy, but has problems doing interval runs. It is important, therefore, that each player is tested, and a training programme devised for him which is specific to both his needs and his role in the game. Such training programmes require constant retesting and updating.

4 DEVELOPING THE BODY: MUSCULAR ENDURANCE

Local muscular endurance is the term used for a performer's ability to sustain activity for a long period, making intensive use of a small number of muscles. Such activity may make only small demands on the respiratory and circulatory systems before the muscles become exhausted. Muscular endurance depends on a number of factors such as strength, efficiency of the blood supply, and the muscles' ability to remove waste products. Some team sports make few demands in this area, but Rugby League is not one of them.

The very nature of the game requires players to make repeated body contact and become involved in heavy collisions; quickly regain their feet after becoming involved in a tackle; and move forwards and backwards in the defensive line.

Since all players, whatever their ability or position, need to possess a high level of muscular endurance, it is necessary to have a more comprehensive understanding of the changes that occur in the muscle.

As a muscle tires, it loses some of its ability to relax. The character of a muscle is determined not only by its ability to produce power over a long period of time, but also by its capacity to remain elastic over the same period. When the muscle works, it replaces the oxygen and fuel which are used up, and at the same time disposes of lactic acid and other waste products. As long as these two processes continue to operate at roughly the same rate, the muscle can continue to work efficiently. However, if for some reason the waste products accumulate faster than oxygen and fuel are supplied, the physiological balance is upset and fatigue results. As this sets in, the reaction time becomes slower, while the muscle becomes stiff and is no longer able to relax sufficiently.

The more a muscle is trained to perform a particular movement which is exactly the same – in terms of range, resistance, frequency and speed – as that required in competition, then the less likely it is to become fatigued by that movement during competition. This improvement is primarily due to functional conditioning as a result of work increase.

This improves circulation by calling more capillaries (small blood vessels) into use, thus providing the working muscles with more oxygen and fuel, as well as facilitating the removal of waste products.

Important considerations

Players, whatever their position, require high levels of muscular endurance. These levels can only be improved by regular training, which should be as specific to the game as possible.

The best way to improve muscular endurance is circuit training.

Circuit training

Circuit training can take place in the

home
gymnasium
weights room, and
club.

Circuits incorporating weights and equipment

have an advantage over others, but as the majority of circuits should take place on non-club training days, the home circuit may often be more realistic because it is less demanding in time.

1   Home circuit

(a)   The body, for simplicity, is divided into three major areas:
   (i)   upper   – arms, chest, and back
   (ii)   middle – stomach, abdomen and lower back
   (iii) lower   – legs

(b)   The home circuit comprises three exercises for each of these three areas, giving a total of nine exercises per circuit.

(c)   The exercises are:
   upper   – press-ups, back press-ups, and dips
   middle – sit-ups, trunk curls × 2, and legs raise
   lower   – step-ups, squat jumps, and squat thrusts

(d)   The order of progression is such that each muscle group has time to recover:
   (i)   step-ups   – lower
   (ii)   trunk curls   – middle
   (iii)   press-ups   – upper
   (iv)   squat jumps   – lower
   (v)   sit-ups   – middle
   (vi)   back press-ups – upper
   (vii)   squat thrusts – lower
   (viii) trunk curls   – middle
   (ix)   dips   – upper

(e)   The number of repetitions for each of the nine exercises is decided during the first session, when the individual works for one minute on each activity. The aim is to perform as many repetitions as possible. After each exercise, the individual has one minute's rest before beginning the next.
   Total time : eighteen minutes
   Important : the number of repetitions for each exercise should be written down.

(f)   For all future training sessions the individual halves the number of maximum repetitions and performs three circuits *without* any rest intervals. The exercises should always be completed in the same order. For example:

Exercise	Maximum (Total in 1 min.)	Circuit (Half the maximum)
Step-ups	40	20
Trunk curls	50	25
Press-ups	48	24
Squat jumps	40	20
Sit-ups	50	25
Back press-ups	46	23
Squat thrusts	60	30
Trunk curls	50	25
Dips	30	15

The individual, therefore, does

   20 step-ups   23 back press-ups
   25 trunk curls   30 squat thrusts
   24 press-ups   25 trunk curls
   20 squat jumps   15 dips
   25 sit-ups

moving from one exercise to the other without any rest as he completes one circuit. Again without rest, the individual completes another two circuits, making three in all.

(g)   The time taken to complete three circuits should always be recorded. The times should eventually improve, and when the circuit can be completed in less than fourteen minutes it is time to increase the number of repetitions.

   Warning: If the time taken exceeds twenty minutes the number of repetitions should be reduced.

The exercises

(Demonstrated by Des Drummond, Warrington and Great Britain)

(i)   *Step-ups* (illustrations 56 a,b,c)
Stand in front of a sturdy chair with hands at the side, and step on to the chair until in an upright position. Using the same leg stand down again for one count. On the next circuit use the other leg.

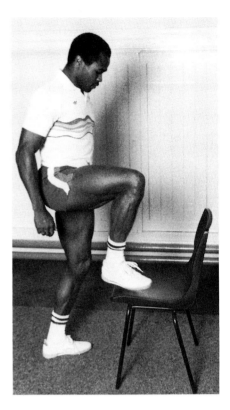

56 a,b,c Step-ups.

(ii)   *Trunk curls* (illustrations 57 a,b)

Lie on the back with legs bent and knees at right angles, feet about a shoulder width apart with soles flat on the ground, and hands clasped behind the head. The player sits up so that his right elbow touches his left knee, and lies down again. This counts as one. Next time up, the left elbow touches the right knee. It is important to twist the trunk as the upper body moves off the ground.

57 a,b   Trunk curls.

(iii)   *Press-ups* (illustrations 58 a,b)
Lie on the stomach with hands a shoulder-width apart
and fingers spread pointing forward. Press up until
the arms are straight, then lower the body until it
almost touches the ground, keeping the body
straight. No part of the body should touch the
ground after the exercise has begun, other than the
feet and hands. The arms bend and straighten for
each count.

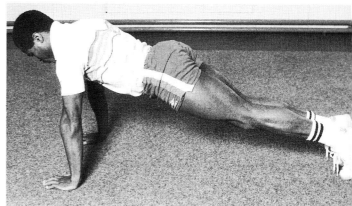

(iv)   *Squat jumps* (illustrations 59 a,b)
From a crouching position spring high into the air,
and down again for one count.

58 a,b   Press-ups.

59 a,b   Squat jumps.

60   Sit-ups.

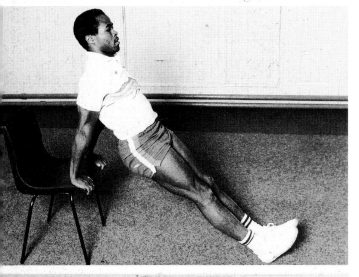

61 a,b   Back press-ups.

(v) *Sit-ups* (illustration 60)
Lie on the back, legs straight and together with heels on the ground. Place your hands on the front of your thighs. Sit up and touch knees with finger tips before lying down again for a count of one.

(vi) *Back press-ups* (illustrations 61 a,b)
Stand with a chair at the back. Place the hands behind the body and hold the chair, with your legs out at 45°. Bend the arms and straighten for a count of one.

(vii)   *Squat thrusts* (illustrations 62 a,b)
Start in a crouch position with knees tucked up between the arms. Thrust out both legs to a press-up position, then spring them back for a count of one. The feet must not slide.

(viii)   *Trunk curls* (illustrations 57 a,b)
This is a repeat of the exercise described on page 235.

62 a,b   Squat thrusts.

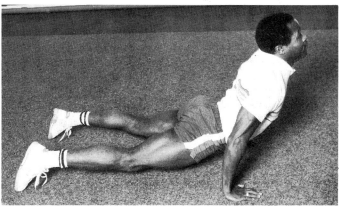

63 a,b   Dips.

(ix)   *Dips* (illustrations 63 a,b)
A variation of the press-up. Start in the press-up position with arms straight. Push back on your arms and raise the backside, then bend the arms and dip your body close to the ground, finally taking the weight forward again to the press-up position for a count of one.

2   The gymnasium

A typical circuit in the gymnasium, organised exactly like the home circuit, will consist of:

(i)   step-ups on to a double bench
(ii)   sit-ups
(iii)   press-ups
(iv)   bench squat: a bench is secured to the top wall bar. The player holds the other end and pushes it above his head, stretching as high as possible. He then squats and the bench is lowered on to the floor, counting one
(v)   trunk curls on an inclined bench anchored to the wall bars, with feet above the head
(vi)   pull-ups, using a beam and underhand grasp
(vii)   shuttle run, across the length of the gymnasium
(viii)   trunk curls
(ix)   inverted press-ups, with feet in wall bars above the head.

3   Multi-gym

Using the same exercises as for the development of strength (see Chapter 5), but with lower weights and higher repetitions (between twelve and twenty repetitions – three continuous circuits).

4   The club

There are several ways of devising circuits specific to the game which the entire squad can perform and which are particularly beneficial therefore. One such is the defence circuit:

The squad is divided into two equal groups

(i) *Defensive line.* Cones are placed ten metres apart from the goal-line to half-way. On a command, both squads move upfield together to the second cone. On reaching it they back-track to the first, then move forward to the third. At all times they move forward two cones (twenty metres) and back-track one (ten metres). It is important that the players always face upfield, maintain a straight defensive line when moving forward and communicate.

(ii) *Press-ups.* The two groups working together, talking and counting, do a set number of press-ups, fifty, followed by a thirty-second rest.

(iii) *Upright rowing.* Group A sit down in line and link arms while group B sit down opposite, close enough to hold the hands of group A, and also link arms. Each group, working together with the other group, perform sit-ups, so members of group A lie on their backs while group B are pulled into a sitting position, and as group A sit up group B lie back. The exercises should be performed quickly, in unison, with all the players calling out the number of repetitions – for example, 100 sit-ups, followed by a thirty-second rest.

(iv) *Shields.* Group A stand in line holding shields, with group B also in line five metres away. On a command, group B move forward in line and hit the shields, using alternate shoulders. The hits should be of good quality, and the line should be maintained at all times. After the required number of hits have been completed the groups change position, to complete three sets of twelve hits with thirty seconds' rest between each set.

(v) *Punching the shields.* The groups align as above, with group A holding the shields. Group B move forward together, punching the shields strongly for thirty seconds before moving back. Alternate,completing three sets with thirty seconds' rest between each set.

(vi) *Upright rowing.* As before.

(vii) *Tackle bags or tubes.* Group A stands in line each player holding a tackle bag or a tube. Group B, maintaining the line, move forward and tackle. Then the groups alternate as before, completing three sets of twelve tackles with thirty seconds' rest between each set.

(viii) *Press-ups.*   As before.

(ix) *Upright rowing.*   As before.

Summary

1   The senior club

Players must be encouraged to accept responsibility for their own fitness, and the indoor circuit will provide them with an opportunity to improve their muscular endurance without unrealistic demands being made on their time. Quite often a club circuit, similar to the defence example, should be incorporated into club training.

2   Other clubs

At clubs where the players are reluctant to train in their own time, some form of circuit training should be included in each week's training programme. The more specific the circuit, the better.

Endurance training summary

1   High levels of endurance can be achieved only if players include:

(a)   A long run
(b)   Interval training, and
(c)   Circuit training

in their weekly programme.

2   The training should be specific to the individual. Tests should be conducted which identify any area of weakness in each player's fitness, and this should be strengthened by a concentration of training.

3   The training should be specific to the game. In season, interval training should consist of shorter, faster runs (for example, 60–120 metres) and club sessions should regularly include circuit training specific to defence requirements .

Strength

1   The value of weight training
2   Multi-weight machines
3   Free weights
4   Weight-training terminology
5   The development of strength

Great advances in fitness training have been made during the last twenty years but British Rugby League has been slow to embrace them.

Nowhere has this improvement been more evident than in weight training. A carefully planned weight-training programme can be beneficial to most sports, but its influence on Rugby League, a sport which is dependent upon speed and bodily collision, has been colossal.

No other training, minute for minute, can compare with the overall results obtained from weight training, and every player over the age of sixteen, whatever his playing position or body size, should be involved in such a programme. *If you are not involved in a weight training programme, the game has progressed too quickly for you.*

1   THE VALUE OF WEIGHT TRAINING

1   Strength

Strength is developed by lifting heavy weights a few times, the aim being to lift a heavy weight tomorrow which is impossible today. Repetitions should be ten or less.

2   Muscular endurance

Endurance is developed by lifting slightly lower weights more often. Repetitions to develop endurance should be in excess of twelve.

3   Speed

The most efficient method of increasing speed is to combine a heavy-weights programme with speed drills.

4   Prevention of injuries

Weight training strengthens ligaments and tendons as well as muscle. Joints are therefore made far more resilient, particularly when the weight training is combined with flexibility work. The growth of tissue size helps to resist tissue injury and prepares the body to handle stress.

5   Co-ordination and agility

Lack of strength is often the major cause of poor co-ordination, leading to early fatigue and loss of agility.

6 Self-confidence

Improved fitness and physical appearance, in addition to the increase in kilograms lifted, causes an improvement in the 'self-image', essential to the confident games player.

2   MULTI-WEIGHT MACHINES

Throughout this section the weight-training exercises are shown on multi-weight equipment. It is recommended that wherever and whenever possible, players should train on these machines because they are quicker and safer for beginners to use and are readily available in most sports centres.

Rules for working on multi-weight machines

1 Always do a warm-up and stretching routine before you start working
2 Breathing: inhale before you lift, exhale at the completion of the lift
3 Use the full range of movement, maintaining flexibility
4 Train fast yet under control – do not crash the weight stack down
5 Keep resistance on the muscle at all times, to gain maximum training benefit
6 Train, don't strain
7 Always finish with stretching to avoid muscle stiffness
8 Keep a training diary of everything you do.

3   FREE WEIGHTS

Similar exercises can be done with free weights, but these can be dangerous when handled by a novice. If free weights are all that is available the player must adhere to the following safety precautions:

Safety factors with free weights

1 Never try to lift a weight that is too heavy
2 Ensure before you lift that all weights are secure on the bar

3 When handling heavy weights always work with a partner
4 Always lift with the back straight, eyes forward, and head up
5 Ensure a thorough warm-up and stretching before handling the weights
6 Ensure correct breathing during the exercise.

4   WEIGHT-TRAINING TERMINOLOGY

Repetition: the exercise from starting position back to starting position.
Repetition maximum: the maximum number of repetitions with a particular load that can be done without rest. This is the *key* to progressive weight loading and development.
Set: the repeating of an exercise (repetitions) a given number of times. Along with repetition maximum (RM), the set constitutes the basic structure by which an individual modifies his routine toward his target.

5   THE DEVELOPMENT OF STRENGTH

1   When to start

Gains in strength should be made during the close season. It is important, however, that the individual has a high level of endurance before he begins. Players who have this should begin a strength training programme immediately the season finishes, but should remember that their endurance levels must also be maintained.

   Those whose level of endurance is not high enough should concentrate for at least a month on developing both energy systems and muscular endurance, as discussed in the last chapter. When these levels have increased strength training can begin, but the new levels of endurance should also be maintained.

2   How many sessions a week?

For any appreciable gains in strength, the individual is required to perform three sessions each week. These should take place on alternate dates, and endurance levels should be maintained on the other days.

3   Does weight training continue once the season starts?

Basically, yes. Otherwise all the pre-season gains will be lost. Care must be taken, however, not to strain the body, or leave all the energy in the weights room. It is recommended that the frequency of weight training in the season is halved to three sessions per fortnight, and that these sessions take place at least two days before a game. In this way strength will be maintained. Immediately the season finishes the individual should revert to doing three sessions each week.

4   What kind of weight training?

Arguably the best results are produced by the 10–8–6 system of repetitions and sets. In this system a weight is selected that will permit not more than ten repetitions during the first set; then the resistance is increased for the second set, to a point that will permit not more than eight repetitions; and in the third set the resistance is increased to an amount that will permit six repetitions. *In all cases the maximum number of repetitions is performed in each set, so muscle failure is always achieved.* Thus, in reality a person will actually only perform 8–6–4 repetitions. When he is able to achieve 10–8–6 the weights should be increased. A 20–12 repetition should be adopted for leg exercises.

The results of this programme are supported by research and experience which show that a definite increase in strength, muscle speed and size will occur if the programme is properly followed.

Recommended exercises
(Demonstrated by Shaun Edwards, Wigan and Great Britain)

1   *Bench press* (illustrations 64 a,b)
Lie on the bench, feet firmly on the ground, with knees bent. Undergrip: the bench should be high, and the chest should be no more than two inches below the bar to secure full movement. The weight should be lifted above the chest until the arms are outstretched.

64 a,b   Bench press.

2   *Trunk curls* (illustrations 65 a,b)
Legs must be bent, almost at right angles, hands behind the head, and feet secured. The right elbow is moved to the left knee, aiming at three sets of twenty. Repetitions are to be done consecutively. No weights.
Programme: 20–20–20

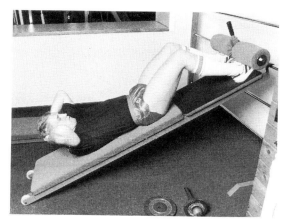

65 a,b   Trunk curls.

3   *Leg press or squats* (illustrations 66 a,b)
The back must be kept straight, so keep the head up. Bend knees to no more than 90°. Control the weights through the full range of movement.
Programme: 10–8–6

66 a,b   Leg press or squats.

4   *Dips* (illustrations 67 a,b)
Bend arms to right angles then straighten. Lock
ankles for greater stability.
Maximum: 10

5   *Lateral pulldown* (illustrations 68 a,b)
Wide grip, pull down behind the neck for maximum
mobility.
Programme: 10–8–6

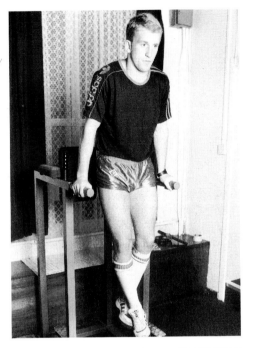

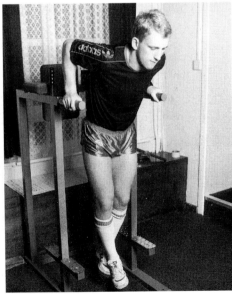

67 a,b   Dips.

68 a,b   Lateral pulldown.

6   *Upright row* (illustrations 69 a,b)
Keep the back straight throughout the exercise, lifting the weight with the biceps.
Programme: 10–8–6

7   *Front shoulder press* (illustrations 70 a,b)
With arms bent to 90°, push upwards until arms are extended. Keep control of the weights at all times and maintain the effort, with back straight.
Programme: 10–8–6

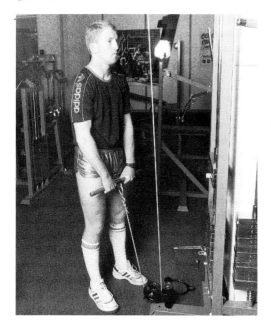

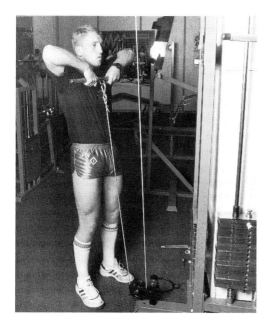

69 a,b   Upright row.

70 a,b   Front shoulder press.

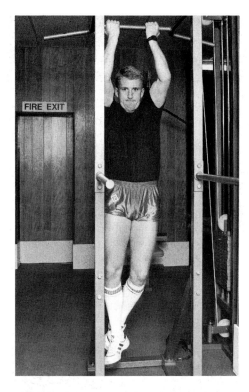

8 *Chins* (illustrations 71 a,b)
With weight on arms at all times, undergrasp and pull until eyes are above the bar, then down until arms are at 90°.
Maximum: 10

9 *Leg extension* (illustrations 72 a,b)
Sit with knees bent and chair supporting. Extend legs fully, hold, and bend slowly. Control the weight stack at all times.
Programme: 20–12

71 a,b Chins.

72 a,b Leg extensions.

10   *Leg curl* (illustrations 73 a,b)
Keeping abdomen and thighs in contact with the
bench throughout the movement, lift the weight by
bending legs to an angle of 90°.
Programme: 20–12

73 a,b   Leg curl.

74 a,b   Abdominal crunch.

11   *Abdominal crunch* (illustrations 74 a,b)
Secure legs and, holding harness, bend at the tummy.
Programme: 10–8–6

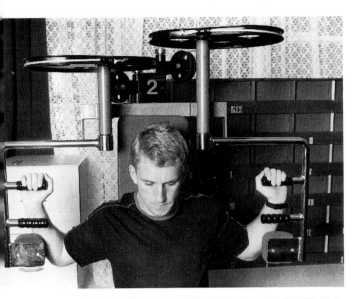

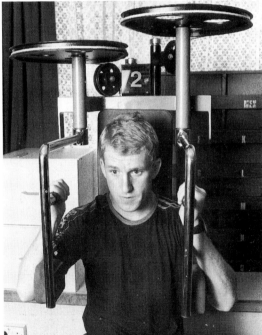

75 a,b   Peck deck.

12   *Peck deck* (illustrations 75 a,b)
Force the weights together, exerting pressure
through the palms.
Programme: 10–8–6

WEIGHT-TRAINING CHART

Name _____   — Warm up before commencing workout – Work to muscle failure – Increase weight after each set

Exercise	reps	sets	Week No. Date	Date	Date	Date	Week No. Date	Date	Date	Date	Week No. Date	Date	Date	Date
1. Bench Press	10–8–6	3												
2. Trunk Curls (Bent Leg)	20	3												
3. Leg Press or Squats	10–8–6	3												
4. Dips	10 max.	2												
5. Lateral Pulldown	10–8–6	3												
6. Upright Row	10–8–6	3												
7. Front Shoulder Press	10–8–6	3												
8. Chins	10 max.	2												
9. Leg Extension	20–12	2												
10. Leg Curl	20–12	2												
11. Abdominal Crunch	10–8–6	3												
12. Peck Deck	10–8–6	3												

You must work to develop strength – your technique and natural ability are not enough

Speed

1   Is speed necessary?
2   Understanding muscle composition
3   Reaction time
4   Strength and suppleness
5   Bounding and hopping
6   Harness running
7   Sprint training methods

76   Speed is an essential ingredient of success: Joe Lydon evades a despairing tackle by Wally Lewis (Australia) by sheer speed in this Wigan v Australians match in 1986.

1   IS SPEED NECESSARY?

Although speed is an essential ingredient of success for wingers, centres and half-backs, it is an advantage for all players to be fast. Speed takes the ball carrier into and through a gap in the defence. It enables the support player to be in position, and a player to follow and gather a kick; it helps the ball carrier to run round the opposition. When defending, speed prevents a player from being vulnerable. There are more players who have not fulfilled their potential because of a lack of speed than for any other reason, so it is common sense for all players whatever their position to increase their running speed.

2   UNDERSTANDING MUSCLE COMPOSITION

Although all muscles work in the same way, they do not contain muscle fibres of the same type. There are two distinct and definite types:

Slow-twitch muscles, which contract and relax slowly, but are resistant to fatigue, and
Fast-twitch muscles, which contract twice as quickly and produce far more force, but tire quickly.

Most individuals average 50% slow twitch and 50% fast twitch. Many marathon runners, however, average as many as 80% slow twitch while most sprinters have a high proportion of fast twitch.

Each and every muscle fibre in a single motor unit is of the same fibre type – slow or fast – and it is the motor nerve which actually dictates the characteristics of the muscle fibre. If the fibre is consistently recruited for slow work, it becomes a slow-twitch fibre. If it is recruited for fast movements it becomes a fast-twitch fibre. It is therefore important that most running is performed at speed. The long aerobic run is essential to develop the cardiovascular system, but once a high level of endurance has been established this run should be restricted to one per week.

The interval runs should be relatively short and fast, while passing drills should more often than not be performed at speed. More important, perhaps, is

that each player follows a sprint training programme which includes actual quality sprinting. In season, players should sprint every week.

3   REACTION TIME

Speed depends on reaction time, that is, the time that elapses between the senses recognizing a signal and feeding the information to the brain, and the brain passing on the stimulus to the muscles. American sprint coaches discovered that the reaction time of the sprinter, from hearing the starter's gun to the first movement of the muscle, reduced with starting practice, but that the greatest improvement occurred when the gun was used in training sessions. This is relevant to Rugby League, and reaction-time drills should be devised which are specific to the actual stimulus the players will receive in a game.

Each coach can devise his own drills, which may include a mixture of standing, walking, and rolling short sprints towards:

(a)   A dropped ball
(b)   A player hitting a shield and turning, making the ball available
(c)   The coach merely bringing the ball into view, and
(d)   Chasing a kick.

4   STRENGTH AND SUPPLENESS

Running speed, which is basically determined by length and frequency of stride, can be improved in a number of ways. Because the propulsive force is created by extension of the driving leg, this should receive some attention when training for sprinting. Any programme to improve this quality needs to be supplemented by carefully structured strength and flexibility work.

Training for speed work should also enable athletes to withstand the build up of high levels of lactic acid in the muscles, and increase efficiency in its removal, in circuit training, for example.

5 BOUNDING AND HOPPING

These have become popular methods of leg strengthening. The Americans call this type of work *plyometrics*.

Plyometric drills

1 Bouncing vertically on the spot for thirty to sixty seconds, using a double arm take-off at maximum speed.
2 Hop over distances of 30–100 metres using long maximum-force efforts. Use first one leg then the other, and both legs, utilizing both single- and double-arm action. There should be one to four repetitions.
3 Bounding, then hopping off one leg and both legs, using maximum speed over distances of 30–100 metres with one to four repetitions.

Typical bounding session

To be completed outside on grass, with all exercises completed over forty metres and repeated three times:

1 Continuous hopping, left foot
2 Continuous hopping, right foot
3 Continuous hop and step
4 Exaggerated strides with high knee lift
5 Continuous double-footed jumps.

6 HARNESS RUNNING

This involves a partner holding a harness round the runner and offering resistance by leaning back, but the resistance should not be so great that the running action is impaired. A long towel can serve the same purpose as the harness.

7 SPRINT TRAINING METHODS

(a) Sprint training should take place at the beginning of training, following a thorough warm-up and stretch, while the players are fresh.

(b) The rest between sprints should be long enough to enable full recovery.
(c) When sprinting, the individual should have the elements in his favour, a following wind, for example, a downhill slope and so on.

Training programmes

(a) 1 Adequate warm-up
    2 10 × 50 metres sprint
    3 3 × 150 metres
    4 Steady 15-minute run
    The sprints should be from a standing start and at maximum speed

(b) 1 Adequate warm-up
    2 5 × 40 metres sprint
    3 3 × 50 metres
    4 2 × 60 metres
    5 3 × 150 metres
    6 Steady 15-minute run
    All sprints should be at maximum speed. The 150-metres sprints should be from a standing start, while a rolling start should be used for the others

(c) 1 Adequate warm-up
    2 Pyramid sprints, all at maximum speed and from a standing start. Each sprint starts at the goal-line and finishes at
        (a) 22-metre line   × 4
        (b) half-way line   × 3
        (c) far 22-metre line   × 2
        (d) far goal-line   × 1
        (e) far 22-metre line   × 2
        (f) half-way line   × 3
        (g) 22-metre line   × 4
    3 Warm down

(d) 1 Adequate warm-up
    2 Positional sprints, as follows:

	metres			
Wingers and full-back (rolling start)	40	50	70	100
	5 →	3 →	2 →	1
	5 ←	3 ←	2 ←	1

	metres			
Half-backs and back row (standing start)	20	30	40	50
	7 →	5 →	3 →	1
	7 ←	5 ←	3 ←	1

	metres			
Centres (rolling start)	30	40	50	60
	8 →	6 →	4 →	2
	8 ←	6 ←	4 ←	2

	metres			
Front row (rolling start)	10	20	30	40
	6 →	4 →	3 →	2
3 Warm down	6 ←	4 ←	3 ←	2

(e)   *Reaction sprints*

Chain sprints.   The whole squad is spaced out at five-metre intervals round the perimeter of the pitch. Players start to jog, then when the coach places the ball on the floor they sprint to try to catch the player in front and continue sprinting until a the coach whistles. The length of sprint can be varied.

Follow-the-leader sprints.   Players in groups of four or five pass the ball without covering any ground. When the coach blows the whistle the player with the ball sprints downfield, and the rest of the group responds by supporting and taking a pass. Every player must handle the ball and this must be done at speed. The sprint continues until the coach again blows his whistle and the players return to passing without moving. The coach controls the practice with his whistle.

(f)   *Sprints, all at maximum speed from a running start,* thus:

5×20 metres, 4×30, 3×40, 2×50, 1×60, 2×150.

Bounding.

SUMMARY

(a)   *General training.*   Although each individual needs to include one long run in his weekly training programme, most running should be performed at speed to create a high percentage of fast-twitch fibres in the muscle.

(b)   *Sprinting.*   Quality sprints should be performed weekly.

(c)   *Reaction time drills.*   Should be specific to the game.

(d)   *Strength improvement.*   Each player should be involved in a heavy-weight training programme (see Chapter 5).

(e)   *Flexibility work.*   To supplement the weight training and increase stride length. Flexibility work should take place before and after every training session.

(f)   *Speed endurance exercises.*   These should be performed each week.

Annual conditioning programme

1   IMPORTANT CONSIDERATIONS

1   The players

The majority of Rugby League players are in full-time employment and are family men. Club training takes place during two evenings a week with match days at week-ends, and care must be taken that the players' training on non-club training days does not make unrealistic demands on their time. Whenever possible the extra sessions should be structured so that training can take place from home at the most convenient times. Home training can include the aerobic run, home muscular endurance circuit, and sprinting.

2   Staff

It is an advantage, when finances allow, for clubs to seek the assistance of well qualified physical educationalists. However, it must be remembered that physical conditioning is specific to the game, so the physical educationalists must be knowledgeable about Rugby League. If they are not, they should act as advisers only. At the same time it is important that the club's head coach makes positive attempts to understand the concept of conditioning, because the responsibility is his.

In order to monitor the training and recognize improvement, tests should be devised to measure suppleness, stamina, strength, and speed.

The tests should be performed periodically, the most important being:

1   *Before the season ends* – to establish training norms and to help in setting pre-season training goals for each player.
2   *The first club training session of the new season* – to monitor the gains made by each player since the end of the season.
3   *Prior to selection for the first game* – to motivate each player to train hard, and to reach the goals set for him by the coach in order to gain selection.

77 Ellery Hanley demonstrates a device which immobilizes the body and measures the flexibility of the hamstrings.

3 Examples of tests

(a) *Suppleness*
A simple device can be constructed which immobilizes the body and measures the flexibility of the hamstring (see illustration 77).

(b) *Stamina (aerobic)*
A strong case can be made for insisting that the players perform two long runs per season, perhaps of 10km or 5km. These are to be completed early in pre-season training time, before the trial games. Twelve-minute tests can then be monitored from time to time throughout the season.

(c) *Stamina (anaerobic)*
5 × 20-metre shuttle runs, or
8 × 200-metre interval runs.

(d) *Stamina (muscular)*
The combined scores of the number of press-ups, sit-ups and squat thrusts completed in one minute per exercise, the three exercises being performed one after the other without a rest.

(e) *Strength*

Sample strength test: for example, bench press and lateral pulldown. Record the maximum weight and repetition number; for example
     Bench press   100kg × 7
     Lateral pulldown   85kg × 6

(f) *Power*
Sergeant jump: the player stands sideways against a wall and stretches up as far as he can. Then with a standing jump he reaches as high as he can, and the distance above the mark is recorded.

(g) *Speed*
40-metre standing sprint.

4 Records

Records should be kept of all the tests. In this way each player's progress can be monitored throughout his time at the club, and norms can be established.

5 Training diary

Each player should be encouraged to keep a training diary. This is particularly relevant if the players are being encouraged to train in their own time. In this case diaries should be handed into the conditioner regularly so progress can be monitored and advice given.

2 BARLA UNDER-19 INTERNATIONAL PREPARATION, 1986

BARLA's Under-19 international squad trained throughout the summer of 1986, in preparation for the tour by the Australian Combined High Schools. Listed on the next page are the results of the August tests, completed before the final trial games. They give an indication of standards.

BARLA Under-19 International Preparation, 1986.   1.   *Stamina tests*

A	*Aerobic endurance – 10 km run, 19 August 1986*		
	Name	Position	Time (min./sec.)
1	Daintith	(FB)	39.11
2	O'Neil, K	(FB)	39.52
3	O'Brien	(SR)	40.15
4	O'Neil, I	(SO)	40.22
5	Hewer	(SH)	40.48
6	Brookfield	(H)	40.58
7	Randerson	(C)	41.20
8	Elgar	(SR)	41.49
9	Connelly	(FB)	41.56
10	Parle	(W)	42.01
11	Butt	(C)	42.03
12	Wilkinson	(C)	42.12
13	Lang	(SH)	42.21
14	Tunstall	(H)	42.33
15	Tennison	(W)	42.58
16	Makin	(SH)	43.16
17	Forber	(P)	43.18
18	Raw	(W)	44.24
19	Maplethorpe	(P)	44.37
20	Boothroyd	(W)	44.39
21	Croston	(SR)	45.53
22	Osman	(H)	46.19
23	Livesey	(SR)	47.26
24	Telford	(SR)	48.44
25	Moran	(LF)	51.49
26	Smales	(LF)	53.34

B   *Muscular endurance, 23 August 1986*
Combined score of press-ups, sit-ups and squat thrusts completed in three minutes without a rest, one minute being spent on each exercise.

	Name	Position	Total
1	Tennison	(W)	203
2	Lang	(SH)	191
3	Hewer	(SH)	190
4	Brookfield	(H)	189
5	Raw	(W)	187
6	Connelly	(FB)	184
7	Reid	(SO)	181
8	Maplethorpe	(P)	179
9	Osman	(H)	177
10	Butt	(C)	175
11	Makin	(SH)	173
12	Boothroyd	(W)	170
13	Livesey	(SR)	164
14	Wilkinson	(C)	163
15	Moran	(LF)	160
16	Randerson	(C)	157
17	Telford	(SR)	156
18	Parle	(W)	156
19	O'Brien	(SR)	154
20	O'Neil, I	(SO)	150
21	Horn	(P)	146
22	Smales	(LF)	146
23	O'Neil, K	(FB)	143
24	Turnstall	(H)	135
25	Phillips	(P)	125

Twelve-minute run grades

It is strongly recommended that, during the season, club training should allow for tests to be conducted comprising 12-minute continuous runs. Standards for these are as follows:

Over 3250 metres	Very good
3065–3249 metres	Good
2878–3064 metres	Average
2692–2877 metres	Poor
Below 2691 metres	Very poor

C *Anaerobic endurance, 23 August 1986*
8 × 200 metres on athletics track, with rest of $2\frac{1}{2}$ minutes between runs
(This took place twenty minutes after the muscular endurance test.)

The following completed the eight runs (times in seconds)

Name	Position	1	2	3	4	5	6	7	8
Hewer	SH	26.41	26.76	27.18	28.19	28.62	30.45	28.83	28.92
Parle	W	25.23	26.96	29.01	29.10	29.85	29.90	30.15	27.25
Tunstall	H	28.01	28.85	29.38	29.43	29.87	29.83	30.13	30.34
O'Neil, K	FB	27.30	28.57	30.53	30.31	30.04	31.69	33.24	28.75
Boothroyd	W	26.46	28.29	29.14	29.55	31.69	32.77	28.51	31.08
Maplethorpe	P	29.55	29.51	31.17	30.25	30.81	31.07	30.67	31.53
Lang	SH	28.30	29.55	29.14	31.01	30.62	33.75	32.55	30.75
O'Neil, I	SO	27.53	28.90	29.37	31.90	30.81	32.87	31.35	33.55
Brookfield	H	30.15	29.95	30.57	30.61	30.93	31.87	32.22	32.18
Connelly	FB	27.48	29.06	29.78	31.30	32.25	31.87	33.49	32.21
Osman	H	29.30	29.71	30.51	30.81	32.18	33.41	34.05	32.24
Moran	LF	28.81	28.53	30.86	30.29	32.58	33.22	35.13	34.60
Telford	SR	27.50	28.91	33.08	29.87	34.12	33.43	35.13	29.06

Ellery Hanley has always seen the need to back his skills with a programme of physical conditioning to gain or improve suppleness, stamina, strength and speed.

D   *Speed test*
Forty-metre standing start, 19 August 1986
(This took place after a warm-up and before the 10km test. Times in seconds.)

	Name	Position	Time
1	Wilkinson	(C)	5.24
2	Parle	(W)	5.33
3	Maloney	(W)	5.35
4	Raw	(W)	5.35
5	Reid	(SO)	5.44
6	Hewer	(SH)	5.46
7	Butt	(C)	5.47
8	Tennison	(W)	5.48
9	O'Brien	(SR)	5.52
10	Boothroyd	(W)	5.53
11	Livesey	(SR)	5.62
12	O'Neil, K	(FB)	5.62
13	Connelly	(FB)	5.64
14	Smales	(LF)	5.64
15	Moran	(LF)	5.65
16	Maplethorpe	(P)	5.71
17	Horn	(P)	5.71
18	Lang	(SH)	5.74
19	Telford	(SR)	5.77
20	Randerson	(C)	5.78
21	O'Neil, I	(SO)	5.79
22	Phillips	(P)	5.83
23	Tunstall	(H)	5.84
24	Makin	(SH)	5.84
25	Osman	(H)	5.86
26	Brookfield	(H)	6.16

3   PHYSICAL CONDITIONING PROGRAMME

(a)   Late season

1   The end of season can be hectic with some clubs being involved in more than one game per week, which often results in a reduction in the quality of training.

2   Clubs not involved in finals should consider encouraging their players to improve their levels of endurance so a weight-training programme can be started immediately the season ends.

3   It is also an advantage to test the players towards the end of the season so that out-of-season preparation can be measured. The players should be weighed and tests conducted to measure suppleness, stamina, strength, power and speed (see page 254).

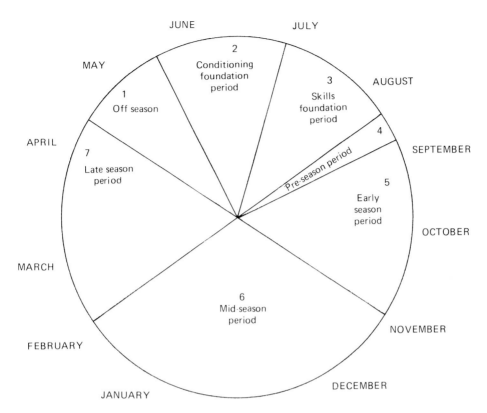

JUNE

JULY

MAY

2
Conditioning
foundation
period

3
Skills
foundation
period

AUGUST

1
Off season

4

APRIL

SEPTEMBER

7
Late season
period

Pre-season period

5
Early
season
period

OCTOBER

MARCH

6
Mid-season
period

FEBRUARY

NOVEMBER

JANUARY

DECEMBER

(b)   Off season: May

(a)   Many clubs do not finish the season until mid-May, so this period may be restricted to two weeks.

(b)   Players require a mental break, but that is no excuse for not performing three long runs a week of approximately thirty minutes duration, and one indoor circuit.

(c)   All training is performed away from the club in a free and relaxed atmosphere. The players are encouraged to complete training diaries which will be handed in at the first club training session.

(d)   The players should warm up before training, and warm down afterwards. Flexibility exercises should be included in both.

(e)   Care should be taken with diet.

(c)   Conditioning foundation period: June–mid-July

(a)   A six-week period with the players doing six sessions per week (total 36 sessions).

(b)   No club training, though facilities should be made available. Half the sessions (18) can be completed from home.

(c)   Content
(i)   *First two weeks.*
Weight training: players new to weights should perform three sessions a week (six in all) in which they develop muscular endurance and acquaint themselves with this form of training (low weights with high repetitions).

Players already on a weight-training programme should intensify their efforts, doing three heavy weight-training sessions each week.
Long runs: players should do three long runs a week. The first five are relaxed runs of around thirty minutes duration, but the final run should be timed over 1600 metres to establish standards for the anaerobic runs to be completed later.

(ii)   Remaining four weeks

Week 1

Two long runs   each of thirty minutes' duration

One long interval session   2 × 800 metres and 4 × 400 metres,
                                                                      using the 1600 metre-time to work out the
                                                                      target time and rest interval (see page 231)

Three heavy weight-training sessions

Week 2

One long run   thirty minutes.

One long interval session   2 × 800 metres, 4 × 400 metres

One of timed runs to establish training norms   1 × 50 metres, 1 × 100 metres,
                                                                     1 × 150 metres, 1 × 200 metres (see page 231)

Three heavy weight-training sessions

Week 3

One long run   thirty minutes

One long interval session   2 × 800 metres, 4 × 400 metres

One short interval session   8 × 100 metres, 2 × 150 metres, 2 × 200 metres
                                                                   using the time recorded in the previous
                                                                   session to work out target times and rest
                                                                   intervals (see page 231)

Three heavy weight-training sessions

Week 4

One long run   thirty minutes

Two short interval sessions   a) 8 × 100 metres, 2 × 150 metres
                                                                      2 × 200 metres

                                                                  b) 4 × 200 metres, 8 × 100 metres
                                                                      8 × 50 metres

Three heavy weight-training sessions

    Flexibility work should be included before and after each session
    Training diaries should record all training
    Training is structured to ensure the best use of the out-of-season period.

---

*(d)   Skills foundation period: mid-July–mid-
    August*

(a)   Club training should begin with identical tests to those conducted in the late season. Improvements should be noticeable in aerobic and muscular endurance.
    Each player should be weighed, and only those on a special diet should have increased weight.

(b)   The training programme is devised to reduce the amount of conditioning time necessary in the club sessions, so skill, decision-making and tactical coaching can take priority.

(c)   Physical conditioning continues with six sessions a week. These include:
    (i)   Two club + four additional sessions, or
    (ii)   Three club + three additional sessions.

(d)   *Content*
    (i)   Strength training – three heavy weight-training sessions a week, performed on non-club training days.
    (ii)   Long runs – one long run per week, performed on a non-club training day.
    (iii)   Interval training – should now be incorporated into club training. Some of the runs can be performed at speed, passing a ball.

Training Diary
Name Joe Saunders ....   Third week in July ....

Monday	Warm-up and flexibility Heavy weights session
Tuesday	Club training:	Warm-up and flexibility Skill Games awareness Interval training Defence circuit
Wednesday	Warm-up and flexibility Heavy weights session
Thursday	Club training:	Warm-up and flexibility Sprint session Skill Games awareness Tactics
Friday	Warm-up and flexibility Heavy weights session
Saturday	Rest day
Sunday	Warm-up and flexibility Thirty-minute run

Training Diary
Name Joe Saunders ....   Club Third week in August ....

Monday	Warm-up and flexibility Heavy weights session
Tuesday	Club training:	Flexibility Sprint Skill Games awareness Defence circuit
Wednesday	Warm-up and flexibility Heavy weights session
Thursday	Club training:	Warm-up and flexibility Skill and games awareness Tactics Interval training
Friday	Rest day
Saturday	Club training:	Warm-up and flexibility Sprint session Tactics
Sunday	Warm-up and flexibility Thirty-minute run

(iv) Muscular circuit training (defence circuit, for example) can now be performed at the club, and made specific to the game (see page 238).

(v) All players should perform at least one speed session a week.

(vi) *Club sessions*: because the players are training on non-club training days, and levels of fitness have already been increased since the end of the season, emphasis can be placed upon:
skill
decision-making, and
tactics.
Above is a typical training diary for mid-July.

(e) Pre-season: mid-August–end of August

(a) Players continue to train on non-club training days.

(b) Strength training is halved, with players now

performing three sessions a fortnight.

(c) Concentration on speed training.

(d) Club training concentrates on team play and tactics.

(e) Trial games may be played.

(f) Identical tests are completed prior to the first trial game. Gains should have been made in all areas since the end of season tests, and gains in strength, anaerobic endurance, and speed should be most apparent since the last tests completed in mid-July.

(Tests are completed during one week's training, spread over three sessions).

Above is a typical training diary for late August.

(f) Early season: September – November

(a) Aims: to produce a winning team, and to improve individual performances.

(b) Conditioning is only one ingredient of preparation, although an important one.

(i)   *Suppleness*:
to be improved, with flexibility exercises before and after each session.

(ii)   *Stamina*:
to be improved, achieving levels specific to the game

(a)   Long run – one thirty-minute run a week in own time.

(b)   Interval training – at least one session per week to supplement skill drills, which can also improve the anaerobic energy system.

(c)   Muscular endurance – to be specific to the game and incorporated into defence circuits.

(iii)   *Strength*:
to be maintained with three heavy-weight sessions every two weeks, in the player's own time.

(iv)   *Speed*:
the major priority, requiring at least two quality sessions per week.

(v)   *Skills, games awareness and tactics*:
to be developed in every club session.

(c)   The training programme will have to be modified to incorporate any mid-week fixtures.

(d)   Occasional physical tests.

A typical diary for a training fortnight in the September to November period is set out in the next column.

(g)   *Mid-season: November – February*

(a)   This period could be much influenced by the weather, and alternative indoor facilities may have to be used, affecting the training programme.

(b)   The players should continue to work six days a week, thereby ensuring that other aspects of the game can be developed in training.

(c)   As important cup games approach, an argument could be made for slightly reducing the quantity of training so players peak at the right time.

(d)   Occasional physical tests.

Training Diary
Name Joe Saunders .... Club October ....

Monday	Warm-up and flexibility Thirty-minute run
Tuesday	Club training: Warm-up and flexibility Skill Games awareness Interval training Defence circuit
Wednesday	Warm-up and flexibility Heavy weights session
Thursday	Club training: Warm-up and flexibility Sprints Skill Games awareness Tactics
Friday	Warm-up and flexibility Sprint session
Saturday	Rest
Sunday	Game
Monday	Warm-up and flexibility Heavy-weights session
Tuesday	Club training: Warm-up and flexibility Skill and Games awareness Tactics Interval training
Wednesday	Warm-up and flexibility Heavy weights session
Thursday	Club training: Warm-up and flexibility Speed Skill, Games awareness Tactics, Defence circuit
Friday	Warm-up and flexibility Twenty-minute run
Saturday	Rest
Sunday	Game

(h)   *Late season: February – May*

(a)   This period may be influenced by important games, and the playing of more than one game a week.

(b)   Training should be slightly tapered off before

important games, with emphasis on re-establishing endurance levels so the annual programme can begin immediately the season finishes.

(i) General points

(a) It is emphasized that this is an ideal system, completely dependent upon the attitude of the players.

(b) If standards of British Rugby League are to improve, the system should be adopted by all professional clubs and top youth teams.

(c) Amateur clubs with standards not quite so high should modify the system, but always ensure that their players are fit enough to play the game, or injuries will result.

(d) Illness, injury, and holiday will cause individual fitness schedules to be modified.

Message to administration

There is little doubt that physical conditioning standards and team preparation would be greatly improved if there was a reduction in the number of fixtures played each season by the leading clubs. Similarly, players need a close season of at least four months for adequate gains to be made in physical conditioning standards.

Kevin Beardmore scores a try against Hull. A game-plan gives each player and the team specific goals which are relatively easy to obtain and, when achieved, will help to produce victory.

SECTION 7

PREPARATION OF THE TEAM

The coach is responsible for improving the performance of each of his players. Match statistics and a detailed study of the game on video will greatly help his analysis.

The game plan

1   DEFINITION

Some teams go on to a pitch without a game plan. They are aware that to win they must score more points than the opposition – but that is the only aim they have. When they lose and things start to fall apart, the coaching and information the players receive is often not specific enough for improvement to be possible.

A game plan gives each player and the team specific goals which are relatively easy to attain, and when achieved will help to produce victory.

Limitations

The game plan is the last part of preparation – the icing on the cake. Success depends on the coaching that has taken place before the game plan is introduced, particularly the four principles of play – control of the ball, defence, support play and kicking – discussed in Section 5.

The coach who develops his game plan without first building proper foundations will struggle for success and wonder why the team:

(a)   Appears incapable of securing positions on the field from which they can put on set pieces – because of a poor kicking game and a poor defence.

(b)   Drop so much ball in the build-up to the set pieces because of poor control of the ball.

(c)   Play set pieces which often split the first line of defence only to fall to a last-ditch tackle because of poor support play.

(d)   Score points but still lose the game because they have a poor defence.

2   BUILDING UP THE STOCKPILE

1   Principles of play:

Because the principles of play are the basis of the game plan, it is essential for the coach to develop the following skills:

A   An aggressive defence   which is well organized, moves forward, tackles hard, and has players with good technique and a high work rate.

B   An intelligent kicking game   using long punts, line kicks, bombs and grubbers into the in-goal area, all combined with a fast determined chase.

C   Control of the ball   with efficient scrummaging, reduction in penalties, and strong, determined, straight running, eliminating handling errors.

D   Support   with continuation of attack and support at every play.

2   Strong, aggressive running

The team must send strong, aggressive runners at the opposition. These will gain ground, tire the tacklers, pressurize the opposition into defensive errors; and physically dominate the opposition.

Timing and direction of the runs is important, particularly when attacking close to the play-the-ball. It is essential that ground is gained.
(a) As one runner is tackled the next should be in position and ready to hit the defensive line from a quick play-the-ball.
(b) The runners should hit the line straight and not angle across field. When they run straight they will make more ground, be more difficult to tackle, and be easier to support.
(c) The runners should receive a quick pass delivered almost straight to enable them to cross the gain-line and make ground.

3   Continuous attacks

The team, when in possession, should have the ability to attack in numbers anywhere on the field of play. This depends on its ability to:

1   Move the ball quickly along the line
2   Mount well-supported attacks around the play-the-ball
3   Attack the blind side, and
4   Have more players around the ball than the opposition (overload).

The team must also be able to string together six plays in order to exert continuous pressure.

The coach may have a problem in ensuring that every drive is well supported, but isolated forages are so negative that a solution must be found. The backs can help to solve the problem. All of them can adopt positions of support, especially the full-back, halves and centres. A useful play is for the centre on the short side to track the ball infield, supporting every handler. Garry Schofield, the Great Britain centre, is adept at this art.

By deploying his troops and using every player to the full, the coach should be able to ensure that every drive in a series of attacks has support.

4   Set pieces

Most coaches will have a collection of carefully worked out set pieces capable of testing even the best organized defences, many of which have been referred to in previous chapters.

Astute coaches, always keen to improve, will be ready to modify and extend their repertoire. They will find studying moves used by others, from both home and abroad, helpful, and this process has been greatly assisted by the use of videos. The coach, however, should never underestimate his own originality, and will find the time he spends devising his own moves well worth while. He has the advantage of knowing his own players so well that he will be able to make the best use of the strengths within his own team.

Each coach should have a collection of plays for every eventuality. He should, for example, have moves:

1   From acting half-back capable of breaking all the varied forms of marker-defences
2   To be used at different places in the line, for example, from first receiver, second receiver, midfield, wide and blind
3   From a scrum to test defences in different areas of the pitch
4   To be used in the opponents' 22-metre area, and others to be used in different parts of the pitch.

Any team which has a wide collection of attacking options can afford to be selective, using those which the coach feels will be best suited to the state of the game at any given moment, to the strength or weakness of the opposition, to injuries to his own team or to the opposition, and so on.

5   Patterns of play

When developing set pieces from a tap or scrum, it is an advantage to string together four or five plays to be used one after the other. It is unlikely that one isolated set piece is going to result in a try, but it can cause the opponents' defence to be moved about. By anticipating this reaction, an astute coach will be able to plan an attack from the next play-the-ball, and perhaps by working on this principle develop a series of attacks for all six plays.

An additional advantage of this system is that all thirteen players will be fully aware of which way the ball is going to move, and from where the next attack will be launched. Anticipation will lead the players to adopt ideal positions of support.

A disadvantage is that the opposition's defence may not react in the way the coach anticipated. This could result, for instance, in the team moving the ball out to the open side into a strongly defended area when an attack down the blind side would have enjoyed more favourable results. This disadvantage can quite easily be nullified by encouraging the players to read the game, and allowing them to overrule any pattern of play if the situation demands it.

Great Britain, in the New Zealand Test series in 1985, had several patterns of six plays to use immediately they received the ball, which enabled the players quickly to combine into a unit. A call immediately possession was secured by Dave Watkinson, Lee Crooks or Deryck Fox allowed the entire team to be aware of the direction of attack for the next six plays. The players, however, were encouraged to read the game and change the pattern by using their own initiative. The overriding call was 'GB', which resulted in the play being cancelled and the ball being passed quickly to the player who had 'called'. The rest of the team, with this knowledge, were able to adopt positions of support around the caller.

6   Use of key players

It is most important to point out at this stage that a game plan should in no way restrict individual flair. Coaches at all times should be encouraged to play to the strengths of the individuals in their squad. Set pieces should not only help in moving the ball to the match winners as often as possible, but also give them the ball in positions and situations in which they are most dangerous.

Although it is usually the coach – perhaps in consultation with his key players – who devises the set pieces, it should be fully realized that it is the players who carry them out. Once the players enter the arena they are in full control, and the coach (unless he is a player-coach of course) becomes a helpless bystander.

Key players fall into two categories: (a) brilliant individuals, and (b) key strategic decision-makers.

78 Ellery Hanley scored the remarkable number of sixty-three tries during the 1986–87 season and proved himself to be one of the greatest Rugby League players of all time.

(a)   Brilliant individuals

It is important that those devising the tactical plan are fully aware of the strengths and weaknesses of the team, and use the team's strengths to the full. A team with devastating runners out wide needs a game plan which not only gives them a lot of ball, but gives them ball at the right time and in the right place. Ellery Hanley's impressive total of sixty-three tries in the 1986–87 season was greatly helped by his coach Graham Lowe, who in his first season at Wigan devised plays which gave Hanley as much ball as possible, and even moved him to loose forward to give him greater freedom.

(b)   Key strategic decision-makers

It has already been emphasized that the success of the game plan is very much dependent upon the players on the pitch. Although the coach devises the game plan, the players carry it out. It is essential, therefore, that they – particularly the key strategical decision-makers – fully understand the game plan and the logic behind it.

Time in training has to be spent in talking, discussing, and educating the players to help them make correct decisions. Each game has to be closely studied, and the decisions made analysed, so the process of improvement can continue.

Although Rugby League is a game in which all the players have to make decisions, it requires a key player or players to control the game plan. It is usual for one of the key players to operate close to the action, often at first receiver, with the duty of organizing the attack and directing it to the correct quarter. This player must not only be aware of all the possible moves and set pieces at his disposal, and fully understand the game plan for each match, but above all must have the ability to read the opposition. It is only by watching the opposition closely that he will become aware of their weakness and understand when and where to strike.

Perhaps it is also worth considering having another key player out wide, to ensure that the team vary

79 Some of the time in training has to be spent talking, educating players to make correct decisions, to take the right options, on the field. The author discusses a point with some members of the Great Britain squad at the Lilleshall National Sport Centre in the summer of 1986.

their tactics and do not become too involved with attacks close to the ruck.

3   ANALYSIS

1   Opposition

An in-depth study of the opposition will help to determine the game plan. Coaches who are experienced within any one league structure will be able to build up information on all the other clubs, updated after every fixture.

English soccer clubs, particularly those in the first and second divisions, employ scouts who each week analyse the next week's opposition. They send a report to the manager giving him a run-down on:

1   Players, their strengths and weaknesses
2   Formations and patterns of play
3   Set pieces, and
4   Any other useful information.

Teams playing within the Sydney competition in Australia, by taking advantage of the league's decision to video all three graded competitions, are able to take the analysis much further. The coaches not only receive video recordings of their own games, but also those of the next week's opponents. The use of these videos enables them to do an in-depth study of each team, and provides all the information necessary to compile a strategic plan for each game. Video analysis of the opposition, and the game plan that results, may seem sophisticated but even so Australian Rugby League is still a decade behind American football.

American football clubs employ a team of technicians whose only function is to analyse the opposition in fine detail. They usually work three weeks in advance of the fixture, and by using 16 mm film of all the matches are not only able to scrutinize the action in fine detail, but can cut the film and present to the coaches edited rolls which depict clearly the key points of play. This is not all: the information is then processed and fed into a computer which is able to predict the tactics and game plan the opposition will use, and their expected reaction to game patterns and set pieces.

Whether Rugby League wants to go that far is open to debate, but no doubt it is an advantage to have a detailed breakdown of the opposition when devising the game plan.

Necessary information will probably include:

1   Type of marker-defence
2   Position adopted by the full-back
3   The use of a sweeper, and reaction to a chip or grubber-kick
4   Speed of the defensive line
5   Type of kicking game
6   Key moves
7   Information on key players
8   Pattern of plays, and
9   Attitude of the team.

2   Ground

Analysis of the playing area will occasionally affect tactics, particularly when playing on a ground which has unusual characteristics. Consideration may have to be given to:

(a)   Width of the pitch
(b)   Depth of the in-goal area
(c)   Slope, and
(d)   Any unusual condition – i.e. muddy, very hard, and so on.

This may be particularly appropriate for the amateur or schools coach whose team wins through to a final played on a senior ground, which may be much wider than usual. When this occurs the coach should consider modifying his training programme to use an area of similar dimensions, which may necessitate making a wide area using the length of their home pitch. Conditions underfoot are also important, and it is essential for players to have a collection of various types of stud. There are few things worse than using studs of a maximum length on bone-hard ground, or, for that matter, short studs in mud.

3   Weather

Weather conditions occasionally affect tactics. A strong wind, particularly when blowing directly downfield, will cause the game plan to be modified for each half.

Unusually high temperatures will also affect strategy, in games played early and in late season. So too will bright sunshine, particularly when the sun is low and behind one of the posts.

It is therefore always an advantage to inspect the playing surface and weather conditions directly before kick-off.

4   The referee

Although referees are supposed to enforce the rules as laid down in the laws of the game, some of them adopt their own interpretations while others have pet dislikes. This is particularly prevalent in games in Britain refereed by foreign officials, which sometimes happens in league matches as well as in internationals. Maurice Bamford, the former Great Britain coach, and his coaching team were taken by surprise during the first Kiwi Test in 1986 when the Australian referee, Barry Gomersall, had a different interpretation from British referees on the length of time a tackled player could be held on the ground. Reports from Australia suggested that their administration was severe on 'holding down', yet Mr Gomersall – who refereed the game excellently – allowed players to hold down for much longer than was normal in Britain.

While Britain quickly released the tackled player, New Zealand held him down until their defensive line had formed. They thus had an advantage which they exploited to the full, and indeed scored two tries directly as a result of a fast play-the-ball. Specific tackle practises were therefore devised before the second Test, which encouraged holding down in the tackle, and the British defence improved markedly with a direct bearing on their victory.

Different interpretations from overseas officials is understandable, but difficult to justify from British referees. Nevertheless, differences occur. Some referees, for example, stand over the tackled player and allow the defence to creep up within the permitted five metres, while others insist that the defence retires

almost ten metres. Obviously the variation in distance has a direct effect on the way the game is played. Other referees have pet dislikes, and penalize certain offences more harshly than their colleagues. Thus, it is often desirable for the coach to learn something about the match officials before devising his game plan.

5   Big-match pressure

Playing in a cup final, particularly at Wembley, or in some other big game, often affects players and the way they react on the pitch. These are further points to consider when devising tactics, particularly for teams possessing a number of inexperienced players.

4   EXAMPLES

When all points have been considered, the coach is in a position to devise a plan of campaign which will assist his team in winning the game. How detailed the plan is will depend upon the philosophy of the coach and the ability of his team to follow the directions laid down.

Although information on the opposition is helpful, it is recommended that the coach always adopts a positive approach to the match, spending more time on developing the strengths of his own team than worrying about those of the opposition. The best way to nullify an outstanding attacker is to give him problems on defence.

Pressure   has to be the key to success. The team must aim to pressurize the opposition at every opportunity, both with and without possession.

Field position   is also a vital consideration. The team which successfully plays the majority of the game in their opponents' half of the pitch will have a decided advantage. When devising the plan, therefore, it is often a help to divide the pitch into quarters.

One suggestion may be:

Own '22'

1   Run hard and straight from acting half-back and off acting half-back

2   Secure centre-field position
3   Kick long
4   Chase fast.

22 to half-way

1   Run hard and straight off acting half-back or first receiver
2   Support
3   Kick
4   Chase fast.

Half-way to opposition's 22

1   Use up the tackle period
2   Secure centre-field position early in the tackle period
3   Attack the weakly defended side with a numerical advantage
4   Support every play
5   Kick for a return of possession.

Opposition's 22

1   Use set moves
2   Attack with five plays
3   Grubber into in-goal on the sixth to regain possession.

An additional consideration may be to divide the game into time zones, perhaps paying particular attention to the first twenty minutes. Instructions in that time may be:

1   Gain physical domination
2   Hold the ball tight – control the ball
3   Use the best players around the play-the-ball
4   Control the ball for six plays
5   Kick on the last.

Many coaches will adopt a far broader plan, which may be a combination of some of the points already made, for example:

1   Discipline to ensure that no penalties are given away
2   Play the game in the opponents' half
3   Control the ball when in the opponents' half
4   Physically dominate
5   Pressurize the opponents' key players
6   Bomb the full-back early – destroy his game
7   For the last twenty minutes – when opposition is tired – run the ball.

Half-time

Once the players are on the pitch they control their own destiny, and must understand the tactics to be used. Half-time gives the coach the only real opportunity he has of changing the game plan. It is, therefore, important that he observes the first half clinically, carefully observing and analysing play. This is impossible if he becomes overexcited, losing his composure and concentration.

Motivation, statistics and video analysis

1 Match day
2 Motivation
3 Match statistics
4 Video analysis

1 MATCH DAY

Match day is the most important day of the week.

For the coach, it is the day that all his hopes, fears and aspirations materialize – the day his work stands up to be counted for all to see. Once the game has started, all the week's planning and preparation depends on the players. It is important that they do not let him down: every one must go out and perform to the best of his ability, so the coach's skill in motivating them is of vital importance.

For the players it is essential that all the year's preparation is channelled into match performance. The dedication required to complete those long lonely runs, the training sessions in the weights room and on the athletics track, the skills work and tactical preparation, all the sweat, blood and tears are of little value if they do not give their all in the game.

It is the coach's duty to help them channel their efforts. During the game he should observe the action and make a detailed analysis of performance. Half-time allows him a brief opportunity to alter the team's tactics and give individual coaching tips to his players.

It is difficult for the coach to fulfil this role if he becomes overexcited or too involved with the emotions of the game. For this reason, more coaches are leaving the sanctuary of the players' bench for the more elevated position of the gantry or top of the stand. The coach should carefully analyse the first half, checking in particular

(a) Whether the team is playing to his instructions
(b) That his pre-match instructions were correct
(c) The individual performances of his own players, and
(d) The weaknesses and strengths of the opposition.

The analysis should be continued after the game. The coach is responsible for improving each of his player's individual performances in addition to that of the whole team. Match statistics and a detailed study of the game on video will greatly help his analysis.

2   MOTIVATION

The coach must motivate his players, and bring each individual to the optimum level of arousal so that they play to the very best of their ability. He should ensure that each player is:

1   Confident of his own ability
2   Confident of the team's ability
3   Conversant with the role he has to play in the game, and
4   Determined to give maximum commitment.

For several years coaches have been aware that motivation is an individual process, and that it is almost impossible to motivate by a team talk alone. Results are better if motivation is a long-term process. It can have at least three stages: a long-term target identified at the beginning of the season, an intermediate level established at the beginning of the week, and a final injection close to kick-off.

A   Long-term motivation

Targets should be identified for the team and for each individual player immediately before the start of the season. These targets should be demanding but realistic, and may have to be modified as the season progresses. The target for the team may be a cup-final appearance, a position in the top eight, promotion, or simply a mid-table position.

The individual may set himself a number of targets, which might include international selection, thirty or more tries in the season, or a permanent place in the top three of the team's tackle count. At the beginning of the season it is often a good idea for each player to identify and write down three individual targets. This may be performed as part of a confidential psychological test, of which the player and coaching staff keep a copy for reference. Players should then be encouraged to refer to these targets from time to time, particularly in individual motivation talks with the coach.

B   Intermediate motivation

Motivation for the coming game should begin as early in the week as possible. It is often best to start with analysis of the previous game, in an effort to improve individual and team performance. Gradually, attention turns to the next fixture, and each player sets himelf new targets. A player who dropped an unusual amount of ball in the last game, may have as one of his targets 'control of the ball'. It is important that the target is positive – 'hold the ball firmly in the tackle' – rather than the negative 'don't drop it'. Other targets may include making more tackles when marker than in the last match, supporting the ball better, and so on.

C   Short-term motivation

As the game approaches each player's level of arousal is brought to the optimum level. This is comfortably achieved when in camp before a big match by personal discussion, but may be restricted in a normal fixture by lack of time. The coach journey can be used before away fixtures, otherwise discussion will have to be brief and restricted to individual dressing-room chats before the game and during the last training session of the week.

Players' meetings and discussions

Motivation can often be achieved by a players' meeting. The best time for this is during the week's first training session when the last game is usually discussed and before concentration moves to the coming fixture. The best results are achieved when the atmosphere encourages the players to take part in the discussion, although the coach must always be in charge.

Such discussions when conducted sensibly can:

1   Foster team spirit
2   Establish a close relationship between playing and coaching staff
3   Make the coach aware of the players' opinions of the game
4   Underline and identify the major coaching points.

It is important at these meetings for the coach to be aware of all the incidents and occurrences of the game. Any bluff will immediately be seen through, which is perhaps another reason why statistics and a detailed study of the match video are essential.

Statistics

The use of statistics can identify specific targets for every player, motivating them to make a greater effort. For example, from a series of tackle counts an average tackle count per player can be arrived at. Each player is then motivated to top his average tackle count in the game. A similar record of the tackles made by the marker defence can motivate the team to improve their defence around the vital play-the-ball area.

Video

Players need to acquire high levels of self-confidence, and this can be increased by recording on video outstanding individual performances. Each player should be encouraged to copy his own outstanding efforts onto video: these, watched prior to the game, help to develop self-confidence.

3   MATCH STATISTICS

It is essential for the coach to give the game his full concentration so he should leave the compiling of statistics to others. Most clubs will have officials or spectators willing to do this in return for free match admission or some other small reward.

To guarantee uniformity, the same people should be used for each game. This is important because statistics from several games will be required in order to make comparisons.

Statistics to be used at half-time should be brief, simple and easily understood. A too detailed analysis is likely to cause confusion.

Once compiled, the statistics provide a useful coaching aid and should be used intelligently. Tackle counts and so on, pinned to the dressing-room wall, without either explanation or discussion, are of little value. Most areas of play can be analysed by statistics so it is the decision of the coach which areas of performance he wishes to concentrate upon. The most common are:

1   Possession count
2   Tackle count, that is, an analysis of defensive work rate
3   Ball-carrying count – an analysis of offensive work rate – and
4   Field position.

1   Possession count

The importance of possession in deciding the outcome of the game has been emphasized earlier in the book, and it appears logical to tabulate this aspect of play.

Scrums, penalties, use of possession, and results of the opposition's handling mistakes can all be tabulated by one statistician, using a simple key, as on Statistics sheet A: Possession Count, which is set out on the opposite page.

Statistics Sheet A

Possession Count

Scrums							Penalties		
Head	Feed	Win					Against	Cause	Player
1			1	2	3	4	1		
2							2		
3							3		
4			5	6	7	8	4		
5							5		
6							6		
7			9	10	11	12	7		
8							8		
9							9		
10			13	14	15	16	10		
11							11		
12							12		
13			17	18	19	20	13		
14							14		
15							15		
16			21	22	23	24	16		
17							17		
18							18		
19			25	26	27	28	19		
20							20		
21							21		

Total
F ......
A ......
Against Head
F ......
A ......
Penalties

Summary
1
2
3
4
5
6

Penalties
F ......
A ......

Total		Errors

Results of Opposition's Handling Errors

1	4	7	10	13
2	5	8	11	14
3	6	9	12	15

Total	Won

.... v

Date .... First/Second Half

Statistics Sheet B

Possession Count

GREAT BRITAIN v AUSTRALIA.
FIRST TEST

Scrums										Penalties		
Head	Feed	Win								Against	Cause	Player
1 Gb	Gb	A	1 ✓	2 4 v	3 4 ✓	4 2 ✗				1 A	OS	
2 Gb	GB	GB	2 Penalty GB	Penalty GB	Penalty GB	P LB 10				2 A	OBS	
3 GB	Gb	Pen A								3 A	Punch	
4 A	A	Pen A	5 1 ✗	6 2 ✗	7 2 ✗	8 4 ✓				4 GB	LT	4
5 GB	GB	GB	LB 4	LB 13	LB 10	to touch 1				5 A	Foot	
6 Gb	GB	Pen A								6 GB	OBS	6
7 A	A	A	9 5 ✓	10 2 ✗	11 4 ✗	12 4 ✓				7 GB	OS	7
8 A	GB	GB	K-Downtown 11	K-offbounds 11	LB 10	K to touch 1				8 GB	Punch	10*
9 GB	A	Pen GB								9 GB	Punch	8
10 A	A	A	13 5 ✓	14 2 ✗	15	16				10		
11			K-Bomb 7	LB 8						11		
12										12		
13			17	18	19	20				13		
14										14		
15										15		
16			21	22	23	24				16		
17										17		
18										18		
19			25	26	27	28				19		
20										20		
21										21		

Total	Summary		tackle Periods : 14	Penalties
F ..3.	1 × 1 : 1		Acceptable (v) : 7	F 4
A ..3.	2 × 6 : 12		Unacceptable (x) : 7	A .5.
Against Head (Feed	3 × 0 : 0			
F ..0.	4 × 5 : 20		Possible Plays : 84	* Sin Bin
A ..1.	5 × 2 : 10		Actual : 43	
Penalties	6 × 0 : 0			OS: offside
F. 1	43			
A. 3.				OBS: obstruction
	Total 14		Errors 7 / 50%	

Results of Opposition's Handling Errors					
1 ✗	4 ✓ (7).	7	10	13	
2 ✗	5	8	11	14	
3 ✗	6	9	12	15	

Total 4	Won 1

OLD TRAFFORD v

Date .....25·10·86..................... First/~~Second~~ Half

A   Scrums

Every scrum is recorded. The end-of-half summary identifies:

Total	won and lost
Against head, and feed	won and lost
Scrum penalties	won and lost

The hooker in particular will value this information, and the entire pack and scrum-half can be motivated by it. The statistics will identify any problems needing additional coaching.

B   Penalties

Similarly, every penalty is recorded identifying:

Total	for and against
Reason for the penalty	
Player responsible	

Each team should not only try to concede less penalties than the opposition, but to concede fewer penalties each game. (The need for uniform decisions by match officials must be stressed here.)

C   Use of possession

A simple analysis in the central column shows how the team uses possession. The record shows:

(i)   The number of tackles in which possession was lost – one to six
(ii)   The player responsible – by recording his shirt number
(iii)   The reason (LB = lost ball, K = kick, and so on)

The summary shows the number of tackles used and the number of handling errors made. The aim in each game is to make fewer errors, and these are best shown as a percentage of the total tackle period – so with twenty tackle periods and five errors, the successful percentage rate is 75%:

D   Results of opposition's handling errors

The number of handling errors by the opposition is noted at the bottom of the analysis sheet. A cross (x)

signifies that the error resulted in a scrum, while a tick ($\sqrt{}$) signifies possession gained. The number in brackets after the tick identifies the player who gains possession.

The aim each week is to force the opposition into a greater number of errors, and to win an increasing percentage of loose balls.

E   Using the possession count

Statistics sheet B, set out on the opposite page, is the official record of the first half of the first Whitbread Trophy Test between Great Britain and Australia, played at Old Trafford on 25 October 1986. It identifies:

(a)   *Scrums*

Wins	GB	3	Australia	3
Against head	GB	1	Australia	1
Scrum penalties	GB	1	Australia	3

(b)   *Penalties*   ⸐GB   4   Australia   5

(c)   *Use of possession by Great Britain*
      Number of possession periods: 14
      Possession used in an acceptable way:
        receive penalties + 3; acceptable kicks + 4
      Possession squandered
        lost balls + 6; unacceptable kick + 1
      Success rate: 7/14 or 50%
      Total plays possible: 14 × 6 = 84
      Plays used   46

(d)   *Australian errors*
      Errors in possession: 4
      GB obtained possession: 1 or 25%

Conclusions

(a)   GB making far too many handling errors. The aim should be 75%, compared with GB's 50%.
(b)   GB losing possession early in tackle count.
(c)   GB conceding too many scrum penalties (2 for feeding).

These statistics not only identify errors, thereby assisting coaches to plan future coaching sessions, but can also help to motivate players to improve individual performances.

Statistics Sheet C

Tackle Count

Date	25·10·86				FIRST TEST	Venue	OLD TRAFFORD			
	GREAT BRITAIN					v	AUSTRALIA			

	Name	Tackle Misses			Tackles	Doubles Trebles			Total
1	LYDON	I	3		Ж I	D	6		11
		II			Ж	T	5		
2	MARCHANT				ЖI		3		3
							0		
3	SCHOFIELD	I	3		Ж II	DD	7		13
		II			Ж I	D	6		
4	HAWLEY	I	1		Ж Ж I	DD	11		15
					IIII	D	4		
5	GILL				III		3		3
							0		
6	MYLER	I	1		Ж I	DD	6		14
					Ж III	D	8		
7	FOX		1		III		3		8
		I			Ж		5		
8	WARD	II	5		Ж Ж Ж I	DD	16		20
		III			IIII		4		
9	WATKINSON		2		Ж Ж IIII	DD	14		30
		II			Ж Ж Ж I	DDD	16		
10	FIELDHOUSE		2		Ж Ж II	DT	12		20
		II			Ж III		8		
11	CROOKS *				Ж Ж Ж III	DDT DD	18		28
					Ж Ж	DDDT	10		
12	POTTER	I	2		Ж Ж Ж IIII	DT DDT	19		28
		I			Ж IIII	DD	9		
13	GOODWAY				Ж III	D	8		23
					Ж Ж Ж	DDDD	15		
14	EDWARDS								
15	PLATT								

* Sin Bin

Time in possession

Stop watches recording the length of time each team controls the ball provide valuable information to be used alongside the possession count statistics. The watch should be running all the time a team is capable of scoring, that is, when

(a) Carrying the ball
(b) Passing the ball, or
(c) Playing the ball.

Both watches stop when

(a) The ball is kicked (until caught)
(b) The ball is out of play (until the restart)
(c) At a scrum (until a team is in possession)
(d) At a penalty (until the tap, or restart kick, has been caught)
(e) When a try is scored (until the restart kick has been caught).

Two watches are required, one for each team, but both can be operated by the same statistician.

The aim should be to increase the time one's team is in possession, and to decrease the time the opposition is in possession. The statistics for the first half of the Old Trafford Test underlined Britain's problem:

Great Britain in possession = 6 min. 19 sec.
Australia in possession   = 8 min. 06 sec.
(Incidentally, these times are unusually low.)

3   Tackle count – analysis of work rate on defence

The best way of monitoring a team's defensive commitment is to carry out a tackle count, similar to the Statistics sheet C: Tackle Count, set out on the opposite page.

Once again uniformity is important. Ideally the same two statisticians should be used at every game, with one recording and the other calling. Each should be clear as to what the coach believes should constitute a tackle. The tackle count provides the dual function of identifying each player's commitment, while motivating him to make a greater effort. It is also necessary for teams using a double-marker system to measure its efficiency (by counting the number of tackles made by the marker).

Tackles missed is an equally important statistic. The aim of each team is to:

(a) Reduce the number of missed tackles
(b) Increase the number of doubles and trebles (tackles from the marker)
(c) Reduce the number of team tackles (by better control of the ball).

Certainly defence in Britain improved during the mid-1980s, but coaches need to be aware of the danger of some players increasing their work rate on defence at the expense of their eagerness to carry up the ball when in possession. An example occurred in the second Whitbread Test against Australia, at Elland Road in 1986, when the player who topped the tackle count handled the ball on only six occasions throughout the entire game. Such a commitment is not acceptable. The players must be determined to work hard throughout the game, both when in possession and defending.

It is therefore sometimes necessary to tabulate each player's work rate when in possession of the ball.

4   Ball-carrying count – analysis of offensive work rate

A simple record of each play-the-ball can be compiled by a statistician during the game, or by a study of the after-match video. At every play-the-ball, the shirt numbers of the players who handle are listed with a circle round those who make ground.

The Statistics sheet D: Ball-carrying Count, set out on the following page, is an extract from part of the first Whitbread Test between Great Britain and Australia played at Old Trafford in 1986.

Ball-carrying count

1   Kick-off
                  12
                  9 - 7 - 11
                  Pen. to GB

Australia in possession

2   Scrum
                  7 - 5
                  6 - 4
                  13
                  3 - 7 - 1 - 6 - 5
                  Pen. to GB

---

3   Tap
                  9 - 8
                  7 - 10 - 4
                  1 - 7 - 12
                  9 - 7 - 11
                  Pen. to GB

---

4   Receive 22m DK
                  1
                  12 - 7 - 11 - 10 LB

Australia in possession

5   Receive line DK
                  6 - 4 LB

Australia in possession

6   Scrum
                  7
                  9 - 11 - 6 - 13 LB

Australia in possession

7   Tap
                  7 - 9 - 11 - 7
                  9 - 11 - 13 - 10 LB

Australia in possession

8   Interception
                  7
                  9 - 8
                  9 - 7 - 11
                  9 - 1 K (into touch)

5   Work summary sheet

The ball-carrying analysis can be summarized on a work summary sheet – Statistics sheet E – which identifies each player's contribution during the team's offensive play. It is set out on the following page.

This is a summary of

1   Tackle Count   – Statistics sheet C
2   Ball-carrying Count – Statistics sheet D

It provides a breakdown of each player's contribution during the game, identifying handling, kicking, tackling and all errors. Thus, his total work rate is recorded, apart from running off the ball.

6   Field position

A game plan, which incorporates obtaining field position with the objective of playing the majority of the match in the opponents' half of the pitch, requires analysis. Did the team obtain their objective, and furthermore did the objective contribute to the match result?

By marking each play-the-ball on a sheet of paper divided into quarters, simple statistics tabulate the result.

Statistics sheet F: Field Positions, set out on page 286, is the summary of the first Test v. Australia, played at Old Trafford in 1986. Australia successfully controlled the areas of the pitch in which the game was played. The further away the play was from Australia's goal-line and the closer to Great Britain's, the more play-the-balls there were.

Using the statistics

Statistics carelessly pinned to a dressing-room wall, particularly after a poor performance, can destroy the relationship between coach and players, have a detrimental effect on team spirit, and cause certain players to lose self-confidence. The coach therefore has to take care how he uses the information he has obtained. His first duty is to analyse the statistics, then carefully consider the best way to present it to the players so as to improve their work rate and decision-making.

There is no doubt that players respond to this information when used intelligently. They recognize its value, and become eager to improve their contribution to the team's effort. By the use of statistics it is relatively easy to set targets for both individuals and the team which help to motivate and improve performance.

4   VIDEO ANALYSIS

The most valuable coaching aid is the video, and every coach should try to have as many of his games recorded as possible. Obviously this is easier for the coach whose team plays in a stadium, but the clubhouse or changing-room roof will also provide a suitably elevated position for the camera.

1   The aims of video analysis

Video analysis enables the coach to make an intensive study of the action. Mistakes can be identified and training structured to improve performance. It is equally important that outstanding play be recognized and widely acknowledged.

2   Analysing the video

It is important to analyse the video before the first training session after the game. This often necessitates study during the evening of the game or at the very latest the day after. If for whatever reason the coach has to delegate this responsibility he must have an assistant whose views he respects totally, and accepts that, after careful analysis, the assistant may have a greater knowledge of the team's performance than he does himself.

The analysis should be performed with a clear head and total concentration. It is a good idea to relax in a favourite armchair with a pad, pen and the video pause button handy. The tape counter should be zeroed before the tape begins.

The detailed analysis should include all relevant information. Team errors and all individual mistakes should be noted, along with positive action. Dropped

Statistics Sheet E – Work Summary Sheet

Player	Passes			Drives					Kicks						DOUBLES
	AHB	LINE	TOTAL	AHB	PASS IN TACKLE	TACKLES	TRIES	TOTAL	TOUCH	SPACE	DOWNTOWN	BOMB	GRUBBER CHIP	TOTAL	DOUBLES

Errors								Involvement						Summary		
LOST BALL	DROP BALL	BAD PASS SCRUM	BAD PASS LOST	OUT OF BOUNDS	TACKLE MISSES	PENALTIES	TOTAL	PASSES	DRIVES	KICKS	TOTAL		TACKLES	OFFENCE	DEFENCE	TOTAL

STATISTICS SHEET F

First Test
Great Britain v Australia
Old Trafford
25th October, 1986

	First		Second	Total
Australia	GB	9	4	
	A	2	3	
		11	7	18
22-metre				
	GB	7	7	
	A	27	12	
		34	19	53
half-way				
	GB	15	17	
	A	23	11	
		38	28	66
22-metre				
	GB	12	15	
	A	15	30	
		27	45	72
Great Britain				

balls, mistackles and other obvious errors must be noted as well as more complex mistakes, such as wrong decisions, incorrect angles of run, mistaken timing, poor support play, failure to move up in the defensive line, and so on. Action which may need further study should be noted, using the tape counter number for easy reference.

The process is time-consuming but invaluable. At the end of the tape the coach will have a long list of points including:

(a)   All positive action, including tries scored, breaks made, good support play, accurate kicks, solid defence, and so on.

(b)   All mistakes, including individual, unit and team errors, faulty technique, incorrect decision-making and poor player combination.

He will also have invaluable information about the opposition's game-plan, set pieces and organization which he will be able to use for the return fixture.

3   Using the analysis

Rugby League is a team sport involving fitness and skill, but above all requiring players to make decisions and combine together to outwit the opposition.

Quite often, administrators and spectators will see players making similar errors of judgement throughout the season. They would be surprised to learn that the players are often oblivious of the errors, and that in many cases, the coach has neglected to analyse, advise or attempt to improve this vital area of play. Video analysis would assist this process. Once the long list of points written from the video has been completed, it helps to clarify thinking if they are transcribed onto a Player Report sheet and a Team Report sheet, set out on pages 288 and 289 and 290 and 291 respectively.

A   Player report sheet

Observations on each player should be written in the space alongside his name. A breakdown of mistakes (lost ball, bad pass, mistackles, and so on), tackles made, penalties conceded and points scored completes the picture.

B   Team report sheet

A complete summary of the game helps the coach to identify areas requiring improvement. Comments on the referee, and the opposition's pattern of play, provide useful information for future reference.

A. PLAYER REPORT SHEET.

DATE: _____ TEAMS
V VENUE

PLAYER	OBSERVATIONS	ERRORS	TACKLES	PENALTIES REASON	PNTS

B. Team Report Sheet

Use of Possession

General Mistakes.	LB	KO	Penalties given in possession	Total

No. of Tackle Periods

	Percentage Errors		Time in Possession
		us	Them

Tackle Count

		Total	Misses
First ½	Second ½		

Remarks on Referee

Mr. ....

Remarks on Game

Weather
Spectacle

Pitch
Control

Team Analysis

	Offence	Defence
Organisation		
Ruck		
Line		
Scrums		
Taps		
Commitment		

Opposition's Pattern of Play

Opposition's Tries

Work and Practice Needed

80 The author and Des Drummond (Warrington and Great Britain) talk through a problem before the start of the Test series against New Zealand in 1985.

4 Team and individual improvement

Before any action is taken, careful thought is needed. First of all, care has to be taken that there is not too much concentration on the negative. Positive play should be acknowledged and strongly emphasized in any team meetings. Training should be structured in such a way that the players' strengths are developed.

Coaching is aimed at eradicating errors, but the coach should not be too ambitious and try to eradicate too much at once. A list of priorities should be devised showing both team errors and individual errors. A useful guideline is to concentrate on no more than three errors at any one time.

The next step is for players to recognize and accept that improvement is necessary. The points should be brought out at the week's first training session, by team discussion or individual talks between the coach and player. It may help if extracts from the video are available, but these should be short and to the point. There is little value in the playing staff and coach sitting through all the action. By all means make the video available for the players to use in their own time, but any coaching should be brief and to the point.

Training should then be devised which develops the points discussed. As far as individual player improvement is concerned, this may require specialist training clinics. These can take place on a normal training night if staff are available, otherwise the coach will have to consider holding them on non-training nights.

5 Videos – other use

A Psychological preparation

Psychological preparation can be assisted by editing videos on a team and individual basis. The team video should contain extracts of the team performing excellently. It should be brief, no more than twelve minutes, with perhaps background motivational music. The video should be all action of tries, breaks and strong defence. An ideal time to show it is on the team bus, or in the clubhouse prior to the game.

The players can edit similar videos of themselves performing excellently. These help to increase self-confidence and are important psychological props.

B Study of opposition

Although the main priority of the coach has to be an improvement of his own team's performance, it is often helpful to watch the opposition in action. A couple of hours watching a video of the opposition's previous game can be most valuable.

Useful information may be:

1 Identification of major play-makers, particularly from the play-the-ball situation
2 Patterns of play in each quarter of the field
3 Identification of kickers
4 Defensive pattern
5 Positions adopted by the full-back and sweeper
6 Set pieces
7 Outstanding individual strengths and weaknesses
8 Possible vulnerability.

Some teams feel that it is an advantage to be handed a brief summary of the opposition's play a couple of days before the fixture.

Psychological preparation of a team

ALMA THOMAS
BA (Psych.), M Phil.
Head of School, Human Movement Studies, Bedford College of
Further Education, Bedford

1 Introduction
2 Communication
3 Motivation
4 Anxiety

1 INTRODUCTION

A successful coach motivates not only the individual players, but also the whole team as a unit. This is easier said than done. Team preparation falls into three categories:

1 Physical fitness
2 Tactical and skills work, and
3 Psychological preparation.

But more often than not the latter is forgotten.

What can the coach do about this area of preparation? Most coaches are intuitively good psychologists by doing what they 'feel' is right at the time. However, this may not be enough in all circumstances, and any knowledge which the coach has regarding psychological preparation of the individual, of the team as a whole, or of himself as coach can only help in the thorough preparation of the team and coach working together as a unit.

There is a school of thought that says, all else being equal, that the team that is psychologically better prepared for the competition will win. Or to put it another way, you are what you think you are. For example, 'we are winners and we've done this before many times', or 'the opposition have not lost this

season, they will be hard to beat.' In a game the first can be the secret of success, the second a hindrance. But both depend on the way in which the coach and players choose to use their minds to prepare themselves psychologically.

It is necessary to limit the content of this chapter to areas about which most coaches show constant concern. This does mean that there are other areas of psychological preparation which cannot be covered, such as the preparation of the individual player as opposed to the team. However, this chapter is aimed at you, the coach, and how you might consider:

1 Communication
2 Motivation, and
3 Anxiety.

within your own role as a team coach. Coaches are powerful and can exert a great deal of influence over players so it is important that the coach examines his own coaching style and characteristics.

2 COMMUNICATION

One of the most important coaching skills which needs to be developed is that of effective communication. All coaches and players understand the importance of having efficient channels of communication. Unless they are open, allowing all individuals to send clear messages about the expectations and goals each has for the other, communication will be inadequate. It is likely too that team relationships and motivation will suffer, as will competitive performance, without effective communication. This can be either verbal or non-verbal.

Verbal communication is mainly used to impart information, while non-verbal communication supports the verbal, but is also used to convey attitudes through gestures, facial expression, and bodily movement. There are times when non-verbal communication actually replaces language in expressing emotion and conveying information about the individual who is communicating.

Consequently, as a coach, it is important to be aware of how you use the different methods of communication. Does your facial expression or gesture say one thing and your verbal communication another? This will cause some concern among the team. The pressure of tight competitive situations challenges the coach to be in control of the information and the emotions communicated.

What are your communication skills like? Try answering the following questions as honestly as you can.

1   Do you have credibility with your players, or do you:
    (i)   never admit making a mistake
    (ii)   find you have problems getting the respect of your players, or
    (iii) usually speak negatively?

    Rate your credibility 1 2 3 4 5. (1 is very low, 5 very high.)

2   Are most of your messages positive or negative?
    (i)   do you think that most of your words and actions are negative and hostile?
    (ii)   do you frequently criticize the players and destroy their self-confidence?
    (iii) do you use praise sparingly and believe that it is not your job as coach to praise?
    (iv)   if you do praise, is it often followed by a negative statement?

Rate the degree to which your communication is positive or negative 1 2 3 4 5. (1 is negative, 5 is positive.)

3   To what extent is the content of your communication high in information or high in judgement?
    (i)   do you constantly evaluate the players instead of giving them instructions?
    (ii)   if something goes wrong, do you place blame rather than give feedback and/or information about how to correct what went wrong?
    (iii) if the team does well and you are pleased with them, do you know how to instruct them to achieve even higher levels of skill?
    (iv)   do you give ample feedback and instruction?

Rate whether your communication skills are higher in information or judgement 1 2 3 4 5. (1 is high in judgement, 5 is high in information).

4   How good a listener are you?
    (i)   Are you constantly giving instructions in practice?
    (ii)   When not shouting advice to the players during a match, are you muttering to yourself on the sidelines?
    (iii) Are you so busy talking that you never have time to listen to the players?
    (iv)   Do you ever allow the players to tell you something about the game, or the practice, or their position, or do you always tell them?

Rate your worth as a listener 1 2 3 4 5. (1 is not good, 5 is very good.)

5   How good are your non-verbal communication skills?
    (i)   Do you show your emotions (smile, wink, or pat the players on the back, scowl or express disgust)?
    (ii)   Are your players able to detect how you are feeling? If not then it may leave some players feeling insecure.

Rate your non-verbal communication skills 1 2 3 4 5. (1 is weak, 5 is strong).

Now add up your score and check it against the totals below:

25–21 You are a good communicator and your teams should enjoy clear two-way communication at all levels.

20–16 Your communication skills aren't bad, but there is room for improvement in some areas.

15–11 Try to be careful about how you say things to the team and individual players. Try to seek some help as to which areas of communication need care and how they can be remedied.

Below 10 Are you quite sure you should be coaching? If so, then try to seek help and guidance on how to improve your communication skills.

Much communication is habitual, and we rarely give conscious thought to the way we do it. All coaches need to work on communication skills, as poor communication is known to be the cause of the majority of personal conflicts and problems in sport. *When communication breaks down between two individuals, motivation, commitment and performance will suffer.*

The most important times for communication with players are:

1 during practice
2 before a match
3 during a match, and
4 after a match.

It is most important that communication at these times is effective. The nature of the communication will be different each time, but the most critical components of its effectiveness are:

1 Consistency. This is critical to the improvement of performance as well as building a healthy team relationship. Make the information consistent, especially with regard to skills, tactics and strategies. Both players and coach should establish consistent communication patterns across all the game, practice and individual situations. Above all, it is important to be aware of how communication can change in different situations.

2 Intensity. This is about how the message is put across. What emotional tones are used to go with the message? Is the message presented in the same manner during both practice and game situations?

If both consistency and intensity change, performance may also change. Some players will learn to cope with the coach's behavioural pattern, but others may find it difficult to adjust. In a stressful situation like a close match, players should not have to constantly readjust to and interpret what the coach is trying to communicate. They should be adjusting to the ever-changing game!

3 Information overload. This can create many communication problems for players. The coach must learn to limit remarks when there isn't much time, for example at half-time, or in tight pressure situations. Consideration should be given to the amount of information the players can absorb and assimilate. Sometimes players may return to the field after being bombarded with so much information that they find themselves distracted by trying to work out what to do with it, and as a result performance may suffer.

4 Negative messages. The players are the first people to know if they are playing well or not, especially if mistakes have been made. They do not need reminding of these by the coach as well. Players require positive reinforcement for their efforts, and communication that is relevant to the situation and if possible help to correct errors. *Encouragement works better than criticism.* An overload of negative messages will not help to correct mistakes or to motivate players. Encouragement is essential in team games, and is a skill which all coaches should learn and practise.

A coach who communicates well:

1 Listens well and understands the messages others transmit, whether intentional or unintentional

2 Transmits consistent messages in a specific way, and gets the right positive message across

3 Knows what message he transmits, whether intentional or unintentional

4 Encourages his players to enter into clear and open communication, both with himself and between players

5 Maintains a relatively consistent form of communication from practice to practice and game to game

6 Watches for signs that communication is not effective.

3 MOTIVATION

This is a major concern in sport. The questions that coaches ask about motivation are, 'How do I motivate individual players to play consistently well?', and 'How do I motivate my team to go on playing well and winning?'

Motivation can be thought of as the need or drive a player has, which helps to arouse, put into action and direct his behaviour. Motivation is two-dimensional, requiring direction towards the goal a person is striving to achieve, and intensity which affects the effort he puts into trying to reach that goal.

Success in Rugby League teams depends on team work and a sense of collective confidence, in knowing that the team is well prepared and fundamentally sound. A coach's major role is therefore to integrate the team into a unit that performs efficiently and well, with a sense of pride, excellence and above all a collective identity. To do this a coach must:

1 Realize that all the players are individuals; they each have different needs as well as the needs of the team as a whole.

2 Enhance the potential of each player whilst at the same time making the entire unit of individuals gel in a co-ordinated manner.

This is easier said than done, but there are techniques which can be used to help the coach to meet this challenge.

Motivation through goal-setting

Goal-setting is known to be one of the effective methods of motivating players at all levels. Even those of the highest calibre will benefit from a goal-setting programme. The following are the main things to keep in mind:

1 Specific, hard, challenging goals are better than specific easy ones.

2 Players must have enough ability to attain or meet the goal.

3 Goals must be specific in terms of what exactly is to be achieved. They cannot remain vague intentions if they are to be effective.

4 Intermediate goals should be used as a link to the long-term or end goals.

5 Feedback is required if the goals are to have maximum effectiveness in improving performance.

6 Goals should be flexible enough to allow for change or revision, yet have structured target times/dates. Without target dates there is no way of measuring progress.

7 Goals should be established together, between the coach and the individual player and between the coach and the team. There must also be commitment to achieving the goals.

8 Goals should also be related to the overall aim of improving or maintaining performance.

Goal-setting is important because:

1 Goals direct attention to the task in hand and motivate continued effort over time. They also re-establish relevant procedures or strategies for goal achievement.

2 Goal-setting allows the player and the team to accept responsibility for their own performance and motivation. If goals have been established which challenge coach and team, little if any other motivational technique will be needed.

3 Goals help in the setting up of better lines of communication between coach and team. By jointly setting goals the coach and team are better able to understand the expectations that each has for the other. Without mutual expectations, conflict, frustration and a resulting decrease in motivation may occur.

Two examples of goal-setting worksheets for use

Goal-setting action steps

1. My primary goal is _____

2. This goal can be structured into immediate, short-term and long-term sub-goals.

    A   Short-term goals are _____

    B   Intermediate goals are _____

    C   Long-term goals are _____

3. Additional goals related to my primary goal are

    A _____

    B _____

    C _____

4. My goals can be measured in the following ways (How I know I have attained them)

    A   Primary goal _____

    B   Short-term goals _____

    C   Intermediate goals _____

    D   Long-term goals _____

    E   Related goals _____

5. Schedule for attaining goals – target date
    A   Short-term goals _____
    B   Intermediate goals _____
    C   Long-term goals _____
    D   Related goals _____

6. Plan for attaining my goals. Procedures and steps
    A. Daily plan _____

    B   Seasonal plan _____

    C   Plan for competition _____

    D   Career plan _____

7. Additional skills, knowledge, opportunities, concerns, and the like that I have to consider in meeting my goals:

    _____
    _____
    _____
    _____
    _____
    _____
    _____

Goal-setting Worksheet

Sport								
			Name			Year's experience		
Area		Specific Goal	Strategies to achieve specific goal	Target date	Weekly goal evaluation			
					1	2	3	
	Strength							
	Average							
	Weakness							

with either the individual or the team are set out on pages 298 and 299. ('Goal-setting Action Steps' is taken from *The Athlete's Guide to Sports Psychology: mental skills for physical people*, by D. V. Harris and B. L. Harris, 1984. 'The Goal-setting Worksheet' is reproduced with the kind permission of the National Coaching Foundation.)

There are many areas in which goals can be set, including individual skills, team skills, tactics, practices, fitness, and discipline.

4   ANXIETY

All players at some time feel anxious about various aspects of their game. This is particularly common in connection with important and crucial matches.

If players feel, for example, that they are not going to do well they easily become anxious. The expectations of the coach and the team may tend to make some players even more anxious, so they worry about what other people may say and in some cases what the media may say and write. The feeling common to all these examples is that the player doubts whether his ability is good enough to stand up to the demands of the situation in which he finds himself. Consequently, *the more worried and anxious a player becomes the greater the disruption of his performance.*

What can the coach do to help reduce anxiety in his players?

1   Know the players well as individuals. The more he knows them, the more able he is to recognize anxiety and help to lessen it in some way.

2   Learn to recognize the symptoms of anxiety. All anxiety is accompanied by physical tension, and the signs are easily recognized, for example:
i   sweaty hands,
ii   dry mouth,
iii   increased heart rate,
iv   feelings of nausea,
v   wanting to go to the toilet often, and
vi   increased adrenalin.

3   The mental or cognitive symptoms of anxiety are much more difficult to detect, for example:
i   the player may seem distracted and unable to concentrate,
ii   he appears lethargic in play and practice,
iii   he appears to be inhibited either in his play or in social exchanges with team-mates and the coach.

4   There may be other mental symptoms which only the player will be aware of, for example:
i   Worrying thoughts about any or all aspects of the game and his performance, or
ii   Memories of a bad or poor performance in the past.

One important fact for coaches to remember is that these different symptoms of anxiety occur at different times in the run-up to an important game. For example, mental anxiety may be quite high in the days or weeks before the game, and be reduced only after the game. On the other hand, the symptoms of physiological anxiety may be quite low during the days before the game but more apparent in the two or three hours prior to the game.

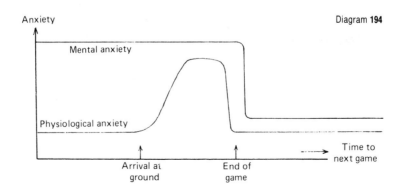

Diagram **194**

Diagram 194 will help to show the time differences.

4   Once it has been recognized that a player is showing anxiety, it is the task of the coach to deal with the problem. Remember, the best players are the ones who can control and maintain their own level of anxiety in order to produce a good performance. This is different for each player, because they are all individuals. Hence the importance of knowing your players well. However, even though they will have developed their own methods of coping with anxiety, which the coach should be aware of, players will need to be taught further methods to help them. The coach can help this by:

i   Making the player feel accepted no matter what the outcome of the game.

ii Encouraging the team as a whole to accept the player, no matter what the outcome of the game.

iii Keeping the negative comments down to a minimum. (Ideally, there should be no negative comments at all.)

iv Encouraging openness, support and enthusiasm from the rest of the team.

These four points are important, because they not only control anxiety but help to maintain and strengthen self-confidence, which is best built up in a positive atmosphere rather than a negative one.

v   Encouraging the players to talk about what makes them anxious. Once the cause is known then coach and player are better able to enter into a supportive programme.

vi   Encouraging players to follow their normal routine, as changing it can add to the anxiety.

vii Encouraging the players to think positively about their performance. Concentrate on the skills that the players perform well, and if possible encourage them to raise their own expectation.

viii Teaching the players to feel 'I've done this before, successfully, many times.' This encourages self-confidence. It will involve players in a mental rehearsal technique known as visualization, which allows the player to see himself performing certain skills, set-plays, tactics or indeed the whole game successfully. Visualization includes a physical feeling as well as hearing, though the physical feeling is said to be the most important aspect. Once the players have mastered this skill, it allows for more confidence in their own personal performance which gives more time to concentrate on other things in the match, for example the opponents' play.

ix   *Teaching the players to relax.* There are two different types of relaxation technique: mental relaxation which reduces anxiety, and physical relaxation which reduces the physiological signs of anxiety. Both are beneficial. It should be remembered that deep relaxation techniques should not be used immediately prior to the game as they could cause players to become too relaxed, adversely affecting their performance during the game.

x   Being careful about *what* you are saying and *how* you are saying it. There are three crucial times:
(a)   immediately prior to the match,
(b)   during the match, and
(c)   immediately after the match.
Before the match, coaches must remember that all the players are individuals and each has a different level of anxiety. Some would prefer to be with fellow players and talk quietly about the game, others prefer to be alone and quietly think about their individual roles in the match, while others may wish to listen to music on their personal earphones.

One 'psyching up' talk may not suit all players. It is worth reminding coaches that there is no substitute for knowing your players well as individuals.

As they have no contact with the coach during a game, it is important that players have enough information and confidence in themselves and their team-mates to make the right decisions during play. Immediately after the match it is important to realize that whatever is said about the team or individual performance should be positive.

Coaches may find the anxiety check-list (adapted from one used in *The Athlete's Guide to Sports Psychology: mental skills for physical people*, by D. V. Harris and B. L. Harris, 1984), set out below, helpful for use with players. It guides the awareness of the feelings associated with anxiety and in turn links them with the resulting performance. Once a pattern has been established both the player and the coach are better able to control and cope with anxiety in order to produce a better performance.

This appendix has outlined some aspects of the psychological preparation for performance. Remember that, like all preparation, it is long term and should not be used as an emergency measure. Psychological skills should be an integral part of the players' training, practised alongside the physical skills.

Check-list for Tension and Anxiety Indicators

SIGNS OF TENSION	CIRCLE FREQUENCY OF OBSERVATION		
	ALWAYS	SOMETIMES	NEVER
Facial grimaces, frowning	3	2	1
Clenching teeth, grinding teeth	3	2	1
General bodily restlessness	3	2	1
Moving body part continuously: foot, hands, knee	3	2	1
Headaches	3	2	1
Neckaches	3	2	1
Backaches	3	2	1
Diarrhoea	3	2	1
Constipation	3	2	1
Irritable bowel	3	2	1
Indigestion	3	2	1
Irritable G. I. tract	3	2	1
Fatigue	3	2	1
Insomnia, disrupted sleep	3	2	1
Restless legs	3	2	1
Restless hands	3	2	1
Pulling, tugging on hair, moustache, eyebrows, etc.	3	2	1
Muscles twitches, spasms, cramps, tics	3	2	1
Excessive sweating	3	2	1
Cold, clammy hands and/or feet	3	2	1
Chewing fingernails	3	2	1
Chewing inside of cheek or lips	3	2	1
General irritability	3	2	1
Heart pounding or racing	3	2	1
Anger, hostility	3	2	1
Shaking hands, tremors	3	2	1
Irregular breathing rates, shortness of breath	3	2	1
Uncontrollable thoughts	3	2	1
Mental confusion	3	2	1
Forgetfulness	3	2	1
Skin rashes	3	2	1
Loss of appetite	3	2	1
Excessive eating	3	2	1
Unexplained fears	3	2	1

TOTAL SCORE _____

Index

Bibliography

Australian Rugby League *Coaching Manual* Patterson & Beck 1980

Australian Rugby League *Coaching Rugby League Level 1* MacArthur Press 1978

Australian Rugby League *Coaching Rugby League Level 2* Australian RL 1981

Allan Bancroft *The Way Forward* Copyprint 1983

Peter Corcoran *Skills Manual* Australian RL 1979

Peter Corcoran *Mini Footy – a game of Rugby League for youngsters* Australian RL 1980

Peter Corcoran and Gordon Treble *I'll Coach Them* Australian RL 1981

Ray French *Running Rugby* Faber and Faber 1980

Ray French *Coaching Rugby League* Faber and Faber 1982

Jack Gibson *Parramatta Players Manual* 1983

Jack Gibson *Parramatta Training Programme* 1983

Jack Gibson *Cronulla Sutherland Players Manual* 1985

Jack Gibson *Cronulla Sutherland Off-Season Training Programme* 1985

Jim Greenwood *Total Rugby* Lepus 1978

Charles Hughes *Soccer: tactics and skills* B.B.C. 1980

Phil Larder *The Rugby League Skills Manual* Stanley Press 1983

Leeds & Hunslet Schools *Manual of Rugby League Coaching* 1948

Malcolm Lewis *Successful Rugby* Charles Letts 1980

Los Angeles Rams *Training Manual* 1984

Rod McKenzie *Conditioning for Rugby League Football – a winning approach* RFL 1984

National Coaching Foundation *Introductory Study Packs*

Geof Gleeson *The Coach in Action* 1984

Rex Hazeldine and John Cadman *The Body in Action* 1984

Dr Lew Hardy and John Fazey *Mind over Matter* 1984

Rod Thorpe *Planning & Practice* 1984
Play the Game for Children in Sport 1986
The Coach at Work 1986
Physiology and Performance 1986

Frank Pyke *Towards Better Coaching* Frank Daniels 1981

Johnny Raper *Rugby League Fundamentals* A.H. & A. W. Reed 1972

Rugby Football Union *Better Rugby* 1973

Don Rutherford *Rugby for Coach and Players* Arthur Barker 1971

John Syer and Christopher Connelly *Sporting Body, Sporting Mind* Cambridge University Press 1984

Thomas Tutko and Jack Richards *Psychology of Coaching* Allyn & Bacon 1971

Thomas Tutko and Umberto Tosi *Sports Psyching* J P Tarcher 1976

Ivan Vodanovich *Rugby Football the All Blacks Way* Orbis Publishing 1982

Allen Wade *F.A. Guide to Training and Coaching* Heinemann 1967

Dr Denis Wartley *The Psychology of Winning* Berkley Books 1979

Ron Willey *Clues on Coaching* Beer Publishing 1982

Ray Williams *Skilful Rugby* Souvenir Press 1976

Eric Worthington *Teaching Soccer Skill* Lepus Books 1975